C000254135

WORLD ADVERTISING REVIEW 1991

MODERN · PUBLICITY · 59

WORLD ADVERTISING REVIEW 1991

MODERN · PUBLICITY · 59

EDITED BY

PHILIP KLEINMAN

CASSELL

Cassell Publishers Limited
Villiers House, 41/47 Strand, London WC2N 5JE, England

© Cassell Publishers Limited 1990

All rights reserved. No part of this publication may be reproduced or transmitted in any form or by any means, electronic or mechanical including photocopying, recording or any information storage or retrieval system, without prior permission in writing from the publishers.

First published 1990

British Library Cataloguing in Publication Data
World advertising review: modern publicity
1. Pictorial advertising. Illustrations.
Serials.
I. Title II. Modern publicity (1930)
659.13

ISBN 0-304-32306-3

Edited and written by Philip Kleinman
Compiled in collaboration with *Lürzer's Archive*, Frankfurt

Typeset by Nene Phototypesetters Ltd, Northampton
Reproduction by Golden Cup Printing Co. Ltd, Hong Kong
Printed and bound in Hong Kong by Colorcraft Ltd.

CONTENTS

INTRODUCTION

ALCOHOLIC DRINKS 1

AUDIO AND VIDEO 2

AUTOMOTIVE 3

CLOTHING AND FOOTWEAR 4

COMPUTERS AND OFFICE EQUIPMENT 5

CORPORATE 6

EXHIBITIONS AND EVENTS 7

FINANCIAL 8

FOOD AND NON-ALCOHOLIC DRINKS 9

HOUSE AND GARDEN 10

INDUSTRIAL 11

JEWELLERY AND WATCHES 12

MEDIA 13

MISCELLANEOUS 14

PHOTOGRAPHIC 15

PUBLIC SERVICE 16

RETAIL AND RESTAURANTS 17

TOBACCO 18

TOILETRIES, COSMETICS, PHARMACEUTICALS 19

TRAVEL AND TOURISM 20

CREDITS

INDEX OF PRODUCTS AND SERVICES

INDEX OF AGENCIES AND STUDIOS

INTRODUCTION

The main difference between this edition of World Advertising Review and its predecessors is the greatly increased number of television commercials included this time. The most innovative pieces of advertising are to be found precisely in these TV films rather than in the print ads selected, though among the latter are many attractive items.

Saatchi & Saatchi Advertising's London agency turned out some impressive work in the period covered, seemingly unhurt by the well publicised financial problems of the Saatchi group. Witness the agency's blockbuster commercial, directed by Hugh Hudson, for British Airways, in which about 4,000 extras are used to create a gigantic face. Witness also the British Rail film, directed by Tony Kaye, in which imaginative manipulation of images combines with Leon Redbone's music to create an enchanting effect.

Tony Kaye's name figures among the credits for yet another outstanding British advertising film, for the Volkswagen Passat. The agency is BMP DDB Needham, born of a merger between Boase Massimi Pollitt and the Omnicom subsidiary DDB Needham, itself formed from two originally independent agencies, Doyle Dane Bernbach and Needham Harper. BMP, previously a public company in its own right, agreed to join the Omnicom group – and take managerial control of it in the UK – after fighting off an unwelcome takeover bid from the smaller but rapidly growing French agency BDDP (Boulet Dru Dupuy Petit). Both BMP and BDDP have strong and justified creative reputations. Both are well represented in this edition of WAR.

BMP's Passat commercial is noteworthy not only for its striking black and white photography but also for the way in which it avoids the hard sell in favour of human interest. Many of the best pieces of TV advertising look increasingly like miniature feature films, with the characters in them counting for as much as, or more than, the products being plugged.

The British advertising industry has become particularly skilled in the production of such slice-of-life mini-movies, but examples in this book come not only from Britain. Among the most noteworthy is the Apple computers commercial by the French agency CLM/BBDO. In it the product message is not stated but only implied; the visual emphasis is all on the pigheaded man who represents the old-fashioned way of running a company.

Another campaign strong on human interest is that by Ogilvy & Mather's New York office for American Express, though the films, whether they are focusing on father and son or on husband and wife, take care to weave the benefits of the Amex card into the story line. From Dentsu in Tokyo comes another engaging father-and-son tale, this time for Clinica Lion toothpaste. In contrast, the Brazilian campaign by Guimaraes e Giacometti of São Paulo for Champion watches goes for a cynical rather than sentimental glimpse of human relationships.

Human interest is perhaps at its most intense in the episodic Gold Blend coffee campaign by McCann-Erickson, London, the actors in which have become almost as well known as the stars of TV soap operas. However, their praise of the product is somewhat too fulsome to preserve the illusion of real life. It is arguable that the Gold Blend series would be more realistic and even more effective if Gold Blend itself took a less prominent part in the script. If realism is to be abandoned, however, it may be preferable to go all out for fantasy, as Young & Rubicam does in New Zealand with its family of car-eaters impatient for their Kentucky Fried Chicken.

As well as devoting more attention to TV, this edition of WAR differs in another respect from its predecessors. The captions on a number of ads and films, though by no means all, exceed the limits on length that have been set in the past. Every ad campaign has behind it a story worth telling, and more space has been allotted to telling a few such stories in slightly greater detail than previously.

In relation to two of the campaigns, those for Hennes clothes and Zeon watches, the story is not so much about the whys and wherefores of the ads themselves as about the attention drawn to them by Britain's Advertising Standards Authority in its investigations into feminist accusations of a harmful use of sexual motifs.

Striking the right balance between illustrations and text in what remains, after all, a picture book is not entirely easy. The task is, ironically, made easier by the lack of publicity sense on the part of many agencies, which fail to take advantage of the opportunity to describe the ways in which their ideas were generated and the marketing problems they were intended to solve.

If the makers of ads really knew how to advertise themselves, there would be many more books published like the one put together by copywriter Richard Phillips and actress Maureen Lipman about J. Walter Thompson's British Telecom campaign (sampled in the Miscellaneous section). The initiative for even that book, it must be said, did not come from the agency. Advertising still has a long way to go.

PHILIP KLEINMAN

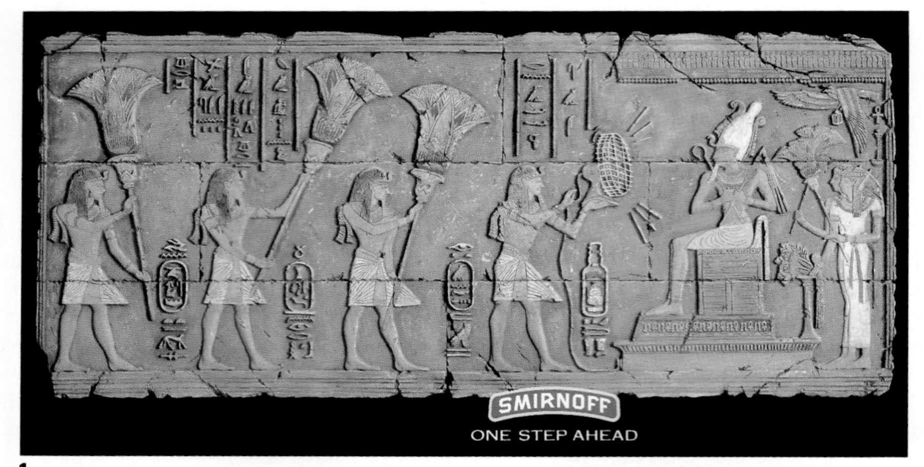

1

2

3

1, 2, 3
Smirnoff vodka
United Kingdom
Agency: Young & Rubicam, London
Y&R's UK advertising for Smirnoff has been through several phases since the historic 'The effect is shattering' campaign which started in 1970. This 'One step ahead' campaign, though perhaps not the funniest, is the most elegant. Notice the supermarket trolley in the cave drawing ad, the electric fan in the Egyptian frieze, and the outboard motor in the mosaic.

4
Kronenbourg beer
France
Agency: Young & Rubicam, Paris
The Eiffel Tower, to which this structure bears a passing resemblance, has become a boring advertising cliché, but being built of Kronenbourg beer mats makes a difference. Copy says: 'Kronenbourg has been a public monument for 325 years. Every day it attracts millions of fans.'

La Kronenbourg
Est Un Monument Public De 325 Ans.
Elle Attire Chaque Jour
Des Millions D'Amateurs.

5
Malibu
United Kingdom
Agency: Burkitt Weinreich Bryant, London

A clip from a TV film with a graphic style somewhat similar to that of BDDP's print campaign for 1664 beer (nos 19, 20). Shot entirely in silhouette, it uses only three colours – brown, white and orange. It shows couples dancing on a Caribbean beach to reggae music. A couple sitting drinking react to the sight of other, incongruous couples – a fat man with a thin woman, a very tall woman with a very short man. When the seated man and woman rise to join in the dancing, she also is revealed to be very tall and he very short. Voice-over: 'Malibu and orange. The special party mix.'

The campaign is primarily pitched downmarket at fun-loving, sociable young people. The tropical theme, defined by the agency as 'the core brand property', has been reinterpreted in line with consumer research that showed target drinkers disliked images of yuppies on tropical beaches. The solution was to show Caribbean people enjoying themselves in a believable but amusing way.

The result is said to have been renewed growth in sales of the product, which had begun to stagnate after its successful 1980 launch by International Distillers & Vintners. The agency says Malibu was for the first half of the decade very fashionable among young adult patrons of night clubs and discos. The problem is that this group, while acutely image-conscious, has little brand loyalty.

6

7

6
Archer's Peach County schnapps
United Kingdom
Agency: Burkitt Weinreich Bryant, London

Look carefully at this engaging picture, and you'll see the glass is full of tiny peaches. The photographer is Jack Bankhead.

7
Johnnie Walker Black Label whisky
United Kingdom
Agency: Collett Dickenson Pearce and Partners, London

A cunning photograph, this, by Neil Barstow. Notice the human hand, hidden chameleon-like, among the smooth pebbles.

8

8
Castlemaine XXXX
United Kingdom
Agency: Saatchi & Saatchi, London
Here the offbeat humour of this well-loved campaign is linked with the client's sponsorship of the Australian cricket tour of England. The man with the big, beer-foamy moustache is Merv Hughes, the most recognisable member of the Australian team.

9, 10, 11
Absolut vodka
United States
Agency: TBWA, New York
Clever stuff here in the latest phase of a campaign that over the years has shown a high level of graphic inventiveness. Past editions of this book have included, for example, illustrations done for Absolut by Andy Warhol and the graffiti artist Keith Haring. The 'Absolut Manhattan' ad places the vodka bottle in a map of Manhattan island. The San Francisco ad depends for its effect on the knowledge that the Californian city is afflicted with frequent mists. 'Absolut Reflection' uses mirror writing.

9

TESTS PROVE AUSTRALIANS WOULDN'T GIVE A XXXX FOR ANYTHING ELSE.
AUSTRALIA
Brewed under licence in the U.K.

ABSOLUT MANHATTAN.
PRODUCT OF SWEDEN. 40 AND 50% ALC/VOL (80 AND 100 PROOF). 100% GRAIN NEUTRAL SPIRITS. © 1989 CARILLON IMPORTERS LTD., TEANECK, NJ.

10

11

12

12
Bavaria beer
Netherlands
Agency: DMB&B, Amsterdam
Headline: 'And now a Bavaria'.
Caption: 'Expert work'.

13
J & B Rare whisky
United Kingdom
Agency: Young & Rubicam, London
The joke of the bottle hidden in a book is pursued through a series of different ads. The copywriter on this one is Neil Patterson, the agency's creative director.

13

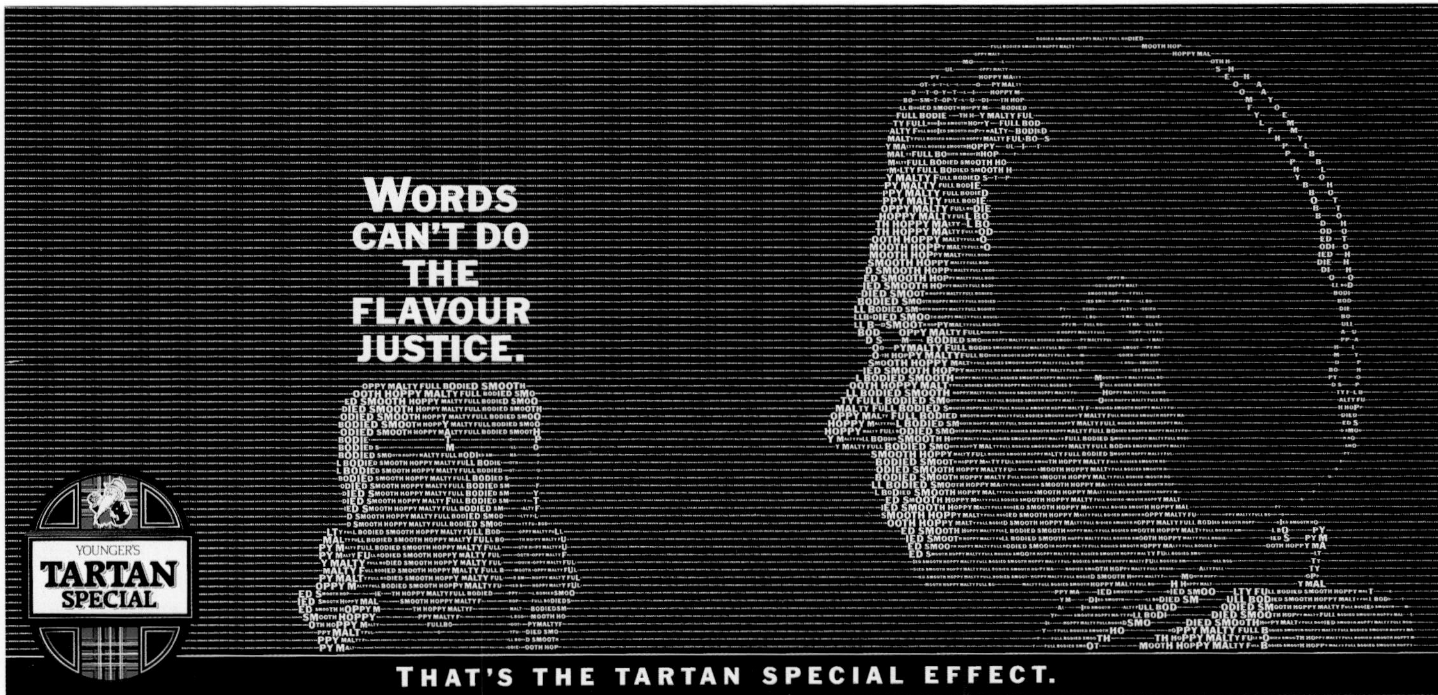

14

15

14
Tartan bitter
United Kingdom
Agency: Burkitt Weinreich Bryant, London

The image of drinker and drink is entirely constructed of the words 'Malty Full Bodied Smooth Hoppy'.

15
Grant's whisky
France
Agency: BDDP, Paris

A particularly pleasing example of an established, visually inventive campaign designed to make the brand appear more fashionable than competitors Johnnie Walker, Ballantine's and Long John. Caption: 'The temptation is great'.

When you can't see what you're drinking, you have to concentrate on flavour.

DO YOUR EYES DECEIVE YOU ? NOT IF YOU'RE A DRAUGHT BASS EXPERT

When William Bass brewed his first pint in 1777, a true individual was born.

An individual whose essential characteristics have been preserved through constant care and diligence in the Bass tasting rooms.

These blue glasses are just one way our experts ensure every pint of Draught Bass we brew tastes as nutty, malty and distinctive as the last.

You've probably noticed that a good-looking pint automatically seems to taste better.

So just one glimpse of a pint like Draught Bass could all too easily impair our flavour-testers' judgement.

To make doubly sure this doesn't happen, they not only drink from blue glasses, but they do so in a darkened room. And only when the flavour of Draught Bass is perfect, will they allow it to see the light of day. ▲

BASS ALE ON DRAUGHT

Bass

You can tell it with your eyes closed.

16
Draught Bass
United Kingdom
Agency: Edwards Martin Thornton, London
Draught Bass is Britain's biggest selling brand of premium cask ale. To back up the contention that 'You can tell it with your eyes closed' this ad relates that the brewer's experts use blue glasses to test-taste the beer so as not to be influenced by its colour.

17
Tennent's Super lager
United Kingdom
Agency: Edwards Martin Thornton, London
From a poster and press campaign featuring various objects fashioned out of beer cans. The caption words, such as 'supercool', 'superstructure', play on the brand name. The copywriter is agency partner Chris Martin.

18
Grand Marnier
United States
Agency: TBWA, New York
Spanish illustrator Gervasio Gallardo continues to supply the surrealistic images for this long-running and attractive campaign.

TENNENT'S
SUPER
tennent's super strong lager
supercool

17

Grand Marnier
Liqueur
ONE GRAND TURN DESERVES ANOTHER.
To send a gift of Grand Marnier® Liqueur (except where prohibited by law) call 1-800-243-3787. Product of France. Made with fine cognac brandy 40% alc/vol (80 proof). ©1989 Carillon Importers, Ltd., Teaneck, NJ.

18

19

20

19, 20
1664 beer
France
Agency: BDDP, Paris
Creative credits for these stylish ads include, surprisingly, the name of a photographer, Nick Knight, and not an illustrator. The campaign is based on a verbal-cum-visual pun, with the slogan 'The greatest number a beer can do for you' referring both to the brand's numerical name and to 'number' in the sense of theatrical turn. The brewer is Kronenbourg.

21
Cuervo tequila
United States
Agency: Young & Rubicam, New York
The margarita (a mixture of tequila and lemon juice) sits atop a Mexican pyramid, as if to emphasise the national character of the drink.

MONUMENTAL MARGARITAS.

CUERVO GOLD MAKES IT.

CUERVO ESPECIAL® TEQUILA. 40% ALC. BY VOL./80 PROOF © 1990. IMPORTED AND BOTTLED BY HEUBLEIN, INC., HARTFORD, CT. UNDER LICENSE FROM THE TRADEMARK OWNERS.

22

No sex please, we're Japanese.

Have you noticed how an increasing number of the television programmes these days leave very little to the imagination?

If you have, we've got some news for you: it's going to get a lot worse.

Especially with all those satellite stations beaming in programmes from other countries.

Like Italy, where deregulated television means practically anything goes.

Why, they've even gone as far as having a regular topless quiz show.

Hardly the sort of thing you would want a young impressionable child to watch.

But what if something offensive came on and you weren't around to keep an eye on your children?

Would a warning that some of the scenes are explicit be enough to make them switch off?

We doubt it.

Which is precisely why Sanyo has introduced the CPB 2554, the first television available in this country you can censor yourself.

All you have to do is press the number of the channel you wish to censor, then press a device we've come up with called the Special Function Key. This effectively prevents anyone from tuning into the channel.

Then finally tap out a 3 digit number on the handset, which acts rather like the combination on a safe.

With a possible 999 permutations, the most persistent child would find it difficult to crack.

So you can go out for the evening and enjoy yourself, safe in the knowledge that even ingenious teenagers won't be able to see a programme you don't want them to.

This isn't all that's special about the Special Function Key. Far from it.

It can also scan through all the channels, so you can see what's on immediately without having to flick through your daily newspaper.

Alternatively, if it's the latest news you're after, why wait for Sir Alastair Burnet?

Thanks to our Fastext facility you have access to all the pages of information from ITV's Oracle and the BBC's Ceefax services in double quick time.

Fastext also allows you to programme the 64 pages that you use most often, from bulletins giving the latest on air, sea and rail travel to the top 100 share prices, bringing them up on the screen before you can say Dow Jones.

Pretty impressive stuff.

But can the quality of the picture match up to it? Naturally it can.

Our Black Filter Tube, for instance, gives you greater definition between darks and lights as well as cleaner, sharper colours.

Whilst our FST (Flatter Squarer Tube) reduces the distortion of the image you get on lesser television tubes, where the screen is curved, a particular problem with larger sets.

And when you turn the television on there's also something most other manufacturers have completely forgotten to include. We've called it Last Settings Memory.

This ensures that the volume, brightness, contrast and channel are the same as when you last turned the television off.

And should you fall asleep during the late night movie this set will stop you waking up with a start to that horrible high pitched tone you always hear after close down.

What more could you want of a television?

How about a dual remote control unit that operates both your Sanyo television and video?

On screen indicators so you can see how loud the volume is as well as hearing it?

Or a Scart socket, so you only need one lead to connect a video or satellite tuner to your television?

This colour television has them all.

Of course, for such high technology you might well expect to pay a small fortune.

On the contrary.

The new Sanyo CPB 2554 will set you back just £449. Thereby proving that on the first censoring television, even the price is modest. SANYO

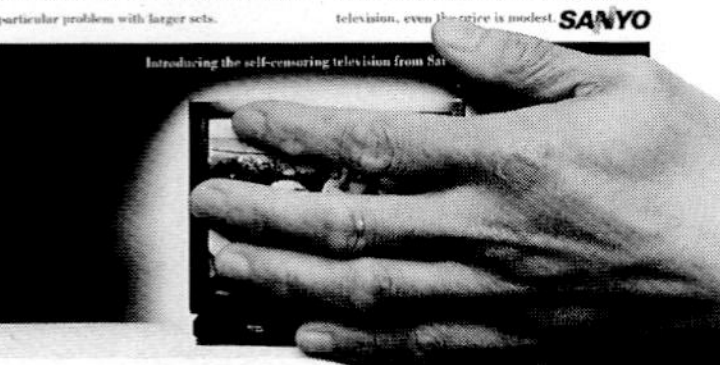

23

Lazy? Stupid? Ignorant? Your video has arrived.

It is not our intention to insult you into buying this video recorder.

On the contrary, this rather blunt appeal is to people sophisticated enough to own up to one of the great universal truths.

Namely, that programming a video is still nigh on impossible for all but a few buffs.

So with the rest of the nation in mind, Sanyo has created a video recorder so simple to programme it requires nothing of you but your index finger.

The VHR 5240E in our picture features something we call Video Text Programming.

This extraordinarily simple device enables you to programme the machine first by converting your television to Teletext, then by using the TV guide information and an on-screen cursor.

Using the remote control, you simply line up the cursor alongside the programme displayed on the screen, press a button and the machine does the rest for you.

Although you, of course, take the credit.

However, should even this exercise seem too demanding, you could try programming the machine using the LCD Remote Control.

Aware of your ignorance in technical matters, it asks you elementary questions via the LCD display panel on the Remote.

What day? What time start? What time finish? What channel?

You merely key in the answers on the Remote Control and point it at the machine.

Press a button and once again the machine is quite happy to do all the work for you.

You can key in up to eight programmes, so you could, for instance, make your selections for the week and programme the lot in one go.

Alternatively, you can tap in eight different selections over a year.

(Just think, you could programme next year's World Cup Final now. Your wife will be pleased.)

This ingenious video also panders to your innate indolence in other ways.

The Digital Auto Tracking, for example, reads the tracking of each tape and then adjusts it automatically.

Which is particularly useful, given that most rented films have different tracking settings.

The Remote Control can operate both your Sanyo video and television.

And if you really can't be bothered to keep track of all your videos, you can now add your own titles to remind you of the contents.

Just in case this still sounds a little like hard work, Sanyo has also added both Quick Start Recording and Fast Response Search functions to help preserve your energy.

Although with Auto Play, Auto Rewind and Auto Rewind Play, the Sanyo VHR 5240E leaves you with almost nothing to do.

Of course, if you are more technically-minded, you could always take a look at the Sanyo VHR D4890E. This offers Super VHS, Nicam stereo sound and all manner of digital effects, complete with an instruction manual that makes War and Peace seem like a short story.

But if you're too lazy to wade through a complicated instruction manual, ignorant about anything electronic and stupid enough to believe that somehow it's you that is at fault, don't worry. You've joined the human race. SANYO

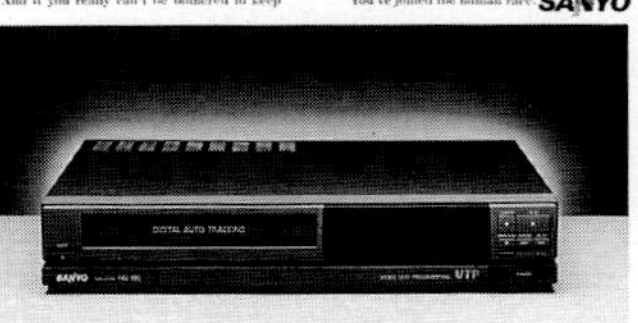

24

A special burglar proof design from Sanyo. (It's ugly.)

The sleek, low design. The clean, angular lines. The sheer minimalism of the object.

You're absolutely right. They're nowhere to be seen.

At Sanyo, we'd be the first to admit that our new MCD950F portable stereo system is unlikely to win a beauty contest.

However, just as a parent sees virtue in the plainest of children, we believe that what the system lacks in looks, it makes up for in performance.

The Peak Music Power Output, or PMPO, is an ear-splitting 100 watts.

A noise level delivered to your ears by something we call an Extended Bass Sound System.

The resulting 'Bassurround' sound has a rich thumping bass effect that really does recreate the atmosphere of a live concert.

Of course, this machine is not just an ugly face.

Behind the Concorde-like fascia, hides a double compact disc player *and* a double cassette player. Something no other electronics company in the world has managed to pull off.

Also, recording both CD-to-tape and tape-to-tape is controlled by Sanyo's new One Touch System.

To record, all you have to do is load the tape (one job we aren't able to help you with) and press the Computer Recording button.

And should you want to skip tracks just push another button for Automatic Music Scan.

But what are all those other controls? We thought you'd ask.

Look carefully and you'll spot a 5-band graphic equaliser. An FM/AM tuner. And for people who don't mind waking up to something ugly, there's even a sleep/alarm automatic timer.

Packed with all these features, it is hardly surprising that our claims of portability have been met with groans. (Not least by the people who have tried picking the machine up.)

So what will you be asked to fork out for this monster? A mere £599.

Which may seem a lot for a machine which isn't exactly an oil painting. But given that it's burglar proof, we think it's definitely a steal. SANYO

25

When you watch the video of your daughter's wedding, does it make you cry?

Where comes the bride? As you settle down to relive your daughter's big day on your video, it's a question you may well ask yourself.

And with good reason. Chances are, you will be watching a picture that's out of focus, badly lit and as jittery as the bridegroom.

Because the trouble with nearly all camcorders around today is that they simply don't deliver the kind of picture quality the glossy publicity brochures and silver-tongued salesmen promise they will.

Why is this?

Well, it probably has a lot to do with the out of date technology that most manufacturers are still using. Most manufacturers, that is, apart from one: Sanyo.

According to an article in the Wall Street Journal, we're way ahead of the field, particularly in the use of digital technology.

Take the new Sanyo VEM S1P, for instance. Not only is it extremely light and compact, it also features something called Digital Auto Focus.

On the Sanyo, instead of focusing on the first thing in its sights, Digital Auto Focus uses a microcomputer and a six image screen system to ensure that small, fast-moving even indistinct background objects are clearly defined.

So should you want to record the bride arriving at church and she's behind the limousine window, the focus will compensate for the glass and give you a daughter to be proud of.

Digital technology doesn't only enhance the focusing. It improves the lighting as well.

Sanyo's Digital Auto Iris automatically compensates for imperfect shooting conditions, when the light is too bright, for example, ensuring that you always get a properly exposed picture.

This function also allows you to shoot outside the church, where hopefully the sun will be shining, then move inside the church without having to resort to the backlight compensation switch you'll find on most other camcorders.

But if this isn't enough to make an honest man say 'I Do', there's even *more*.

Like a 1/1000 of a second shutter speed so you can film fast moving objects, such as the wedding car speeding away.

A power focus capable of going from telescopic to wide angle and a macro zoom function so you can come in close and capture smaller objects like the bride's bouquet.

And to add a final professional touch to your home videos there's a Fade In/Fade Out button, which allows you to fade the sound and the picture at the same time.

At £800, the Sanyo VEM S1P certainly is a most innovative camcorder.

And even if it's a little more than you wanted to pay, we reckon it's worth it.

After all, you'll probably shed enough tears at the wedding itself, without crying your eyes out all the way through the video.

SANYO

22, 23, 24, 25
Sanyo audio and video equipment
United Kingdom
Agency: The Leagas Delaney Partnership, London

The copy is the main thing in these ads, two of which ('Lazy? Stupid?' and 'It's ugly') were written by agency partner Tim Delaney. The 'Lazy? Stupid?' headline refers to the simplicity with which the VHR 5240E video recorder can be programmed. 'It's ugly' sits over a text that declares that what the MCD950F portable stereo system lacks in looks, it makes up for in performance. 'No sex please' refers to the special function in a Sanyo CPB 2552 TV set enabling parents to prevent children from tuning in to any particular channel. The 'Your daughter's wedding' ad concerns the alleged superior focusing of the VEM S1P camcorder over others that produce blurred pictures.

26, 27
Philips car stereo equipment
United Kingdom
Agency: Ogilvy & Mather, London

Strong and relevant images drive home the sales messages. The LSO (London Symphony Orchestra) can be 'fitted perfectly' into a tiny car by means of a Philips compact disk player. Wide frequency loudspeakers enable the driver to hear very high and very low frequency signals on a car stereo and thus remove the gags from singers whose voices are not properly reproduced by less sensitive equipment.

26

27

Con i videoregistratori professionali Grundig, i perfezionisti vedono ciò che volevano.

Cari pignoloni, avete finalmente trovato quello che cercavate da sempre: il SuperVHS Grundig. Oltre ad avere tutto ciò che potete chiedere, il VS 680VPT e il camcorder S-VS180 riproducono con una nitidezza impressionante anche particolari molto sottili e altrimenti invisibili; possono infatti lavorare con il nuovo sistema nato dal VHS per migliorare la qualità delle immagini. Quelle che otterrete potranno essere elaborate dal videoregistratore qui riprodotto più e meglio che da qualsiasi altro. Nessuno, infatti, ha la sua memoria digitale. L'audio è stereo e hi-fi: per avere un'incisione impeccabile potete regolarlo manualmente, e sonorizzare quel che volete con il miscelatore incorporato. Quando fate un montaggio, la settima testina vi permette degli inserimenti senza disturbi anche su scene preesistenti. Un nuovo sistema, con decodificatore teletext ad alta capacità, porta il Televideo su qualunque televisore e semplifica ancora di più la programmazione automatica delle registrazioni. La titolatrice vi offre, oltre a trentanove caratteri, la possibilità di elaborarli. E il telecomando pieghevole pilota sia il decodificatore che la titolatrice. Insomma: qualsiasi confronto possiate fare, il SuperVHS Grundig lo vincerà (e non certo per un pelo).

GRUNDIG

28

Finora, solo un miracolo poteva farvi vedere due programmi alla volta.

Molti vi avevano promesso due immagini sullo stesso schermo (tacendo che fosse indispensabile l'ausilio di un altro apparecchio). Poi, è arrivato il nuovo Jumbo Grundig M95 S/PiP: il primo televisore ad avere due sintonizzatori. Solo le sue dimensioni, d'altronde, permettono di sfruttarli adeguatamente: quando sul cinescopio da trentasette pollici fate comparire un secondo programma in formato minore, lo vedete comunque grande come su una TV portatile. Potete ingrandirlo a tutto schermo premendo il tasto di inversione. Spostare l'immagine ridotta nei quattro angoli. Incorniciarla in sette colori. Fermarvi su un fotogramma. Ricevere trasmissioni in Pal, Secam e Ntsc. Collegarvi anche a videoregistratori e telecamere che usano il nuovo sistema SuperVHS. O scegliere, se volete, l'altro Jumbo della serie S/PiP: trentadue i pollici, M82 il nome. Nel caso vogliate saperne di più, venite a parlarne con un rivenditore Grundig: a quattr'occhi ci si intende meglio.

GRUNDIG

29

28
Grundig video recorder
Italy
Agency: Bozell e Associati, Milan
The Italian saying 'To look for a hair in an egg' refers to the obsessive search for perfection. This ad says 'Thanks to Grundig's professional video recorders, perfectionists can see all they want'.

29
Grundig M95 S/PiP TV set
Italy
Agency: Bozell e Associati, Milan
The product is claimed to be the first TV set which can be tuned to two channels simultaneously, with one picture viewed in a frame inside the other. Copy says 'Up till now only a miracle could let you see two programmes at once'. This provides the excuse for showing St Lucy, an early Christian martyr believed to protect those with eye trouble. She is represented holding a dish containing her eyes, which according to legend were torn out after she refused to break a vow of virginity.

30
Grundig portable TV set
Italy
Agency: Bozell e Associati, Milan
The sexy picture is accompanied by a punning copy line that means both 'What are people wearing this summer?' and 'What are people carrying this summer?'

31
Toshiba C3 TV
Hong Kong
Agency: Ball WCRS Partnership, Hong Kong
A neat visual device backs up the message about a static-free screen.

Cosa si porta
quest'estate?
Portatili
GRUNDIG

30

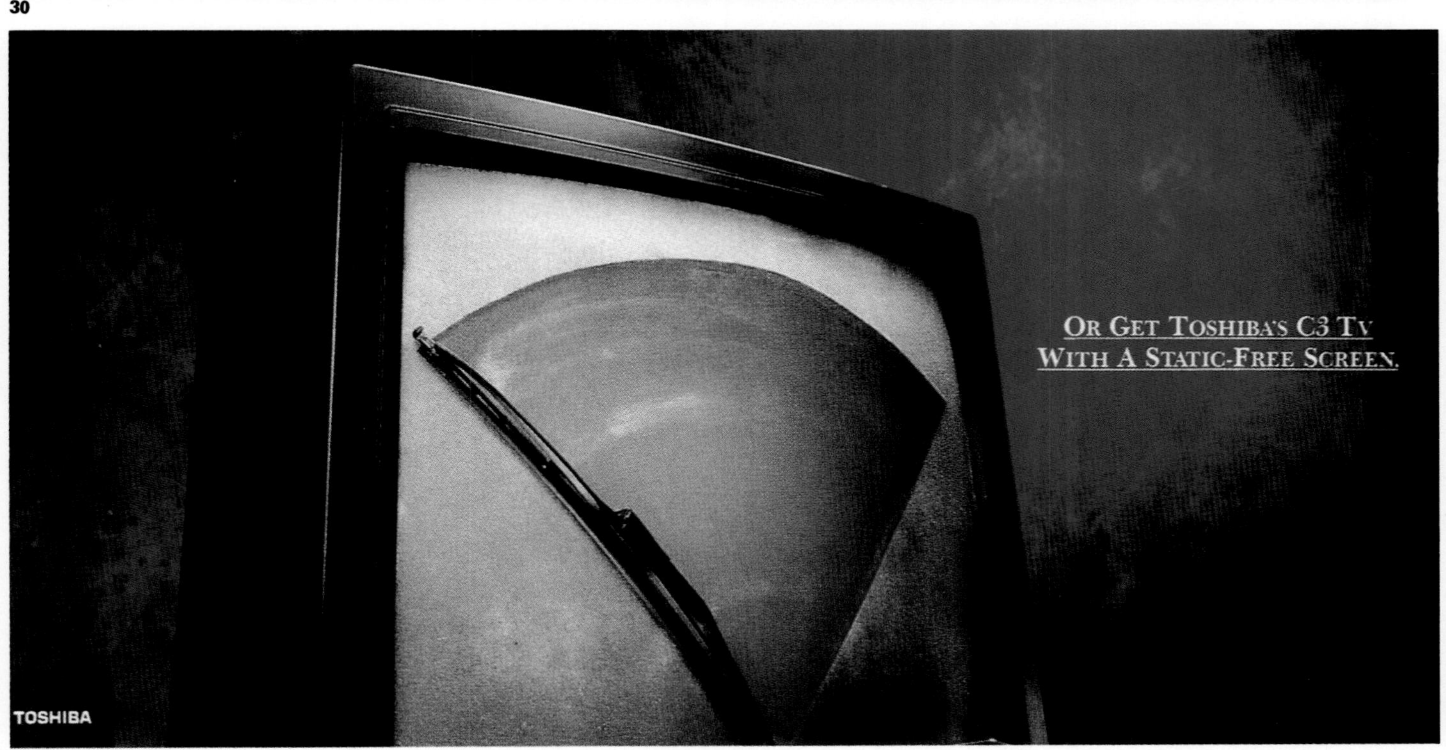
OR GET TOSHIBA'S C3 TV
WITH A STATIC-FREE SCREEN.
TOSHIBA

31

32

33

32, 33
Maxell audio tapes
United Kingdom
Agency: Howell Henry Chaldecott Lury, London
This much admired campaign shows men holding sets of boards on which are written nonsense phrases resembling the words of pop songs. In each commercial, as a song is sung, a man is seen discarding his boards one by one until he reaches the last two boards saying 'I think that's what he says' and 'But I need to hear it on a Maxell'.

34
Vivivideo video cassettes
Italy
Agency: Bozell e Associati, Milan
'With Vivivideo you'll find out life isn't just a film' says this ad. That is because the product range includes cassettes devoted to science, sport, art and other subjects as well.

35, 36
Solidaire TV sets
India
Agency: Insight, Madras
Unusual and skilful combinations of real leaves and petals and drawn living creatures translate the campaign slogan into memorable visual terms.

34

NATURA
SPORT
MUSICA
CINEMA
MANUALISTICA
EDUCAZIONALE
FANTASIA
ARTE

Con Vivivideo scopri che la vita non è solo un film.

Il vostro videoregistratore sta per entrare nell'età della cultura.

Da oggi potete soddisfare le sue passioni artistiche e coltivare i suoi hobby preferiti.

Dovete solo sedervi in poltrona, scegliere una cassetta Vivivideo e viaggiare col telecomando e con la fantasia.

Potete scegliere tra i tanti titoli del cinema, con capolavori di ogni genere e generi di tutti i colori: dal giallo al rosa, dalla commedia all'horror. Ma potete anche avventurarvi nel mondo della cultura, della scienza, dello spettacolo.

A vostra disposizione, nuove straordinarie serie di videocassette dedicate all'arte, alla natura, allo sport, al fai-da-te, alla didattica e al mondo del fantasy. Non è solo un volo della fantasia, è la realtà di Vivivideo.

Se fosse una favola potremmo chiamarla la scelta infinita.

VIVIVIDEO
CINEMA, CULTURA, SPETTACOLO.

Solidaire adds life. To colour.

Yes, in fact Solidaire adds a new dimension to everything it does.
To give you the extraordinary. Everytime.
With an eye for detail, painstaking efforts for perfection, and years of R&D. And a sheer commitment to excellence.
Which is what earned Solidaire international recognition. In the form of large export orders for colour TVs from leading East European, Middle East and African countries.
As the final touch, Solidaire also believes in adding one more thing to your viewing pleasure: value.
So that you get a value-added, value-based product. Everytime.

Solidaire TV

35

Solidaire adds life. To colour.

Yes, in fact Solidaire adds a new dimension to everything it does.
To give you the extraordinary. Everytime.
With an eye for detail, painstaking efforts for perfection, and years of R&D. And a sheer commitment to excellence.
Which is what earned Solidaire international recognition. In the form of large export orders for colour TVs from leading East European, Middle East and African countries.
As the final touch, Solidaire also believes in adding one more thing to your viewing pleasure: value.
So that you get a value-added, value-based product. Everytime.

Solidaire TV

36

37

38

VOM PORSCHEFAHREN
»Nicht nur über den Wolken kann die Freiheit grenzenlos sein.«

Ein Porsche 911 Cabriolet vereint das Erlebnis des Porsche- wie des Cabriofahrens auf vollendete Weise. Wer pure Faszination und grenzenlose Freiheit sucht, sollte diesen Porsche kennenlernen, bei dem begeisternde Sinneseindrücke und unvergleichliches Fahrvergnügen inklusiv sind. Auch gelegentliche Eintrübungen können dem keinen Abbruch tun: Auf Wunsch gibt es jetzt für das Porsche 911 Carrera Cabriolet ein Faltverdeck, das sich elektrisch öffnet und schließt, einfach auf Tastendruck. Hatten Sie nicht noch immer einen besonderen Wunsch offen?

PORSCHE
FAHREN IN SEINER SCHÖNSTEN FORM

39

VOM PORSCHEFAHREN
»Vom Unterschied zwischen funktionalem und überflüssigem Luxus.«

Eine Langstreckenfahrt im Porsche 928 S4, und der Unterschied ist klar: Sogar nach mehreren hundert Kilometern werden Sie den Fahrersitz erstaunlich ausgeruht verlassen. Nichts Überflüssiges lenkt vom Genuß des Fahrens ab. Der Porsche fährt sich wie ein Einzelstück nach Maß, so genau lassen sich Sitz und Bedienungselemente auf Sie einstellen: Es ist eben nicht nur die sportliche Faszination des 928 S4, die deutlich auf die Herkunft dieses Wagens hinweist. Beratung, Probefahrt und Leasing-Angebote: Bitte schicken Sie Ihre Visitenkarte an die Dr. Ing. h. c. F. Porsche AG, Verkaufsleitung Inland, Postfach 1108, 7140 Ludwigsburg.

PORSCHE
FAHREN IN SEINER SCHÖNSTEN FORM

37
Porsche 944 S2
United Kingdom
Agency: The Leagas Delaney Partnership, London
Copy explains how the car's air management system prevents it from being lifted off the ground at speed.

38, 39
Porsche Cabriolet 911 and 928 S4
West Germany
Agency: Wensauer & Partner, Ludwigsburg
Nicely photographed by Dietmar Henneka, these two ads are headed respectively 'Not only above the clouds can freedom be unbounded' (the seaside mountain scene, fronted by a Porsche Cabriolet 911) and 'Concerning the difference between functional and superfluous luxury'. Functional luxury is – of course! – what a Porsche has.

40

When driving and road conditions are beyond even the driver's ability, the Galant itself takes control to offer comfortable drive at every stage. Simply another facet of Mitsubishi Motors' easy-drive philosophy at work. The dynamic performance offered by Mitsubishi's superior 4WD technology, coupled with the beautiful flowing bodylines, our so-called "Organic Styling", symbolize truly pleasant and comfortable driving. Only Japanese craftsmanship can offer driving performance which is perfectly in tune with our innermost sensibilities.

40
Mitsubishi cars
Japan
Studio: Takayuki Itoh Design Office, Tokyo
One of a series of attractive posters, using human movements as analogies for motoring performance. They make garments, rather than cars, look beautiful.

41
Ford Transit
United Kingdom
Agency: Ogilvy & Mather, London
The ad is really selling Ford Transit vans. However, by printing the story of 24 hours in the life of an ambulance version of the same vehicle, it gets its message of reliability across in an interesting and attractive manner.

41

You can depend on a Ford Transit Ambulance right around the clock.

2200 HOURS: Crew change. Full vehicle and kit inspection.

2207 HOURS: Call out to an overdose. Arrive Manchester Royal Infirmary (MRI) 2235 hours.

2240 HOURS: Return to station.

2244 HOURS: Call out to a second overdose. Arrive MRI 2300 hours.

2310 HOURS: Return to station.

2312 HOURS: Call to transfer maternity flying squad from St. Mary's Hospital to Birch Hill Hospital, Rochdale.

Arrive Birch Hill 0015. Return to St. Mary's 0143.

0204 HOURS: Return to station for a half-hour meal break.

0304 HOURS: Call to alcohol overdose. Patient did not require hospitalization.

0323 HOURS: Return to station.

0511 HOURS: Call to female haemorrhaging. Arrive MRI 0531 hours.

0537 HOURS: Return to station.

0545 HOURS: Clean vehicle.

0600 HOURS: Crew change. Full vehicle and kit inspection.

0743 HOURS: Call to Road Traffic Accident (RTA). 51 year old female with head injuries and suspected fractured leg.

0833 HOURS: Return to station.

0943 HOURS: Call to elderly man fallen out of bed. Arrive at scene 1002. Patient did not require hospitalization.

En-route back to station called to bank robbery. Four patients taken to MRI suffering from effects of ammonia fumes.

Arrive hospital 1032. Crew receive treatment at hospital for effects of ammonia.
Take a half-hour break. Leave MRI 1145.

1153 HOURS: Return to station.

1231 HOURS: Full alert – airport. Plane with failed light on landing gear.
Arrive rendezvous point at airport 1243.
Stand down 1305.

1327 HOURS: Return to station.

1350 HOURS: Vehicle cleaned.

1400 HOURS: Crew change. Full vehicle and kit inspection.

1438 HOURS: Call to fall in city centre. Female with possible fractured femur.

Arrive at MRI 1500 hours.

1521 HOURS: Return to station.

1531 HOURS: Call out to man with respiratory problems. Arrive at MRI 1609.

1619 HOURS: En-route back to station diverted to RTA. Van involved in collision with cement mixer.

Arrive at MRI 1742. Hand patient over, clean vehicle and check equipment.

1843 HOURS: Return to station.

1848 HOURS: Call to a 70 year old man with angina.

Arrive at Withington Hospital 1921 hours.

1953 HOURS: Return to station.

2032 HOURS: Call to an assault. Female with lacerations and abrasions to face.
Arrive MRI 2034 hours.

2038 HOURS: Return to station.

2145 HOURS: Clean out vehicle.

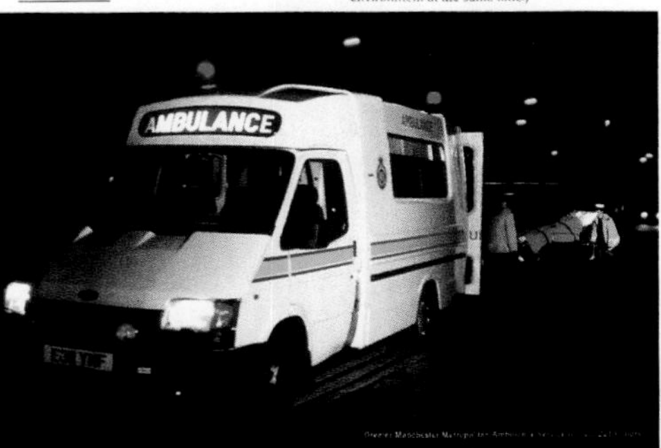

There were over thirty eight front-line runs – it was a typical day.

The 2.5* litre Direct Injection Diesel coped admirably, just like the 2.0* litre petrol we usually drive.

When the new 2.9 litre models arrive they will help us to achieve even better response times.

The new five-speed gear boxes, which are now on all engines, are also a great help when fighting through busy traffic. And the new high-support seats stop your back taking all the stick, especially on long shifts like today.

They've even refined the suspension to give the patients a more comfortable ride on those bumpier routes – this also allows us to carry more life-saving equipment.

(As both the 2.0 and 2.9 litre engines will be running on unleaded petrol, we'll be able to save the environment at the same time.)

But the best thing about the Ford is that you feel it can take the punishment, especially when it's backed up by a fast spares network that makes sure it keeps working.

After all, when people's lives depend on you turning up, it's comforting to know that you can depend on a Ford not to let you down.

2200 HOURS: Crew change.

Lady
with dalmatian
seen from
the window of
a Volkswagen
Corrado.

42

Policeman
with bicycle
seen from
the window of
a Volkswagen
Corrado.

43

44

42, 43
Volkswagen Corrado
United Kingdom
Agency: BMP DDB Needham, London
Lester Bookbinder's hilarious photographs, illustrating the speed of the Corrado, are in line with the high standard of creative work the agency has been achieving for Volkswagen.

44
Motorcraft service centre
United Kingdom
Agency: Ogilvy & Mather, London
One of a series denigrating independent mechanics as dishonest and unreliable.

45
Volkswagen competition
United Kingdom
Agency: BMP DDB Needham, London
The car pictured is an old VW Beetle, but the competition prize offered is a new Golf. The competition, stated to be open to anyone who ever owned a VW car or is due to take delivery of one, requires entrants to guess when Beetles first appeared in Britain. 'Beetlemania' is, of course, a punning reference to the cult of the Beatles pop group. Artfully contrived to grab the attention of the 'flower power' generation.

Remember Beetlemania?

Remember the heady days of flower power?

Remember all those freaky trips?

In your Volkswagen Beetle, of course.

True, it may not have been the hairiest car around.

But, for many, it really was the fab four wheels.

Well, if you're into free festivals, you could soon be getting into something else.

A free Volkswagen Golf CL.

And not just any new Golf but the two millionth Volkswagen in Britain.

Cosmic.

To take part in the competition, just complete the entry form.

You can enter if you've ever owned a Volkswagen or if you're due to take delivery of one before the end of August.

The car is actually blue but also, in a way, green.

It comes complete with a catalytic converter.

Because we still cleave stubbornly to that old hippie notion that the world is a beautiful place.

In fact, very soon we hope to be able to offer a ready-converted version of every model in our range.

Could any yogi bear to be without one?

46

47

46, 47
Fiat Uno
Germany, Netherlands, Belgium, Austria
Agency: Michael Conrad & Leo Burnett, Frankfurt

Something of a sex sell going on here, but done in a pleasingly imaginative way. The headlines are respectively 'Profile new? Logical' and, over the painted lady, 'Rear new? Logical'.

48, 49
Fiat motor oil
Italy
Agency: Bozell e Associati, Milan

'In the last 75 years it's not just engines that have come a long way' says the headline on the ad comparing a 1912 can of Fiat oil with a modern one. One may question, however, whether any progress has been made in the standard of on-can illustration. The other ad is headed 'The most frequently opened can in Italy after Coca-Cola'. Not a mere empty boast. Fiat is brand leader in the country's lubricating oil market.

50
Peugeot scooters
France
Agency: Young & Rubicam, Paris

The press version of a TV ad that is not so much sexy as impudent. Headline: 'Life is so beautiful when one has time to gaze at nature's stirring sights'. Sign-off: 'Peugeot scooters. A unique view of the city.'

51
Dunlop tyres
Australia
Agency: Campaign Palace, Melbourne

Unlike the British commercial for Pirelli (no. 63), this ad does not say 'gripping stuff', but the magnets make exactly the same point. It would be tedious to point out that, with magnets in place of tyres, a car would not get very far.

52
BMW financing
France
Agency: BDDP, Paris

Interesting. Looking – and reading – almost like a fashion ad, this one pitches directly at the woman car-buyer. The picture is captioned 'This morning I bought a little co-ordinated outfit: a car with matching insurance and maintenance'. Copy says BMW is the first car-maker to offer such a financial package.

53
BMW Series 3
France
Agency: BDDP, Paris

The teddy bear is meant not to reassure adults about child safety but to remind them of the comfort of their own childhood cradles. Headline: 'If the gentle sensations of the cradle seem to you a little hazy, sitting in a BMW may refresh your memory'.

48

La lattina più aperta in Italia dopo Coca-Cola.

Rispondete senza pensarci troppo: che olio c'è nella coppa del vostro motore? Forse non lo sapete, ma c'è una probabilità su quattro che si tratti di un prodotto della Fiat Lubrificanti. E ci sono buone probabilità che anche i vostri freni, le vostre trasmissioni, i vostri giunti, i vostri cuscinetti, i vostri radiatori siano protetti da oli, fluidi, grassi e liquidi antigelo, antiruggine e anticorrosione della Fiat Lubrificanti. Perché Fiat Lubrificanti è il numero uno, in Italia, in questo settore. Ed è, per dimensioni e organizzazione, una vera multinazionale che esporta in 35 paesi, grazie a 75 anni di ricerca, sperimentazione e produzione a stretto contatto con la Fiat: una che di motori se ne intende. Qualunque sia il vostro veicolo - automobile, furgone, camion o trattore. Fiat o non Fiat - fatevi aprire le nostre lattine o i nostri bidoni, la prossima volta che avete bisogno di manutenzione. Perché tutto vada come desiderate.

Fiat Lubrificanti
E tutto va.

49

50

51

POUR LA 1ᴱᴿ FOIS, UN CONSTRUCTEUR PROPOSE LA VOITURE, LE FINANCEMENT, L'ASSURANCE ET L'ENTRETIEN DANS UN SEUL CONTRAT : FINANCE 3.

"Ce matin, j'ai acheté un petit ensemble coordonné : la voiture avec l'assurance et l'entretien assortis."

52

Si les douces impressions du berceau vous paraissent un peu floues, s'installer à bord d'une BMW peut vous rafraichir la mémoire.

Ce sentiment de sécurité, de confort, de plaisir que vous ressentiez jadis dans votre berceau. Cette facilité déconcertante avec laquelle vous saisissiez les petits objets que vos parents avaient placés tout autour de vous. Retrouvez toutes ces douces impressions à bord d'une BMW 325 i. Tout d'abord le poste de pilotage est exclusivement tourné vers vous. Toute possibilité de confusion entre les différentes fonctions est exclue. Comme dans un couffin, il faut être installé le plus confortablement possible. L'assise et le dossier sont parfaitement anatomiques. Les garnissages textile ou cuir garantissent une atmosphère cossue et totalement silencieuse. Après le confort, il faut maintenant parler sécurité : sur la 325 i, l'ABS est de série. De plus, en un seul coup d'œil, l'indicateur de maintenance vous précise l'échéance des prochaines révisions et c'est en fonction de votre façon de conduire qu'il la calcule. Ainsi équipée et avec la qualité des matériaux utilisés, la Série 3 vous bercera pendant longtemps. Le modèle photographié peut comporter des options.

Si vous désirez des informations ou un rendez-vous d'essai Série 3, vous pouvez nous contacter au (1) 45 54 20 39.

SERIE 3
AUCUNE VOITURE N'EST PENSEE COMME UNE BMW

53

THE CASE FOR OWNING A 210KPH ALFA ROMEO IN A 110KPH WORLD.

Over the past two decades car engines have dramatically increased in efficiency. Power output per litre of fuel has gone up and petrol consumption and pollution have plummeted.

Alfa Romeo have been at the forefront of this research. Today the Alfa 75 is one of the world's most advanced production cars.

Its 2 litre engine is the most powerful of its type. A fuel-injected twin-overhead-cam four, it uses 2 plugs per cylinder and a world-patented, electronically-controlled camshaft timing variator to optimise torque, deliver more horse power and increase fuel economy.

Car Australia wrote . . . "to say the Alfa's engine sets a new benchmark in the normally aspirated two litre category is no exaggeration." And when powered by the Alfa 3 litre engine BMW described as 'wonderful', the 75 is capable of awesome performance.

As such even at 110kph an Alfa 75 is using barely half its power. So running costs are miserly, wear and tear is much reduced, service intervals are extended and reliability is enormously enhanced.

Alfa 75s are also made special by unique styling. High performance superbly appointed luxury sports saloons, they have rare aerodynamic efficiency and amazing road holding.

Financially too the Alfa 75s have no competition. At $39,090 rrp* for the Twin Spark and $49,288 rrp* for the 3-litre, they are exceptional value for money. And being Alfas, as a recent study showed, their depreciation will be notably better than most of their competitors.

Alfa 75s then not only reflect rare individuality but also unusual astuteness. They are cars for demanding drivers. And for demanding times.

ALFA ROMEO

PERFORMANCE. STRENGTH. STYLE.

54

54
Alfa Romeo 75
Australia
Agency: Brand Management, Sydney

Most of us believe that the reason for owning a 210kph car in a 110kph world is to indulge the owner's vanity. No, says the body copy of this ad, 'at 110kph an Alfa 75 is using barely half its power. So running costs are miserly, wear and tear is much reduced, service intervals are extended and reliability is enormously enhanced.' So now we know.

55
Toyota
United Kingdom
Agency: Collett Dickenson Pearce & Partners, London

The car is pictured in an 'old Zen garden'. Copy emphasises that 'Even the best can always be improved'. One man's Zen philosophy is another's sales patter.

WHY WE'LL NEVER MAKE A PERFECT CAR.

"If perfection could be attained, it would not be worth having."

The car in the old Zen garden is a Toyota Supra Turbo: voted What Car?'s Coupe of the Year in 1989.

If it attracts you, by all means compare its performance figures with those of other famous sports cars.

But far more important, in our view, is the attitude that went into its making: a way of looking at things that owes much to Zen.

Thus, on our assembly lines you'll see total concentration, minute attention to detail.

But most importantly, a refusal to accept that there's such a thing as perfection. Even the best can always be improved.

Fine words. To turn them into reality we spend £1 billion a year on research and development.

Toyota have won the Japanese Society of Mechanical Engineers' Award for engine design four years in a row.

We pioneered the multivalve engine.

Today, every Toyota passenger car has one of these deep-chested engines, which can also run on lead-free petrol.

We were the first to introduce catalytic converters to this country.

So cleanly does the Supra Turbo run that its platinum spark plugs need changing only once every 60,000 miles.

We're just as pernickety about build-quality. Some leading marques proudly advertise that their cars are made from galvanised steel.

Galvanised is not good enough for us. Its zinc coating tends to flake when the metal is folded at the factory.

So we developed galvannealed steel. Exclusive to Toyota, it's every bit as effective against rust but not prone to flaking.

Still not satisfied, we patented Excelite, a multi-layered ferro-zinc steel which offers unsurpassed rust protection.

The pursuit of perfection means thinking about every aspect of a car's construction.

Even the sound the doors make. (Each Toyota factory has a panel of experts who do nothing but tune doors till they make the perfect clunk.)

BMW once ran an advertisement saying that one of their cars carried 134lbs of sound proofing to ensure a quiet ride.

At Toyota, instead of making a noisy car quiet, we'd rather make a quiet car.

So in an effort to achieve the sound of one hand clapping, we refine shapes and fine-tune engines until the cars whisper.

We literally design noise out. The weight thus saved can go where, for safety's sake, it is most needed – into the chassis.

Toyotas have other safety touches that several manufacturers seem to have overlooked.

Ram scoops to suck in fresh air: even when the heating is on you can still have cool air on your face.

For ages now rear seat belts have been standard on all our cars, and anti-lock braking on many.

That's enough things you never knew about Toyotas. (Call 0800 300 700 free, for more details, tax-free sales and your local dealer's address.)

One thing you don't need telling about Toyotas is how reliable they are.

So let us return to the Supra Turbo. What do you imagine this near perfect machine should cost?

As a benchmark, consider that the Supra accelerates from 0-60mph faster than a Ferrari 328 GTB.

We don't say this to demean the Ferrari which, as anybody who has driven one can affirm, is a beautiful car.

Just to point out that our no less beautiful car is about £25,000 less expensive. Even the price is perfection.

Well, near perfection.

TOYOTA

56

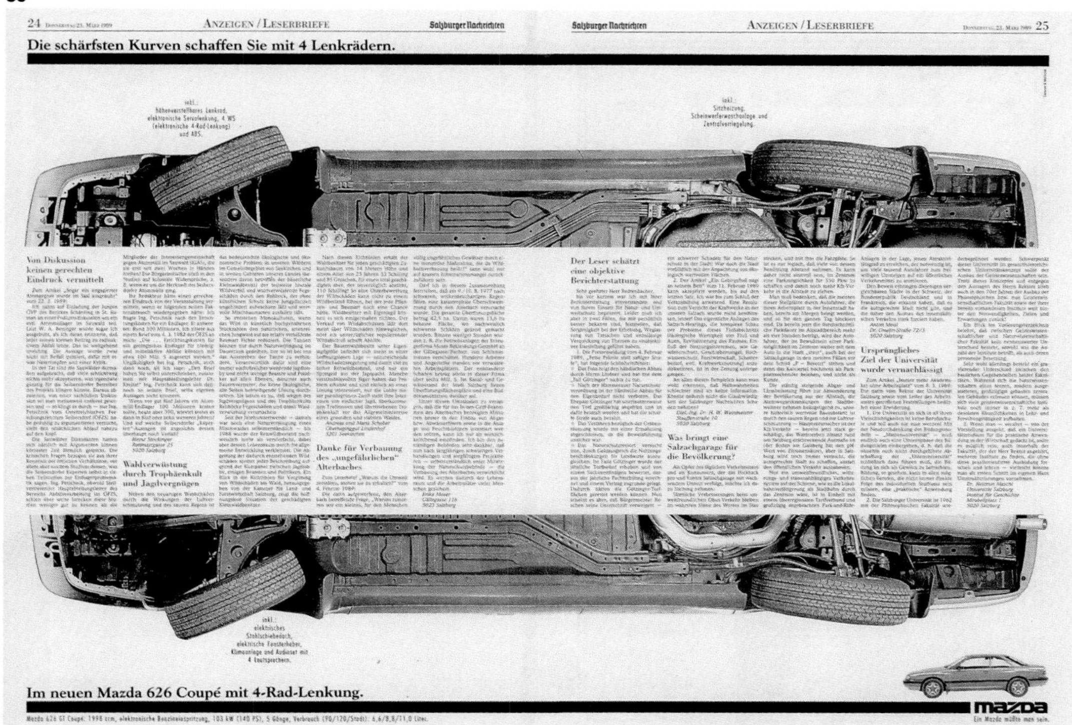

56
Mazda 626
Austria
Agency: Demner & Merlicek, Vienna

The most striking thing about this ad is the unusual use of newspaper space, with the car chassis divided by readers' letters to the *Salzburger Nachrichten* newspaper. The ad is headed 'With four steering wheels you master the sharpest bends'. The underside view of the car helps to make the technical point.

58
Mazda 121
Switzerland
Agency: Advico Young & Rubicam, Zürich

That 'at a price of 12,990 Swiss francs, the Mazda 121 is almost a gift' is only half the truth, says body copy. The rest of the truth concerns the car's 1.3 litre engine, outstanding fuel economy etc. The half-of-the-truth notion is graphically illustrated by printing what looks like only half of an ad.

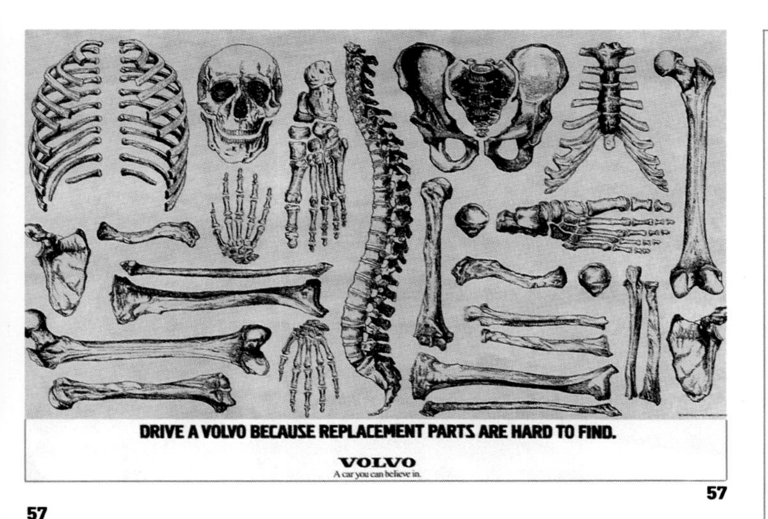

57

57
Volvo cars
USA
Agency: Scali McCabe Sloves, New York

Unnecessary to show a car in this very witty, but hard hitting, ad, which majors on Volvo's reputation for safety.

Die Preise für den Mazda 121 können sich sehen lassen: der I. kostet Sie nur

Der Mazda 121 für Fr. 12 halb geschen

Es ist nur die halbe Wahrheit, der Mazda 121 sei für 12 990 Franken schon fast geschenkt. Die ganze ist, dass Sie dafür einen 1,3-Liter-Motor, fünf Gänge, eine Strassenlage wie bei einem Grossen, dafür einen Verbrauch mit 6 Litern auf 100 Kilometern wie bei einem Kleinen, mehr Parkplätze, da mit 3,475 m Länge das Parkproblem halt kleiner ist, sechs getönte Scheiben, viel Platz, dazu noch was es sonst zu einc Auto braucht, und das a schön verp bekomme Weil Si jetzt bestir am Mazda doppelt interessiert sin sollten Sie in den nächs Tagen bei Ihrem Mazda

58

The submarine will rust before the Audi.

59

The Audi Avant.
Light enough to be carried by a helicopter.
Strong enough to carry one.

60

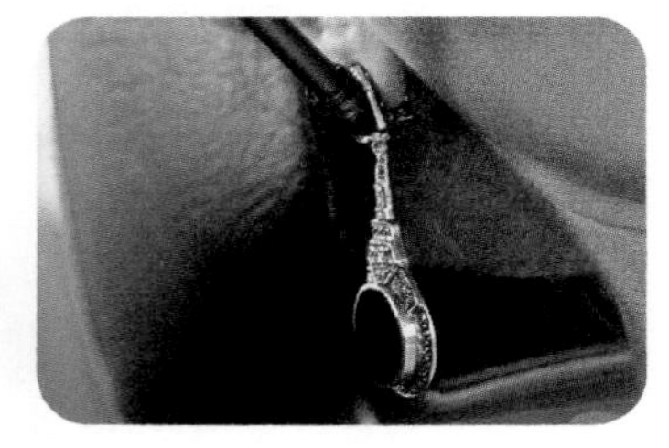

61

61
Volkswagen Golf
United Kingdom
Agency: BMP DDB Needham, London
John Webster, long-time creative supremo of Boase Massimi Pollitt, takes both the art directing and copywriting credits in this amusing film. Webster must relish the chance of working on Volkswagen, formerly the jewel in the crown of Doyle Dane Bernbach before it lost its independence. Like the Passat film, it applies a very human touch to the sales message 'If only everything in life was as reliable as a Volkswagen'.

The sun rises above the bare hills of southern Spain. One by one the night inhabitants of the road leave, sensing danger. The cicada urgently. The tumble weed gently. The snake reluctantly. ***Audio:*** SFX: *Squeak squeak throughout.*

A plume of dust on the horizon confirms their foresight. The Golf GTi approaches driven hard over the rough road. Inside the young man is worried. There are bits of streamer on his DJ. His bow tie is loosened. It was a good party. The girl asleep beside him still looks like a million dollars. Fabulous dress and jewellery. But all he can think about is the squeak. He hunts high and low. The mirror, the lighter, the ashtray. Volkswagens don't squeak. And yet it persists. Somewhere close. Door handle? Sliding roof? – It's driving him mad.

A sign hanging ahead says 'garage'. It's a place forgotten by time. A rusty antique pump, a shack at the back, lots of junk, chickens. ***Audio:*** SFX: *Squeak stops.*

Through the window the young man wakes an old old man. He explains about the squeak. The old man comes to the car with a huge oil gun that looks as if it was meant for locomotives. He sees it is a Volkswagen and scratches his head. There must be some mistake. Volkswagens don't squeak. The young man knows that, but when he rocks the car it's there sure enough. The old man is puzzled. ***Audio:*** SFX: *Squeak squeak.*

Suddenly he lights up.

He opens the door and leans across to the girl still asleep. Gently he flicks her large pendulum earring, it swings and there it is. He laughs. ***Audio:*** SFX: *Squeak squeak.*

Delicate as a surgeon, he applies a single drop to the earring. He flicks it again. Silence.

He stands by the road holding the oil can laughing as the car disappears. Ha ha, I know about life, Volkswagens don't squeak. If only everything in life was as reliable as a Volkswagen. Suddenly the squeak returns. The smile disappears from his face. He looks up. It's his sign blown by the first breath of wind of the morning. ***Audio:*** SFX: *Squeak squeak.*

59, 60
Audi
United Kingdom
Agency: Bartle Bogle Hegarty, London

The submarine and the helicopter make a great change from most print advertising for cars.

62
Volkswagen Passat
United Kingdom
Agency: BMP DDB Needham, London

Not an American film, though shot in New York by director Tony Kaye. It's a beautifully made vignette, in grainy black and white, of a little girl overawed by the sights and sounds of midtown Manhattan. She is rescued from the urban maelstrom by a Passat. One of the most lauded UK commercials of the last couple of years, it was made by a creative team including Tony Cox, creative director of the agency formed from the merger of Boase Massimi Pollitt and DDB Needham. The latter was itself the result of a merger, between Doyle Dane Bernbach and Needham Harper.

62

1. **Visual:** A little girl . . .

2. . . . gripping her daddy's hand in the middle of the urban chaos of Manhattan. ***Audio:*** *Horns honking, sirens screaming, then Billie Holliday starts singing 'God Bless The Child'.*

3. **Visual:** (Cut): Close up of some lunatic pestering passers-by with his feverish visions of the imminent end of the world.

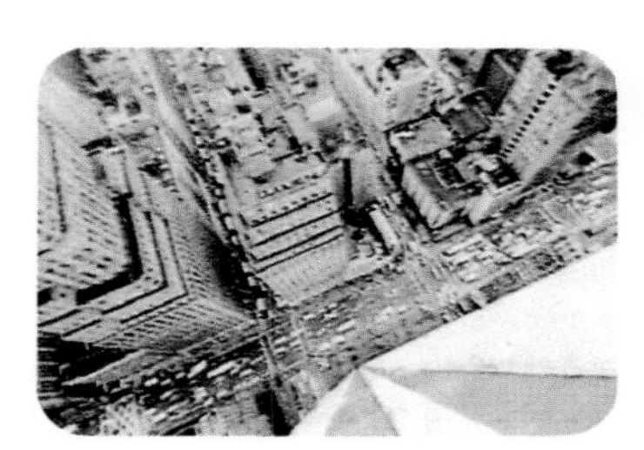

4. (Cut) Cut to bird's eye view of the streets of Manhattan.

5. (Cut) Some suspects are arrested by the police.

6, 7. (Cut) The little girl takes all this in, all the while growing more and more bewildered.

8. (Cut) Bird's eye view of streets is superimposed on the girl's face.

9. Cut to skyscrapers from her perspective.

10. (Cut) But relief from the urban nightmare is at hand. A VW Passat pulls up . . .

11. (Cut) . . . the girl's mother at the wheel.

12. (Cut) Confidently she manoeuvres the car through the rush-hour traffic.

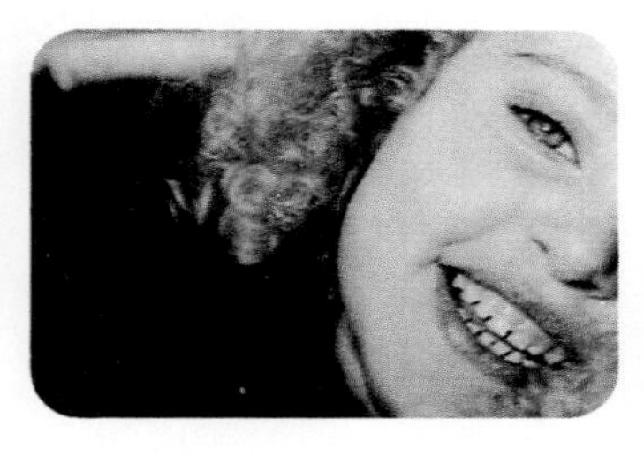

13. (Cut) Buckled up on the child's seat in the back of the car, the little girl feels now at ease again.

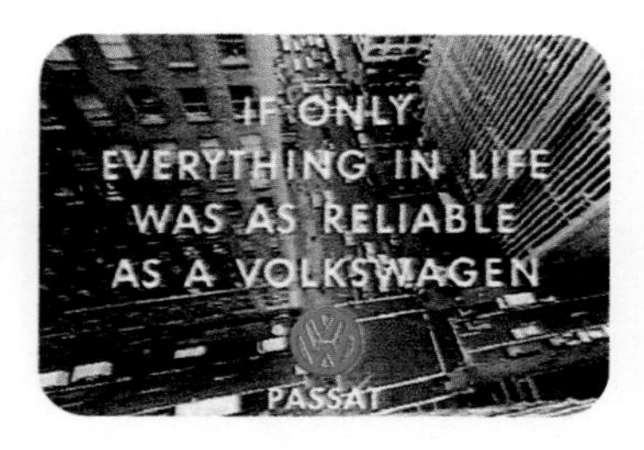

14. (Cut) VW logo and super over bird's eye view of streets: If only everything in life was as reliable as a Volkswagen.

63

63
Pirelli tyres
United Kingdom
Agency: Woollams Moira Gaskin O'Malley, London

As arousing – and as puzzling – as many feature film thrillers, this commercial, written by agency partner Gerry Moira, is dubbed by the agency 'The day the earth stood still'. It appears to suggest that a set of Pirelli tyres saves the earth from destruction. Positioning tyres as the element of security in a frightening world is a novel, and the agency believes effective, approach to their marketing. A previous film showed a man's tyres saving his life after his unfaithful wife tried to kill him by damaging the brakes of his car.

Visual: Open on newsreel footage of an earthquake in somewhere like Tokyo. We see people running as buildings crumble and roads crack. ***Audio:*** MUSIC: *(Turandot: Nessun Dorma)* Cut to Japanese newsreader, the news (whatever it is) doesn't look good. NEWSREADER 1: *(Japanese)* Cut to English newsreader, his face looks just as sombre. NEWSREADER 2: *. . . World will cease to spin on its axis at 4 o'clock Greenwich Mean Time. Citizens are advised . . .* NEWSREADER 3: *(Italian)* Cut to Italian newsreader. He wipes screen to reveal newsreel footage of deserted streets and abandoned cars. Cut to our own footage. We see a gang of youths pushing a supermarket trolley laden with TVs and stereo equipment along the street. They pass scenes of despair and resignation. Little old ladies in black hurry to a nearby church. A young couple take their last embrace. A group of men in a pavement cafe are drinking and counting down aloud. Through all this walks a striking pre-Raphaelite figure. She is barefoot and seemingly oblivious to her surroundings.

She stops at an abandoned Ferrari Testarossa. We notice it is shod with Pirelli tyres. She gets in and starts the car. Cut to TV in the bar. We see a satellite picture of the globe turning imperceptibly.

Cut to the lads' supermarket trolley, running ahead of them and tumbling down some steep steps (Odessa-style). The Ferrari takes neat avoiding action.

Cut back to the church bells ringing. In front of the church the Ferrari rushes through the frame.

SFX: *Church bells.* Cut to girl's POV as the car climbs a steep and winding road. We see the Pirellis flex as they keep the car on the road.

Cut back to the shuttered and deserted streets of the town. Masonry begins to tumble. Cut back to the Ferrari as it reaches the top of the hill. The girl positions the rear wheels of the car over the end of what looks like a giant ball-point. Slowly as the Ferrari revs frantically, the Pirellis begin to turn the giant brass ball. Cut to TV satellite image of the still world, it begins to turn. TITLE: Pirelli (logo). Gripping stuff.

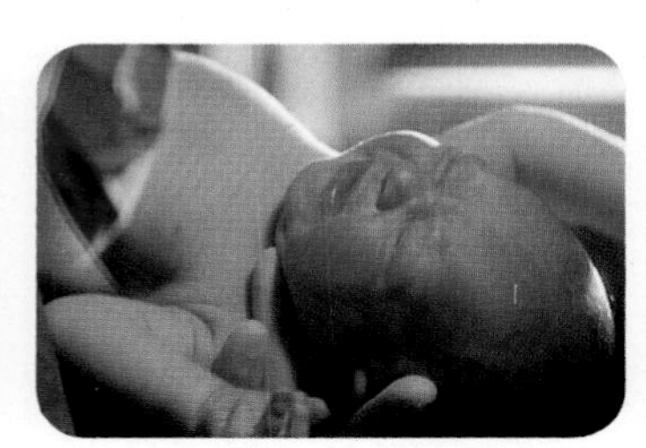

64

64
Audi
United Kingdom
Agency: Bartle Bogle Hegarty, London

Like BMP's films for Audi's sister Volkswagen, this commercial combines human interest with a precise product claim. It almost reconciles one to the use of the German-language slogan.

Visual: Open on a receiver hurriedly being thrown down. A man quickly grabs a jacket. His son, aged six, struggles to do up his own shoelaces in time. ***Audio:*** MVO: *Life is full of decisions. Some of the head, some of the heart.*

Cut to outside. It's late afternoon, early evening. The man and his son hurry to their parked and gleaming Audi 90 Quattro. *Take your next car.*

They drive off through the German countryside. The sun gets lower and lower. *Will it have a catalytic converter that removes 95% of toxic pollutants?* They enter an elegant, yet deserted, German city. It begins to rain. The rain gets heavier and heavier.

They come to a set of lights. They seem to be stuck on red for an eternity. The man drums his fingers on the steering wheel. Eventually the lights change and they set off. *Will it be clean, yet lose nothing in performance?* They continue down the lonely streets past a series of shops. One shop has its burglar alarm going.

They eventually come to a large, imposing turn-of-the-century building. We have no idea what its function is. *Will it have all this at no extra cost?* The man parks the car outside the main entrance. He rushes up the stairs.

He realises he's forgotten something. He rushes back down and lets his son out of the car. They rush inside. We see their POV of a long empty corridor. They get to a pair of swing doors.

Cut to an arm holding up a baby. It's crying. *In short, will it be one of the advanced new generation of Audis?* ***Audio:*** SFX: *Smack and baby cries.*

SUPER: Vorsprung durch Technik.

Cut to blank screen. SUPER: Audi (logo) *Vorsprung durch Technik. As both your head and your heart would say.*

65

66

65
Hansen knitwear
United States
Agency: Frankenberry Laughlin & Constable, Milwaukee
Unusual to see an ad for garments without a glimpse of either the product or someone who might wear it.

66
Elbeo men's socks
West Germany
Agency: R. G. Wiesmeier, Munich
One of a series of engaging black and white pictures of all sorts of men wearing socks around their necks. Headline: 'Ties for the feet'. One would admire them even more if the idea had not already been used by RCP Saatchi & Saatchi in Barcelona. One of the latter agency's ads for Punto Blanco socks was reproduced in the 1988 edition of this annual. It had the copy line 'Choose your socks as you choose your ties' but differed from the Elbeo campaign in focusing on the male model's neckline without showing his face.

67
Kookaï
France
Agency: CLM/BBDO, Paris
Addressed to the cheeky teenage girl rather than, like Rodier's ads, to self-confident women, this one has the line 'It's hot. (Bring us) some nice, fresh boys, please.'

68
Rodier women's clothes
France
Agency: BDDP, Paris
One of a whole series of funny, feminist cartoon ads on the theme that women 'are confident in Rodier' clothes. Here the queen bee is saying 'If I wasn't a woman I would certainly not be a man'.

69
Scandale underwear
France
Agency: BDDP, Paris
The copy line is 'I love to be sent flowers, don't you?' The flowers, of course, are on the garment.

67

68

BDDP

"SI JE N'ÉTAIS PAS UNE FEMME, JE NE SERAIS CERTAINEMENT PAS UN HOMME."

ELLES ASSURENT EN **RODIER**

69

70

PINGOUIN

KIT-PULL.

VOUS N'AVEZ PLUS QU'A LAISSER FAIRE VOS MAINS.

5 PELOTES POUR 1 PULL.

PINGOUIN

IMAGE DE PINGOUIN

71

70, 72
H & M Hennes clothing
United Kingdom
Agency: In house

The Swedish firm Hennes sells a range of garments for men, women and children through its UK shops, but its prime market is youngsters aged 16 to 24. Liz Sheppard, who runs the firm's UK advertising, using freelance creatives, believes the poster campaign that broke in October 1989 was commercially its most effective ever. Among the posters was one, shown here, picturing the Swedish pop group Abba in 1974 and 1989, but it was the 'au pair' ad for women's underwear that brought down on the firm's head a storm of publicity. The Advertising Standards Authority received 34 complaints about the allegedly offensive portrayal of a woman as a sex object.

The ASA upheld the complaint, rejecting the firm's submission that the ad was humorous and that a management containing a high proportion of women could hardly be accused of sexism. Even before that ruling was published, however, the ad had been featured in several newspaper articles reporting the results of a survey commissioned by the ASA into public attitudes to sex in advertising. The survey, using the questionable technique of asking more than 2,000 people to agree or disagree with various general propositions, found that 62 per cent of men and 76 per cent of women regarded the use of sex in ads as offensive. They were also asked to comment on a number of particular sexy ads. The Hennes poster was not among them, but that did not stop the newspapers from using it as an illustration. It is not at all unlikely that the publicity did Hennes considerably more good than harm.

71
Pingouin wool kit
France
Agency: BDDP, Paris

The pack, as shown, contains five balls of wool, enough to knit one jumper. Headline: 'You have nothing left to do but let your hands get on with it'.

73
Pretty Polly stockings
United Kingdom
Agency: Bartle Bogle Hegarty, London

The simplest visual devices are often the most effective, as in this campaign where putting the brand leader's stockings on arms instead of legs demonstrates of what transparently fine (sheer in the jargon of the trade) material they are made.

1974.

The Swedish have always been at the height of fashion.

1989.

H&M HENNES: FÅSHIÖN FROM SWEDEN.

72

73

74

New Kickers.
French lessons in style.

Kickers Kickers

Lesson No.7: Post Impressionism.

Lesson No.11 Romanticism.

Lesson No.21: Surrealism.

75

OUR SHOES OUTLAST THE MEN WHO MAKE THEM.

How long should a good pair of shoes last?

If they come from Italy, probably just long enough to see out the latest fashion.

If they're made in France, likewise.

If they're from Taiwan, the answer depends on whether you consider trainers to be shoes.

Wherever the shoes come from, it seems that nowadays manufacturers are more interested in enduring profits than they are in long-lasting shoes. With one notable exception.

In the small town of Hampton in New Hampshire, U.S.A., there is a shoe company that does not pander to fashion, thinks trainers are people who coach athletes and still believes that the best way to protect its bottom line is to protect its customers feet.

OUR SOLID BRASS EYELETS ARE RUST RESISTANT

The company is called Timberland.

And what do we do that makes us so different from other shoe companies?

Just about everything.

For a start, we don't use mass-production techniques to make shoes quickly and cheaply.

We employ craftsmen, sitting at benches, to produce them slowly and expensively.

They're craggy old men, with the kind of faces that look like they know a thing or two.

Which, of course, they do.

Particularly when it comes to choosing the leathers that make a good pair of shoes.

No point scouring the world for tanneries who can give us bulk discounts and will deliver yesterday. 'Let the big boys deal with them,' is their opinion on the subject.

Leaving Timberland to search for leathers that are soft and supple, yet still strong enough to last a lifetime. (Preferably yours.)

Fortunately for us, we can still find tanneries out there that meet our ridiculously high standards.

And when we do, we gratefully relieve them of every hide in the place.

Naturally, neither the standards nor the hides come cheap these days.

However, we figure if our shoes are still around in years to come, there's a good chance we will be too.

WAXED STITCHING WITHSTANDS THE ELEMENTS.

The next thing the old boys do to prolong the life of our shoes is to impregnate them with silicone oils.

This prevents the leather turning into a sponge every time it rains.

Then just to make sure our shoes really do withstand the wet, we bring in the military.

On a machine designed to test waterproof leathers called a Maser Flex, our leathers must withstand a minimum of 15,000 flexes, which is equal to the highest standards demanded by the Pentagon.

And how do our shoes hold on to their good looks as they get on in years? Well, unbeknown to their customers a lot of our competitors paint the colours on their shoes.

We'd rather dye than do that. In fact, that's exactly what we do, all the way through.

Ensuring that even after years of regular use, the colour won't scuff or flake off.

Ultimately, though, it's the way that we put Timberland shoes together that stops them coming apart.

Which is why each leather is moulded by hand on a special geometric last.

We then use this one piece of leather to construct the uppers, an idea we stole from the Red Indians' original moccasin design.

Apart from having the effect of breaking the shoes in, it means that all Timberlands live to a ripe old age.

Of course, the top jobs in our famous workshops are reserved for those men who know how to handle a needle and thread.

As you'd expect, they're pretty thin on the ground these days. (And the ones we have got aren't getting any younger.)

Even so, they still turn out a hand-sewn shoe that will probably last longer than they will.

HAND-TOOLED IS TOUGHER THAN MACHINE-MADE.

Each shoe is sewn with a high strength nylon yarn using a double knot, pearl stitch which will not come undone even if it's accidentally cut, or in the unlikely event that it breaks.

Many of the seams are then sealed with two coats of latex to stop any water sneaking in the needle holes.

Then, using one of Timberland's many patented processes, the uppers are permanently bonded to the one part of the shoe that should last an eternity: the soles.

Ours are made either from a highly-resistant dual-density polyurethane or a high abrasion rubber.

Even little things are built to last.

Solid brass eyelets. Self-oiling rawhide laces. And four rows of nylon stitching, where other manufacturers make do with one. But that's the old boys at Timberland for you.

Always prepared to go to any lengths in order to protect your feet and the reputation of the company.

Even if it kills them.

Timberland

76

74
Adidas Torsion sports shoes
Germany, France, United States
Agency: Young & Rubicam, Frankfurt
From a series of strong, stylised action photographs relating to various sports.

75
Kickers shoes
United Kingdom
Agency: Ogilvy & Mather Partners, London
From a poster campaign which has helped with a limited budget to rescue the brand, popular in Britain in the 1960s, from a period of decline. The solution, exploiting the fact that Kickers are designed in France, was a series of artistic jokes with high visual impact. They are designed, says the agency, to appeal to the creative instincts of the kind of people attracted to the brand.

76
Timberland boots
United Kingdom
Agency: The Leagas Delaney Partnership, London
Both visuals and copy, written by agency partner Tim Delaney, are strong on information. An excellent example of the approach that says: if there's a good story in the product, tell it.

77, 78
Inter sports shoes
Netherlands
Agency: TBWA, Amsterdam
'You can make a quick getaway with sports shoes from Inter' is the copy line on these very funny illustrations by Maurice Rosy.

77

78

79

80

81

79, 80
Dormeuil cloth
United Kingdom
Agency: BBDO, London

There has been a noticeable international trend in recent years towards the use of nude males in ads, mostly with an eye on female buyers. However, over a period of two years Britain's Advertising Standards Authority received only three complaints about sexploitation of men – none upheld – while organised feminists bombarded it with hundreds of compaints about the supposed degradation of women through nudity and sexual innuendo.

Dormeuil's eye-catching campaign, by its recently hired agency, BBDO, is in fact aimed not at women but at upmarket men who buy their own expensive suits. The message (disguised knocking copy) is that without Dormeuil cloth a suit is no more than a few buttons. As well as cloth for tailors, the Dormeuil name is now to be found on ready-made suits.

81
Chantal Thomass stockings
France
Agency: Saatchi & Saatchi, Paris

The attention is captured here not so much by the picture as by the few words of copy. 'The next day he again preferred to wait for the next day', they say. Who is he, and is the seated woman waiting for him? We shall never know.

Naughty
but
very
nice.
Aristoc
The cream of stockings and tights.
'10 Denier Stayputs', stockings you'll feel comfortable with.

82 83

82, 83
Aristoc stockings and tights
United Kingdom
Agency: WCRS Mathews Marcantonio, London

The idea of this campaign, for the number two brand in the UK market, is to compare Aristoc hosiery to skin cream. Typical is the ad headed 'Apply every morning for wrinkle free skin'. The other example here, aimed more at the trade, is a self-parody which deliberately alludes to the slogan 'Naughty but nice' used for several years by Ogilvy & Mather and the Milk Marketing Board to advertise a different kind of cream – cream cakes.

84
Levi's chinos
United Kingdom
Agency: Bartle Bogle Hegarty, London

This dramatic picture comes from a series that majors on the garments' World War Two credentials.

85, 86
Levi's jeans
Spain
Agency: Bassat, Ogilvy & Mather, Barcelona

The guy with his jeans around his ankles is illustrating a pun. The word *rebajas* means both 'price cuts' and, literally, 'lowerings'. The poster on the hoarding, adorned with a pair of jeans, says 'Orange Alert. New Orange Tag. The label of the 90s.'

84

85

86

87
Etam underwear
France
Agency: Bélier/WCRS, Paris

'In the daytime nobody can guess what I am at night' says the headline. The pay-off line is a pun, recalling the phrase *Je suis dans tous mes états*, meaning 'I'm overwrought'.

88
Schaffhauser wool
Switzerland
Agency: Impuls, Küsnacht

'Because it's the only thing you don't think I can do, Peter' is the copy line on this ad, which invests humdrum knitting wool with a dash of glamour. The agency is part of the Saatchi & Saatchi network.

89
Candy shoes
Australia
Agency: Campaign Palace, Melbourne

The slang use of the word 'tasty', meaning attractive, inspired the zany visuals in this campaign, liable to amuse young women of the age depicted in the ads.

Le jour, personne ne peut deviner ce que je suis la nuit.
Etam
Je suis dans tous mes Etam.

87

Weil es das einzige ist, was Du mir nicht zutraust. Peter
schaffhauser
schaffhauser
WOLLE · LAINE
LANA · WOOL
Deine Handschrift.

88

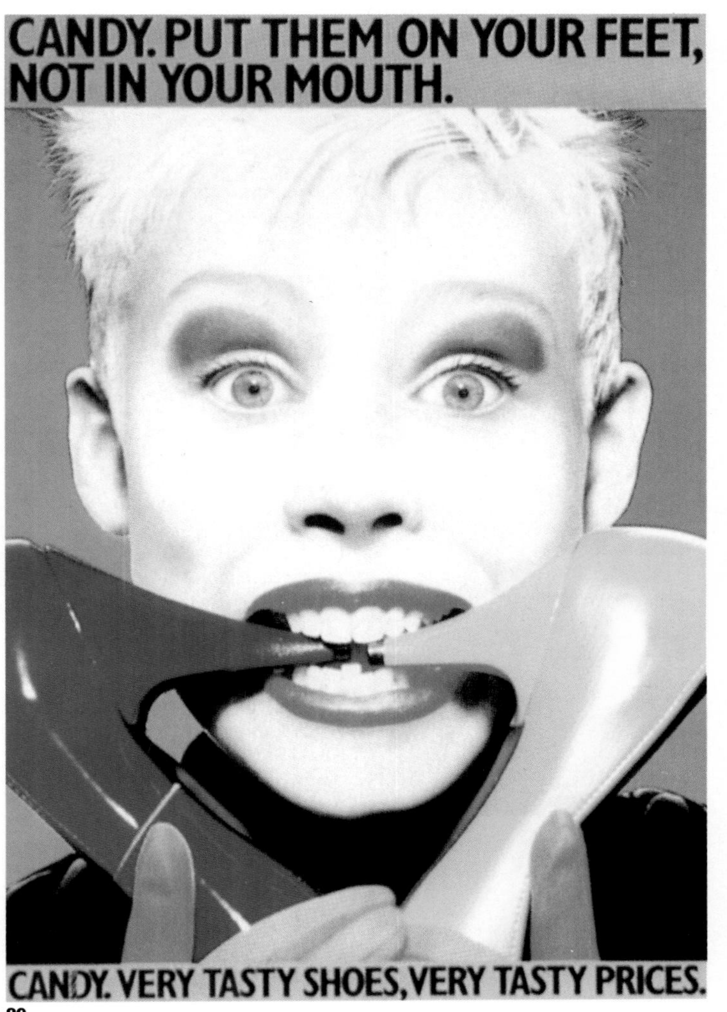
CANDY. PUT THEM ON YOUR FEET, NOT IN YOUR MOUTH.
CANDY. VERY TASTY SHOES, VERY TASTY PRICES.

89

90

90
Cotton
United States
Agency: Ogilvy & Mather, New York
In 60 seconds this Cotton Incorporated film tries tugging at almost all the heart strings. The sentimentality, in a very American style, is skilfully handled but might work less well in another country. The commercial aim is both to encourage consumers to look for the Cotton Seal on garments and to persuade manufacturers and retailers that the Seal will help sell their goods. The fast-changing sequence of slices of emotional life is accompanied by a poem, as follows.

In the silent dawn
A golden sun.
Soft kiss, warm smile –
the day's begun.

In the rising mist
A quiet rain.
One whisper, a sigh –
How to explain?
The touch, the feel, the fabric of our lives.

In the moonlit night
A cold blue haze.
Gay laughter, sad cries –
These mark our days.
The touch, the feel, the fabric of our lives.

91

91
K Shoes
United Kingdom
Agency: Bartle Bogle Hegarty, London
Pitched fairly and squarely, is this film, at the new-style, self-confident career woman.

Visual: We open on the interior of smart offices. A well-dressed executive is sitting at his desk. He is talking to a colleague who reacts to events throughout script. An elegant female reporter dressed in a suit and red K Shoes bursts purposefully into his office, brushing aside his secretary. ***Audio:*** SFX: *Selected heightened sound effects.*

She strides determinedly across the hard marble floor to his desk. She's carrying her contract which she proceeds to tear up in front of his face. SUPER: *Whatever you.* She picks up a stapler and staples a sealed white envelope with 'PRIVATE AND CONFIDENTIAL' onto his tie. Then she picks up a pair of scissors, cuts off two of the strings of a Newton's cradle and two of the balls fall off. SUPER: *Break off.* As she storms out of his office one of her heels becomes lodged in a small decorative heating vent in front of his desk. SUPER: *It won't be.* A slight smile of satisfaction traces across his lips at her predicament. However, with a determined tug of her foot she dislodges her shoe along with the grate. SUPER: *Our heels.*

Cut to our heroine outside his office. She hands the metal grill to the secretary who looks at her with an 'I've always wanted to do that' look and follows her out of the door.

Cut to CU of our heroine's shoes walking towards camera and super. *K. Shoes for the well-heeled.*

92

92, 93
Pingouin jumpers
France, United Kingdom
Agency: BDDP, Paris

The client having carved out a fashion marketing niche for itself with its jumpers, the agency's task was to create a corresponding advertising niche from which competitors would be excluded. Result: these offbeat films. The voice-over in one says 'Since Pingouin started making ready-to-wear jumpers, Miranda wouldn't dream of missing her Saturday shopping expeditions'. The final frame contains the words 'So many jumpers. So many jumpers. Ready-to-wear and made to measure.' In the other commercial we are told 'Suddenly Roberta had a strange feeling her ready-to-wear jumper was being observed'.

93

94

Kontoret är öppet
dagligen 8.30–17.00.

Lunchstängt 12–13.

SVENSK
MÖBEL
CENTER

95

SHARP SUIT

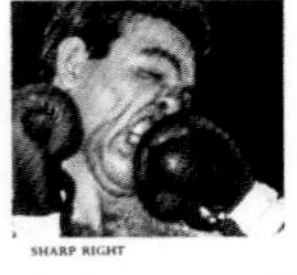

SHARP RIGHT

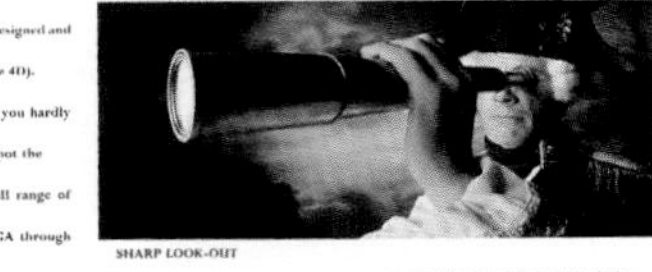

SHARP LOOK-OUT

We've given a whole new meaning to sharpness.

1 O'CLOCK SHARP

NEC
COMPUTER
PERIPHERALS

96

Il computer è il nocciolo. Bull vi dà anche la polpa.

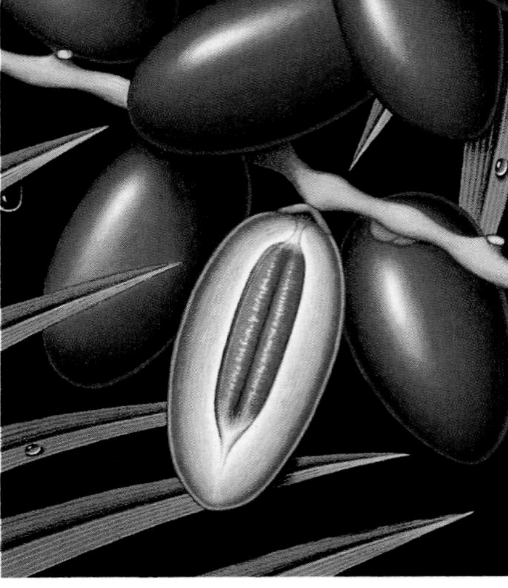

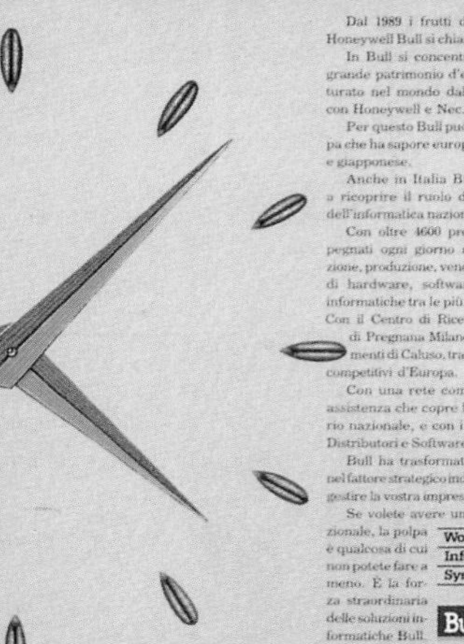

Dal 1989 i frutti dell'informatica Honeywell Bull si chiamano Bull.
In Bull si concentra così tutto il grande patrimonio d'esperienze maturato nel mondo dalla partnership con Honeywell e Nec.
Per questo Bull può darvi una polpa che ha sapore europeo, americano e giapponese.
Anche in Italia Bull continuerà a ricoprire il ruolo di protagonista dell'informatica nazionale.
Con oltre 4600 professionisti impegnati ogni giorno nella progettazione, produzione, vendita e assistenza di hardware, software e soluzioni informatiche tra le più avanzate.
Con il Centro di Ricerca e Sviluppo di Pregnana Milanese e gli stabilimenti di Caluso, tra i più moderni e competitivi d'Europa.
Con una rete commerciale e di assistenza che copre l'intero territorio nazionale, e con i più qualificati Distributori e Software House.
Bull ha trasformato l'informatica nel fattore strategico indispensabile per gestire la vostra impresa.
Se volete avere un'azienda eccezionale, la polpa è qualcosa di cui non potete fare a meno. E la forza straordinaria delle soluzioni informatiche Bull.

Worldwide
Information
Systems

Bull

I frutti dell'informatica.

94
Office furniture
Sweden
Agency: Hall & Cederquist/Y&R, Stockholm
On the left 'The office is open daily from 8.30 to 5 pm'. On the right: 'Closed for lunch 12–1 pm'. A neat juxtaposition of pictures puts over the essence of the selling message on behalf of the Swedish Furniture Centre. The agency is part of the Young & Rubicam network.

95
NEC MultiSync 4D Monitor
United Kingdom
Agency: BMP Business, London
The agency has managed to squeeze not one but four verbal-cum-visual jokes into one ad promoting the 'sharpness' of the high resolution MultiSync screen.

96
Bull information systems
Italy
Agency: RSCG Mezzano Constantini Mignani, Milan
'The computer is the core (or date stone). Bull also gives you the flesh of the fruit.' So says the headline over this visually pleasing ad, which goes on to talk about the range of information technology services available from the company.

97
Hewlett-Packard personal computers
United Kingdom
Agency: Primary Contact, London
This campaign intelligently puts the emphasis on the back-up service provided by Hewlett-Packard rather than going on about qualities its computers share with other brands. The picture is a stock photograph which has been coloured by hand.

AND FOR HIS NEXT TRICK,
HE'LL BUY A PC
WITHOUT PROPER SUPPORT
He doesn't care that Hewlett-Packard offer the industry's best support service.
He doesn't want next-day engineer call-out, with 90% of problems solved on-site, within minutes.
He doesn't need a free HELPLINE service, for software problems.
He's not impressed that Hewlett-Packard quality means a cost of ownership that's half that of the industry leader.
And he's unmoved by our free one-year, on-site warranty.
But then, he enjoys living dangerously.
You may not.
Vectra range of IBM-compatible PCs.
hp
HEWLETT PACKARD
A more intelligent approach to computing

98

Caro notaio di Forlì, caro commercialista di Vercelli, caro avvocato di Roma, caro assicuratore di Messina: la libertà è un bene prezioso, lo sappiamo tutti. Quella di un professionista, a maggior ragione, non ha prezzo. Sono indispensabili rapidità di azione e capacità di stare al passo con i tempi. Con l'aiuto di macchine su misura, tutte Olivetti, in modo da risolvere cento problemi con un unico interlocutore: il Concessionario Olivetti. Libertà personale. Per il tuo lavoro quotidiano, per la contabilità, l'archivio clienti, le scadenze dei pagamenti, Olivetti ti offre una vasta gamma di personal computer. Dal nuovo e potente portatile M111 ai modelli di base, versatili, economici e di facile impiego (M200 - M250). Da quelli più potenti e flessibili come M290 alla serie M380, indicata per esigenze più sofisticate. Libertà di stampa. La videoscrittura elettronica Olivetti semplifica e migliora l'edizione dei documenti. E puoi scegliere tra vari modelli di word processor, dal compatto e facilissimo CWP1 a sistemi integrati e multifunzionali come ETV 2700 ed ETV 3000.

CARO LIBERO PROFESSIONISTA, VUOI DIVENTARE ANCORA PIU' LIBERO?

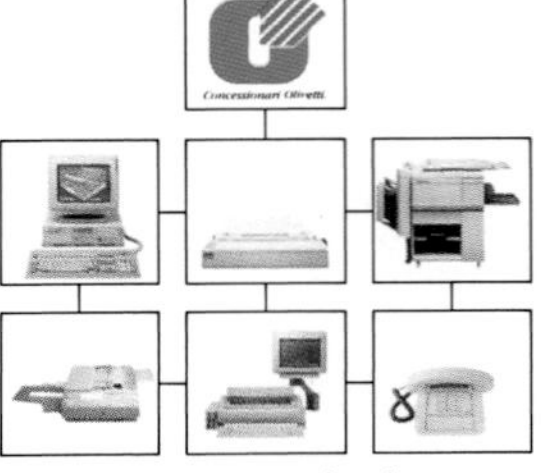

E se già possiedi una macchina da scrivere elettronica, la puoi integrare con un video (ETV 2900 - ETV 500) per controllare in diretta tutto il testo. Libertà di trasmissione. Telefoni dal design elegante e moderno, intercomunicanti multifunzionali e fax per ogni budget: dal modello di base OFX 315 ai modelli programmabili e con memoria come TLM 910, in grado di ricordare numeri telefonici e intere pagine di testo da trasmettere in modo selezionato e differito. Libertà di copiare. Copiatrici belle, facili, intelligenti. Dal bianco e nero al colore. Per ridurre e ingrandire a piacere. Una gamma completa, dal personal copier 7005 ai sistemi di copiatura della serie 7060, velocissimi e dotati di funzionalità sofisticate. Libertà di parola. Caro libero professionista, parlane con un professionista come te: il Concessionario Olivetti. Ascolterà i tuoi problemi, concorderà con te le soluzioni, ti assisterà prima, durante e dopo la fornitura con professionalità e con competenza e ti proporrà una gamma di soluzioni finanziarie molto vantaggiose.

olivetti

I PRODOTTI STUDIATI PER LE ESIGENZE ITALIANE SONO FIRMATI olivetti ITALIA E SONO DISTRIBUITI DAI CONCESSIONARI OLIVETTI.

98, 100
Olivetti computers and other office equipment
Italy
Agency: Bozell e Associati, Milan
No false modesty about this client, judging by the picture in which a big man, representing Olivetti itself, cradles a small one in his arms. Headline: 'Dear small company, would you take some advice from a big one?' Copy goes on to explain how small firms can benefit from various Olivetti products, including not only personal computers but copiers, telephones and fax machines. The other ad is headed 'Dear professional, do you want to become more free?' This literal translation hides a pun, since the term *libero professionista* (what in English used to be called member of the liberal professions) contains within it the word meaning 'free'.

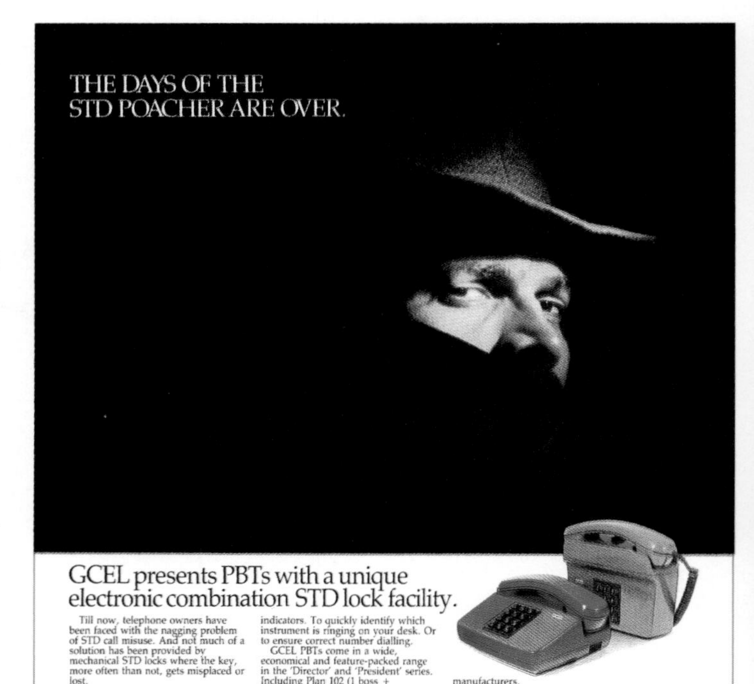

Till now, telephone owners have been faced with the nagging problem of STD call misuse. And not much of a solution has been provided by mechanical STD locks where the key, more often than not, gets misplaced or lost.

Now, GCEL push button telephones (PBTs) offer an easy, economical and foolproof solution. With a first ever electronic combination STD lock facility.

Just select your own 3-digit code number and feed it into the key pad. Thereafter, you and only you can operate STD calls. You can even change your code number at will.

You can opt for 'ring' or 'dial' LED indicators. To quickly identify which instrument is ringing on your desk. Or to ensure correct number dialling.

GCEL PBTs come in a wide, economical and feature-packed range in the 'Director' and 'President' series. Including Plan 102 (1 boss + 1 secretary). The system with features ideally suited for small and medium sized organisations as well as senior-level executives in big companies.

As a Siemens licencee, GCEL has the unique distinction of manufacturing critical PBT components and casings to their specifications. It is also the major supplier of PBTs to MTNL/DOT and various EPABX manufacturers.

No wonder, with GCEL, you'd be settling for a company whose PBTs are referred to as industry norms today.

GCEL
GUJARAT COMMUNICATIONS AND ELECTRONICS LIMITED
Plot No. A/42, GIDC Electronics Estate
Gandhinagar: 382 015 (GUJARAT)
Phone: 21629/21630 • Telex: 1203 208

Dealers at: AHMEDABAD: T.E.C.S., Phone: 446100, Telecare, Phone: 20089, Trinity Marketing, Phone: 363569, Veearsons, Phone: 409919, 403596, 469347 • **BANGALORE:** Microna Corpn., Phone: 602915, United Teletronics, Phone: 624069, 225477 • **BARODA:** Marketing & Products Services, Phone: 0-320597/ R-325650, Aroona Telecom Services, • **BIKANER:** Gahlot Scientific Stores, Phone: 4449 • **BOMBAY:** Veearsons, Phone: 258940/ 258704/ 251700, Ajmera Brothers, Phone: 310591/ 315962/ R-4926222, Chandramauli Corpn. Phone: 6494330/ 6147626/ 259356 • **CALCUTTA:** Market Creators, Phone: 277961, Dunics, Phone: 48 1338/ 47 9257 • **CALICUT:** Galaxy Business Systems, Phone: 52600/ 64100 • **HYDERABAD:** Mythri Marketing Pvt. Ltd., Phone: 223147 • **IMPHAL:** Manipur Electronics, Phone: 20555 • **INDORE:** Devendra Electricals, Phone: 0-31142/ R-34166 • **JABALPUR:** Triveni Engg. Co., Phone: 22342 • **JAIPUR:** B.S. & Co. (Telecom Division), Phone: 66109 • **JORHAT:** D.R. Brijmohan, Phone: 20057 • **KANPUR:** Orison Electronics, Phone: 243343/ 214953 • **MADRAS:** Shrivatsa Associates, Phone: 444846 • **NAGPUR:** Sudhir Electronics, Phone: 32853 • **NEW DELHI:** Ankay Associates, Phone: 606128 • **PUNE:** Index Trading Co., Phone: 35843 • **RAJKOT:** Maruti Electronix & Electricals, Phone: 32124, Modern Radio House, Phone: 26024 • **SURAT:** Parul Electronics, Phone: 46740.

CONTOUR ADS-GCEL-206A/89

99

100

Cara seteria del Comasco, caro pastificio foggiano, cara carpenteria di Cagliari: le dimensioni di un'impresa moderna si misurano dalla sua capacità di comunicare e integrare i diversi servizi. Così, qualunque sia il tuo fatturato, puoi essere più grande di quanto sembri. Con l'aiuto di macchine su misura, tutte Olivetti, in modo da risolvere cento problemi con un unico interlocutore: il Concessionario Olivetti. Personal consigli. Olivetti ti offre una gamma di personal computer che va dai modelli base, versatili, economici e di facile impiego come M250, a quelli più potenti e flessibili come M290. Per la tua amministrazione, il marketing, la ricerca e lo sviluppo, il magazzino. O personal più sofisticati per la direzione commerciale: come la serie M380 in cinque differenti modelli. Videoconsigli elettronici. Puoi scegliere tra vari modelli di word processor, dal compatto e facilissimo CWP1 ai sistemi integrati e multifunzionali come ETV 2700 e ETV 3000. Se già possiedi una macchina da scrivere elettronica la puoi integrare con un video (ETV 2900 - ETV 500) per controllare in diretta

CARA PICCOLA AZIENDA, ACCETTERESTI QUALCHE CONSIGLIO DA UNA GRANDE?

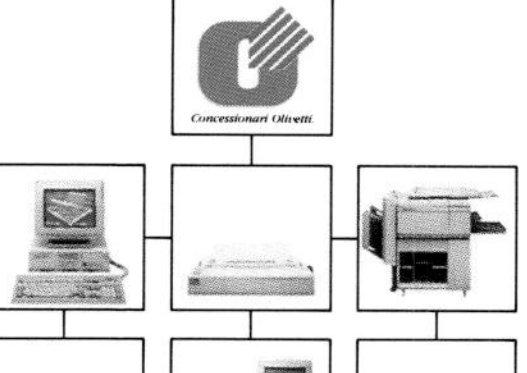

tutto il testo. E con i sistemi di Desk Top Publishing Olivetti, basati su personal computer e stampanti laser, in grado di integrare testi, grafica e immagini, puoi assicurare alle tue comunicazioni verso l'esterno una straordinaria qualità tipografica e una elegante forma editoriale. Teleconsigli. Telefoni dal design moderno ed elegante, intercomunicanti multifunzionali e fax per ogni budget: dal modello di base OFX 315 ai modelli programmabili e con memoria come TLM 910. Fotoconsigli. Copiatrici belle, facili, intelligenti. C'è solo l'imbarazzo della scelta tra i modelli più piccoli della classe 7005 - 7020, i modelli di fascia media (7039 - 7041 - 7047) che ottimizzano il costo copia e i potenti sistemi di copiatura della classe 7060 ricchi di funzionalità sofisticate e capaci di velocità di oltre 40 copie al minuto. Consigli pratici. Cara piccola azienda, ora accetta qualche consiglio da una più piccola di te: il Concessionario Olivetti più vicino. Ascolterà i tuoi problemi, concorderà con te le soluzioni, ti assisterà prima, durante e anche dopo la fornitura con professionalità e competenza. E ti proporrà varie soluzioni finanziarie molto vantaggiose.

I PRODOTTI STUDIATI PER LE ESIGENZE ITALIANE SONO FIRMATI olivetti ITALIA E SONO DISTRIBUITI DAI CONCESSIONARI OLIVETTI.

99
GCEL telephones with electronic locks
India
Agency: Contour Advertising, Bombay
The product offers office managers the ability to prevent the wrong people ('poachers') using the phone. To make a call via STD (subscriber trunk dialling) a three-digit code must first be keyed in to the phone.

101
Panasonic FX-RS505 image scanner
United Kingdom
Agency: Grange Advertising, Berkhamsted
The giant eyeball is a witty but also perfectly relevant device for introducing computer users to the scanner's capabilities.

COMPUTERS HAVE ALWAYS BEEN ABLE TO THINK. NOW THEY CAN SEE.

Ever wished computers could see things your way? Simple! Just hook a Panasonic Image Scanner onto your PC* and it will behave as if it had eyes, opening a whole new dimension in computing for you.

It will, for example, read text documents (no keying in–think of the saving in labour!) or scan graphic images at an excellent 400 dots per inch resolution and not 300 dpi like many other, more expensive scanners. These captured images or text documents can then be transported directly into your wordprocessor, Desktop Publishing or CAD/CAM application. Under their control, scanned files can be viewed and manipulated to achieve your perfect result.

Then again, if you add a Panasonic FaxBoard to your PC, your system will become a powerful facsimile station capable of sending and receiving documents direct from your desk. Last but not least, optical filing becomes a real possibility with the FX-RS505.

You may think that giving your computer sight is expensive. It's not. At £1195+VAT, the Panasonic Scanner comes complete with all necessary hard and software to "plug in and play"–in minutes! We also include OCR software in the price–unlike some manufacturers.

Seeing is believing. Find out more about the range of Image Scanners by filling in the coupon or dial 100 and ask for FREEFONE Panasonic.

FX-RS505 Image Scanner

*IBM PC/XT/AT or compatible

Panasonic OA

For more information on the FX-RS505 Image Scanner complete the coupon and send it to Julie Everard, Panasonic Business Systems UK. A division of Panasonic UK Ltd, Panasonic House, Willoughby Road, Bracknell, Berks RG12 4FP. Tel. 0344 853915. Telex: 847652. Fax: 0344 862075

I would like more information on the FX-RS505 Image Scanner please.

Name ______ Company ______
Address ______
______ Post code ______ Tel. No. ______
Are you a dealer ☐ or end user ☐?

101

PC AX 3 s.
LA GUERRE ECONOMIQUE DEVIENT UNE PARTIE DE PLAISIR.

MICROPROCESSEUR 386 SX, MÉMOIRE VIVE DE 1 MO. DISQUE DUR ULTRA-RAPIDE : LE PC AX 3S EST LE GENRE D'ARME QU'ON PRÉFÉRERAIT ÊTRE LE SEUL A POSSÉDER. PAS LA PEINE DE FORCER SON TALENT ; AVEC CE PC, LE COMBAT DEVIENT FRANCHEMENT INÉGAL, VOIRE DÉLOYAL. QUEL PLAISIR QUAND TOUT VA SI VITE, QUE TOUT EST SI FACILE ! UN CONSEIL TOUT DE MÊME : RESTEZ VIGILANTS. LE PC AX 3S EST UNE ARME A NE PAS METTRE ENTRE TOUTES LES MAINS. SURTOUT CELLES DE VOS CONCURRENTS.

EPSON INFORMATION : 3614 CODE EPSON.

EPSON. MIEUX VAUT L'AVOIR DE SON COTE.

102

102
Epson PC AX 3s computer
France
Agency: BDDP, Paris
Sticking to the established caricatural style of BDDP's Epson campaign, this ad is headed 'Economic warfare becomes a pleasure outing'. Copy says the Epson gives its owner an unfair advantage over competitors. And there on the wall are the heads of competitors bagged by the lucky Epson man.

103
Bene office furniture
Austria
Agency: Demner & Merlicek, Vienna
'Disorder was for her yesterday's word', begins the copy. Note that the word *Unordnung* (disorder) is printed in disorderly fashion. Copy continues, tidily, 'A line as clear as it was well thought out penetrated the room and left more time for the important things of office life'.

103

104
Apple computers
France
Agency: CLM/BBDO, Paris

Remarkable. A computer commercial which shows no gadgetry and says nothing about information technology. Instead it conveys vividly how an old-fashioned pre-IT firm is run. All CLM's TV advertising for Apple, number two in the French computer market, suggests that its machines help people make the best of their own potential rather than usurping their role. This is computing with a human face. Technical details are left to print ads.

104

1. **Visual:** Reflected in a rain puddle, a big black limousine is driving across a vast industrial tract.

2. (Cut) In the back of the car, the owner of the venture and his teenage son.

3. Cut to father. ***Audio*** (FATHER): *'One day all this will be yours . . .'*

4. **Visual:** Cut. ***Audio*** (FATHER): *'. . . the factories, the machines, the people.'*

5. **Visual:** Cut to son who is listening to his father's monologue with a stony expression on his face. ***Audio*** (FATHER): *'But always remember that when it comes down to making decisions, you'll be all alone.'*

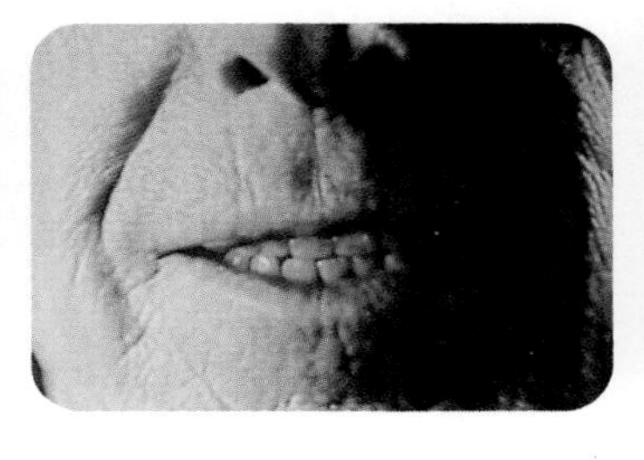

6. **Visual:** Cut. ***Audio*** (FATHER): *'You won't be able to depend on them. Their interest is not the same as yours. All these people who will be working for you are there to execute tasks and not there to think.'*

7. **Visual:** Cut. ***Audio*** (FATHER): *'If they ever started to think, they would want to start changing things. And that is not within their ability. Never forget that they owe you everything.'*

8. **Visual:** Abrupt cut to a young worker . . .

9. (Cut) . . . watching the limousine drive past. ***Audio*** (MVO): *'There are various ways of running a business and this is one of them. Luckily there are others.'*

10. **Visual:** Cut to Apple logo.

„Die klassische Familie ist museumsreif"–

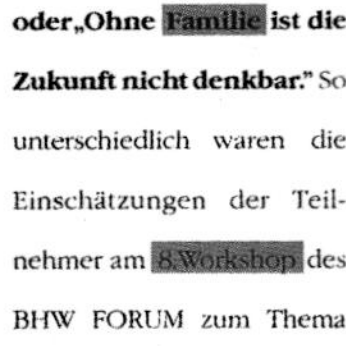

oder „Ohne Familie ist die Zukunft nicht denkbar." So unterschiedlich waren die Einschätzungen der Teilnehmer am 8. Workshop des BHW FORUM zum Thema „Familie ist Zukunft" – oder: Zukunft ohne Familie?" Wenn Sie an dieser Diskussion interessiert sind, können Sie die Dokumentation der Veranstaltung bestellen: BHW FORUM, Postfach 10 01 55, 3250 Hameln 1. Bitte DM 5,– in Briefmarken beifügen.

BHW: Engagement für die Zukunft

Thomas Kuhlenbeck zum 8. Workshop des BHW FORUM

BHW FORUM

EINE INITIATIVE DER BHW GRUPPE

105

TODAY'S STATE-OF-THE-ART
IS TOMORROW'S JUNK.

In today's fast-changing world, one scientific breakthrough is soon outdated by the next. IBP, a successful public sector undertaking, is built on this discovery.
The aim of scientists and researchers working at IBP is simple: pursuit of scientific excellence.

The result is major contributions in critical areas like petroleum products, vacuum engineering systems for defence and space applications, cryocans for the dairy industry, and even freeze-dryer plants for the pharmaceutical industry.
To name a few.
Despite these achievements,

IBP is ever on the move.
Because if you rest even for a moment, chances are you may be dumped in the dustbin of tomorrow.

IBP Co. Limited
(A GOVERNMENT OF INDIA ENTERPRISE)
Not a moment of rest

106

EEN GOED FREE-LANCE TEAM GAAT DOOR TOT HET GROTE IDEE IS GEBOREN.

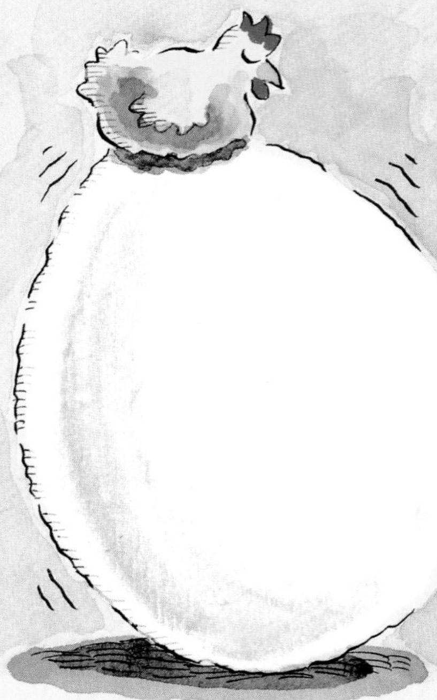

Goede reklame is reklame met een idee. Want een goed idee geeft het produkt een eigen gezicht. Waarmee het zich kan onderscheiden van andere produkten in de markt.

Maar goede ideeën dienen zich zelden zomaar aan. Er bestaan immers geen formules of trucjes voor. Elk goed kreatief team weet dat je er soms lang op moet broeden.

Streven naar het Grote Idee. Dat is het wantrouwen tegen de lege prullenbak. Het is niet alleen een kwestie van kreativiteit. Het is ook vaak een kwestie van doorgaan. Van dingen weg durven gooien die je vijf minuten daarvoor nog rijp achtte voor een lamp. Of minimaal een eervolle vermelding.

Het is de enige manier die leidt tot dat ene idee. Het idee dat na een dag zelfkritiek nog overeind staat.

Dat is dus waar een goed free-lance team altijd naar streeft. Want u weet hoe het gaat met reklame zonder een idee. Daar kraait geen haan naar.

Herman Feberwee 023-294387
Peter Meijburg 01720-74571

HERMAN FEBERWEE (ART), PETER MEIJBURG (COPY), HAZEVELD 2, 2405 AE ALPHEN A/D RIJN.

107

Allt sem þarf
til að gera
árangursríkar
auglýsingar

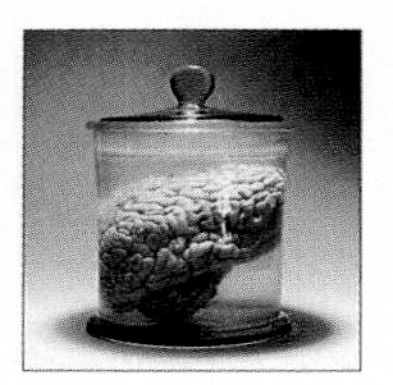

-rúmast í einni krukku

108

105
BHW building society
West Germany
Agency: ABC/Eurocom, Düsseldorf
BHW's publicity efforts are centred on the BHW Forum, the conference it sponsors on social and economic problems. The subject of the Forum's eighth workshop was the future of the family, on which opinions were divided. The picture illustrates the headline contention that 'The conventional family is ready for the museum'. That was one opinion expressed in the discussion, but another, quoted in the text of the ad, was that 'the future is unimaginable without the family'.

106
IBP Company
India
Agency: ASP, Bombay
Computer stationery takes the place of the waste paper normally used to wrap gram in India. The message that state-of-the-art technology is continually being replaced is intended to reinforce IBP's image as a science-based innovator.

107
Freelance creative team
Netherlands
Creative team: Herman Feberwee & Peter Meijburg, Alphen
Art director Feberwee and copywriter Meijburg took space in the Dutch trade press to advertise their services with this striking image. Headline: 'A good freelance team carries on until the great idea is born'.

108
GBB advertising agency
Iceland
Agency: GBB/Hvíta Húsið, Reykjavík
Here's a message of special interest to readers of this book. 'All you need to make successful advertising', it says, 'fits into a jar.' This witty self-promotion ad was produced by the Reykjavík ad agency GBB, which has since changed its name to Hvíta Húsið (White House).

109
Safeway
United Kingdom
Agency: Ogilvy & Mather, London
As part of the new wave of 'green' advertising and publicity, we have here a supermarket chain attempting to establish its ecological credentials. The two pieces of ice the company says in the headline it wants to prevent melting are the Arctic and Antarctic regions, supposedly threatened by Greenhouse effect warming of the planet. The new refrigerator is a huge central storage unit which copy says uses an ammonia gas coolant instead of the CFCs which break down the ozone layer and thus contribute to the Greenhouse effect.

109

110

111

112

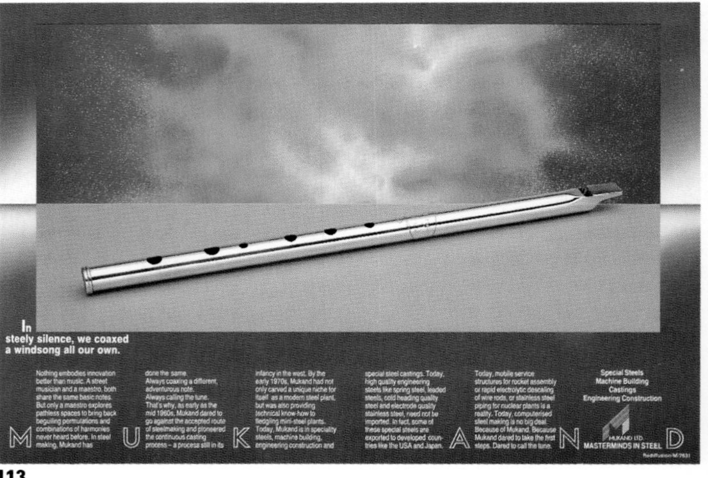

113

110
Water industry
United Kingdom
Agency: DMB&B, London
Strong image and strong headline work together to make clear the importance of water. The real purpose, however, of this ad and others like it paid for by 'the 10 water and sewage businesses of England and Wales' is to persuade the British public that the recent privatisation of the water industry is a good thing. Many British citizens are, however, rightly suspicious that the replacement of a public monopoly by a group of private ones may turn out to be not a good thing at all.

111
Mazda
Worldwide
Studio: Nakamoto Design Office, Tokyo
One of a series of artistic pictures by photographer Nob Fukuda to have appeared in the company's house magazine *Mazda World*.

112
Saatchi & Saatchi
East Germany
Agency: Saatchi & Saatchi, London
A stunning piece of media selection – on the eastern side of the Berlin Wall – even if short on pictorial imagery. Art director and copywriter credits both go to the agency's creative director, Paul Arden. As he says, the opening up of the wall provided an ideal opportunity to gain maximum publicity at very low cost. Paradoxically it is rare for ad agencies, whose business is publicity, to go about publicising themselves with this kind of panache.

113
Mukand
India
Agency: Rediffusion, Bombay
Mukand is, among other things, a steel manufacturer. The picture of the steel recorder is supported by copy comparing the firm's progressive steel-making methods to music – 'always coaxing a different, adventurous note. Always calling the tune.'

114
Toray Industries
Japan
Agency: Dentsu, Tokyo
A frame from a TV film in which the company's 17 different activities are represented by the tines of a music box. A voice-over says: 'If any one of these tines were missing, this music box would not play. With Toray the strength of the 17 fields of enterprise . . . are brought together to play one beautiful melody. Each one in crystal harmony, that's Toray.'

115
BP
United Kingdom
Agency: Saatchi & Saatchi, London
The curious animal-like creature pictured is a road 'cat's-eye', seen in close-up. The message of the ad is that British Petroleum is introducing new, safer petrol tankers less likely to swerve out of a straight path and run over the cat's-eyes.

116
AT&T
United States
Agency: Ayer, New York
One of four factually based slice-of-life mini-movies designed to show the range of AT&T products and services in use, this concerns the arrival in a small American town of a visiting Soviet dignitary. It cuts rapidly between scenes such as the town newspaper covering the event, a school band taking part in the ceremonies, a motorcade watched over by police helicopters. As the story proceeds we see computers, fax machines and telephone links all playing their part – thanks, of course, to American Telephone and Telegraph.

114

115

116

117

118

117
Vienna Festival
Austria
Agency: Demner & Merlicek, Vienna

'Time for Freud' is the headline on the giant poster bearing an unusually angled portrait of the father of psychoanalysis. The copywriter is agency partner Mariusz Jan Demner. A Freud exhibition formed part of the Vienna Festival Week.

118
Bristol Animation Festival
United Kingdom
Agency: J. Walter Thompson, London

The most animated character at the festival will be you, promises this light-hearted ad with its comical photo by Charles Settrington.

119
Nob Fukuda photographic exhibition
Japan
Studio: Keizo Matsui Design Office, Osaka

Fukuda, whose work is to be seen in several places in this book, is one of Japan's best known photographers. A native of Osaka, he set up his own Studio Nob there in 1971.

119

120

120
Basketball matches
United States
Agency: Martin/Williams, Minneapolis

The agency's client was First Bank Systems, which sponsored a series of 'record attendance nights' at basketball matches when the local Timberwolves team was trying to boost the number of its spectators. Even old ladies, as the poster graphically makes clear, can help sportsmen achieve that kind of record.

121
The Empress Place
Singapore
Agency: Ball WCRS Partnership, Singapore

One of the shows put on by the Historical & Cultural Exhibitions company at Singapore's Empress Place was the Treasures of Qing Exhibition. This poster promises an insight into the life of a royal consort during the Qing dynasty in China.

121

The Prince of Wales has complained he can't see St. Paul's. In 1708, people complained because they could.

It's hard to credit, but 280 years ago Sir Christopher Wren was an avant-garde radical. His first designs for St Paul's cathedral were rejected because they were just, well, too way out. The most ambitious early plan, 'The Great Model', is still exhibited in the crypt of St Paul's. To our eyes it doesn't look way out at all, it looks rather splendid.

But the bishops of the day had different ideas. It just didn't seem like a cathedral.

Why the strange columns like some sort of ancient Greek temple? And what about that extraordinary, almost carbuncular, dome affair on the top?

It was only thanks to the support of King Charles II that the cathedral we see today was built. A truly magnificent creation it remains, but less bold than it could have been.

Even so, poor old Wren had to erect an 18-foot wall around the building site to prevent his critics spying on the work and scuppering his ultimate plans.

Compare modern London with Canaletto's 1750 painting and you'll find St Paul's is hidden, once again. But now by a dense forest of concrete and glass towers.

The spread of buildings like these has prompted the future King Charles III, in his own words, to: 'Throw a royal brick through the inviting plate glass of architects' pompous professional pride.' Maybe he's got a point.

Take the new Lloyds insurance building. It's been hailed as one of the great triumphs of 20th century architecture.

But why do London taxi-drivers refer to it as 'The Dalek'? And why did a MORI poll find that 70% of the stripey-shirted underwriters prefer their previous, conventional building?

If the public disagree with architects about what constitutes good architecture, the profession itself is even more divided.

A list of the different styles they work in reads disturbingly like the entry register of the 1989 Pseuds All-comers Championship.

There's International, Modernist, Brutalist, Constructionist, Neo-Classical, Post-Modernist, Neo-Vernacular, High-Tech, and, wait for it, Deconstructionalist!

Some people think all this variety gives us diverse, exciting cities.

Others feel the result is a messy hotch-potch of buildings that relate neither to their surroundings nor to each other.

These are the people the Prince of Wales speaks for when he calls for a return to more familiar styles of architecture.

But could the Prince be accused of being a Stick-in-the-mud?

His critics point out that many of our finest historic buildings were, in their own time, revolutionary designs. And like St Paul's, they stuck out like massive sore thumbs.

But Prince Charles insists he's not 'anti' modern architecture, just against buildings that are ruthlessly functional and inhuman.

The fact is, there's a bloody style war raging in British architecture, and with his series of speeches and 'Omnibus' TV film, Prince Charles is right at the heart of the conflict.

Leading, as it were, a daring frontal assault on enemy positions, the Prince now presents his personal view of architecture in a controversial new exhibition at that home of controversy, the Victoria and Albert Museum, South Kensington.

Entitled 'A Vision of Britain,' the exhibition is possibly the most frank and outspoken contribution to a public debate ever made by a member of the royal family.

(Coinciding with the start of the exhibition, Doubleday are publishing a book of the same title, price £16.95.)

Whether you're a Deconstructionalist, a Post-Modernist or just a Neo-Stick-in-the-mud, to appreciate the debate fully, this is one V&A show you should not miss.

"A view of the city from the river", painted in 1750 by Antonio Canaletto. The great dome of St. Paul's cathedral dominated the scene for another 200 years. But by 1970 it was fast disappearing behind modern office blocks.

H.R.H. THE PRINCE OF WALES'S 'A VISION OF BRITAIN' 8th SEPT. TO 19th NOV. V&A

122
Vision of Britain exhibition
United Kingdom
Agency: Saatchi & Saatchi, London
The exhibition, at London's Victoria & Albert Museum, expressed the architectural opinions of Prince Charles, who has led the criticism of the ugliness of many modern buildings. The picture, by Canaletto, shows an 18th-century view of St Paul's Cathedral dominating the City of London. Nowadays it is almost hidden by office blocks.

123, 125
Berlin Film Festival
West Germany
Studio: Volker Noth Grafik-Design, Berlin
Two quite different posters for the 1990 International Film Festival in Berlin. One, with the starkly beautiful photograph of post-war deprivation, draws attention under the heading 'The Year 1945' to a retrospective collection of movies. The other advertises the children's section of the festival. The elements of the cartoon face include the number 13 because, though the main festival was the 40th of its kind, this was only the 13th children's festival. Volker Noth set up his own studio after leaving the Noth & Hauer firm at the end of 1989.

124
Takashi Kanome exhibition
Japan
Studio: Takashi Kanome, Tokyo
Takashi Kanome designed this extraordinary 'bird animal installation' for an exhibition sponsored by the Seibu retail chain.

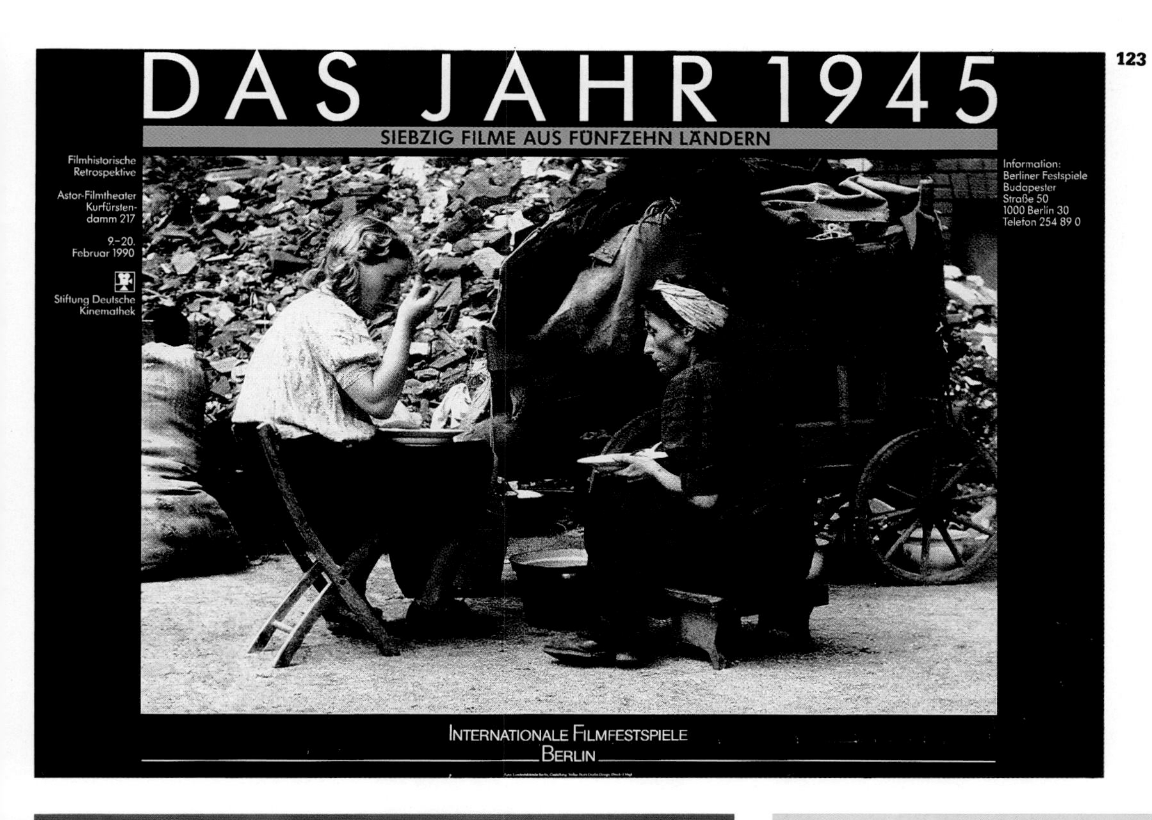
DAS JAHR 1945
SIEBZIG FILME AUS FÜNFZEHN LÄNDERN
Filmhistorische Retrospektive
Astor-Filmtheater Kurfürstendamm 217
9.–20. Februar 1990
Stiftung Deutsche Kinemathek
Information: Berliner Festspiele Budapester Straße 50 1000 Berlin 30 Telefon 254 89 0
INTERNATIONALE FILMFESTSPIELE
BERLIN

123

124

13. KINDERFILMFESTBERLIN
10.-20. FEBRUAR 1990
Unter der Schirmherrschaft von unicef
Urania, Kleiststraße 13, Berlin 30, täglich 14.00 und 16.00 Uhr
Colosseum, Schönhauser Allee 123, Berlin, Prenzlauer Berg, ab 11. Februar täglich 14.00 Uhr
Adria, Schloßstraße 48, Berlin 41, täglich 15.30 Uhr
Vorbestellungen für Gruppen für Urania und Adria, Telefon 261 52 53
Landesbildstelle Kinosaal, Wikingerufer 7, Berlin 21, 12.-16. Februar 1990, nur mit Vorbestellung, Telefon 390 92 317
40. INTERNATIONALE FILMFESTSPIELE
BERLIN
Berliner Festspiele GmbH, Budapester Straße 50, 1000 Berlin 30, Telefon 254 89 0

125

7

126

127

If you had been standing here reading a poster on June 27th 1944 it would have been the last thing you ever did.

In the early hours of June 13th 1944 four stubby winged aircraft making a noise "like a giant raspberry blown from obscure great lips" were spotted, apparently on fire, over Kent.

Shortly afterwards one crashed on a bridge in Bow killing 6 people and making 200 homeless.

As usual the rescue workers were quickly on the scene, but they searched in vain for members of the crew.

They found none. There were none.

It was London's first flying bomb, the "Doodlebug" as it came to be known; one of Hitler's "secret weapons" designed to terrorize the people of Britain into submission.

In the following weeks few parts of London escaped its effect.

They dropped on the 'royals' in St. James's Palace, the porters in Lewisham market, the nuns in Tyburn, Bayswater, even the animals in the zoo.

One even landed pretty near to where you're standing right now.

In fact, 1,074 V1s fell on or near railway property. "A train is coming in on platform 2 and a flying bomb is approaching platform 6" is rumoured to have been a common announcement.

At first, following minor incidents, Londoners typically picked themselves up, dusted themselves off and got on with reading their papers, their reserve and humour infuriating the Germans.

As the bombardment wore on it became anything but a joke. It became a permanent nightmare.

People would lie awake at night tense, rigid, their hearts racing. In a cold, trickly sweat they'd listen for the drone, and then the "deafening silence" – convinced each bomb was on a predestined course for them.

As you can imagine sudden noises weren't popular that summer. Even milkmen were warned not to clatter their churns as it was playing havoc with people's nerves.

By August nearly a million had left London, and more were leaving every day.

However, September saw the advent of much new technology allowing anti-aircraft guns greater success in shooting down the bombs.

Faster fighters were also proving adept at intercepting them, by flying behind and blasting with their guns, or in some cases, when they'd run out of ammunition, by resorting to "tipping" them off course with their wings.

Even the previously unglamorous barrage balloons had their finest hour, becoming known as the Goalkeepers of London.

At 12.43pm. on Thursday 29th March 1945 the last V1 flying bomb was shot ignominiously into the English Channel.

With that solitary splash died much of the spirit of the German High Command.

The Allies had won the battle of the flying bomb, but, it had cost the lives of over 6,000 people, left nearly 18,000 injured and damaged 20,000 homes, not to mention the psychological scars it inflicted upon millions.

But how can we imagine what the people of London must have felt like during such a time?

They travelled on the same railways, drank in the same pubs, worked in the same offices and even read the same poster sites as you do today.

At the Imperial War Museum, which has just reopened, you won't find us trying to glorify the war, we want to give you an impression of what it was like to be part of it.

That's why as well as the thousands of exhibits, with as many intimate stories behind them, you'll find interactive videos, films, and special displays like the "Blitz Experience," designed to let you feel what it was like then.

After all, it's only when you've tasted what it was like to live through a war, that you can appreciate what it's like not to.

IMPERIAL WAR MUSEUM **Part of your family's history**

The Imperial War Museum is open daily 10am to 6pm from Friday 30th June. Walking distance from Lambeth North and Elephant & Castle Tube Stations.

128

1. **Visual:** A black screen. ***Audio:*** *Music that suddenly stops due to an apparent electrical breakdown.*

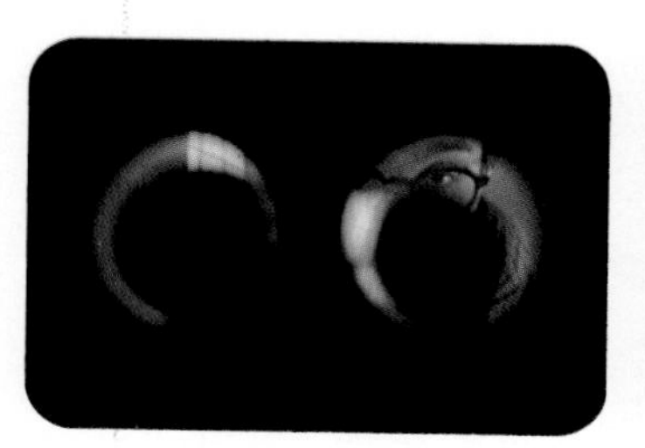

2. **Visual:** Two circular openings slowly emerge from the black screen and it becomes evident . . .

3. . . . that the camera is placed inside a socket, looking out into the room. A man gazes into the socket's two holes sceptically.

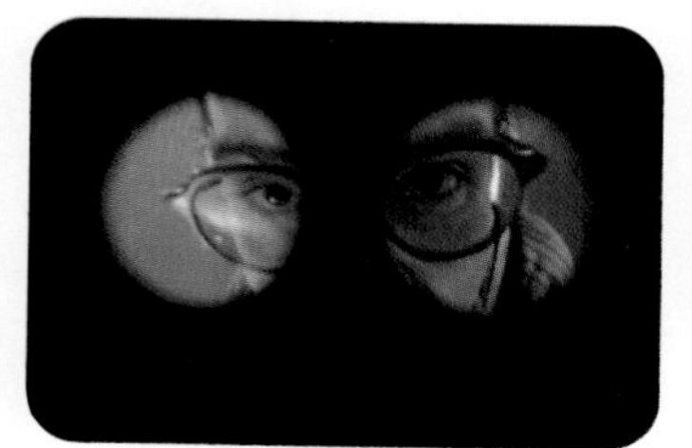

4.

5. He takes off his glasses and tries . . .

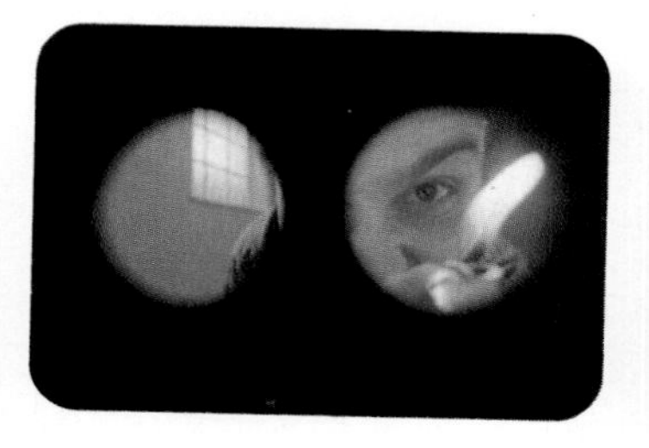

6. . . . to shed some light on the matter with the help of a cigarette lighter. He succeeds only in burning his eyebrows.

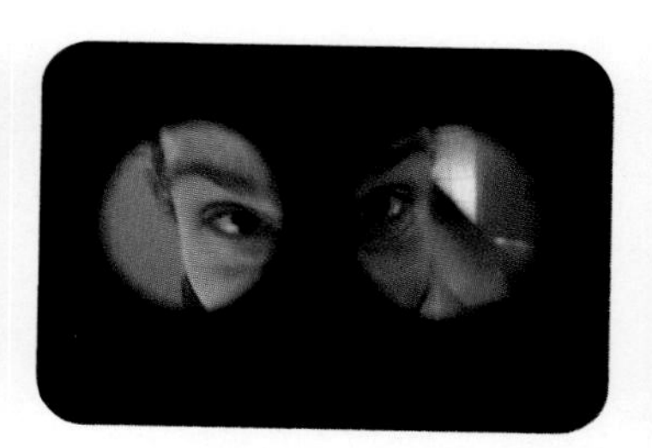

7. Then he takes a pen and fumbles around the outside of the socket.

8. No result. He thinks long and hard . . .

GIOVANNA D'ARCO
DI EMILIO ISGRÒ
PROGETTO OTTONOVE NOVEDUE - TETRALOGIA DELLA SANTITÀ
MILANO TEATRO DI PORTA ROMANA DALL'8 AL 28 MAGGIO 1989

129

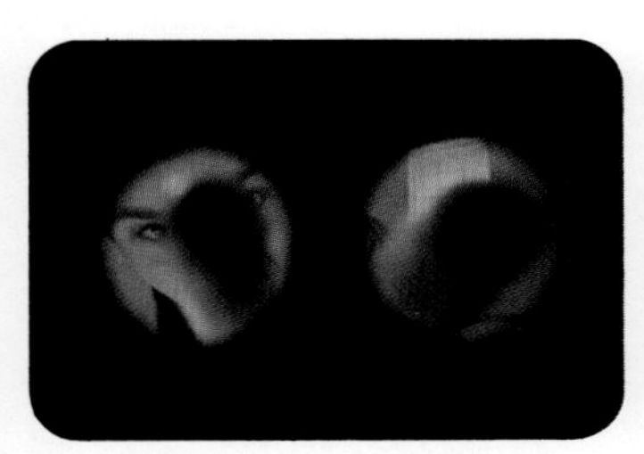

9. . . . and then he winds up making a big mistake.

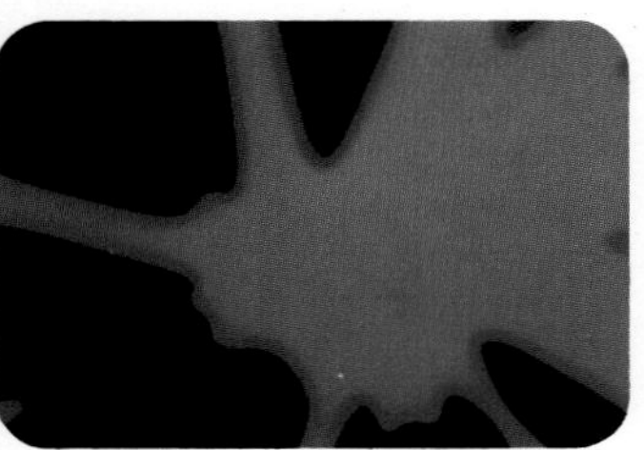

10. ***Audio:*** *Scream of pain. Sizzling.*

Das SiemensMuseum München
Prannerstraße 10

11. **Visual:** Cut to Super: The Siemens Museum, Munich. Prannerstraße 10. ***Audio*** (MVO): *'If you want to find out more about electricity, come to the Siemens Museum Munich. The Siemens Museum, Munich, Prannerstraße 10.'*

126
International Design Exhibition
United States
Studio: Keizo Matsui Design Office, Osaka

Keizo Matsui designed the bottles shown in this poster for the 1989 International Design Exhibition in Osaka, Japan. The sponsor was the Suntory liquor company. Photos by Nob Fukuda.

127
Imperial War Museum
United Kingdom
Agency: Ogilvy & Mather, London

The sinister object pictured is one of Germany's World War Two flying bombs, or Doodlebugs, with which London was attacked in 1944 and 1945.

129
Giovanna D'Arco, theatre play
Italy
Agency: Armando Testa, Turin

Posters for the play *Giovanna D'Arco* (Joan of Arc) by Emilio Isgro, at the Porta Romana theatre in Milan, carried this striking image, halfway between a female icon and a representation of the sun.

128
Siemens Museum
West Germany
Agency: MC&D, Munich

The Siemens Museum in Munich is devoted to the subject of electricity. This funny little film puts the viewer inside an electrical socket, looking out. When a man sticks his two fingers in it he naturally meets with disaster.

130

Nico iba a cumplir 16 años.
Y me devanaba los sesos pensando qué regalarle a un monstruo de su edad.
Era viernes. Y habíamos quedado en almorzar juntos.
A la una en punto, cosa rara en él, me pasó a buscar por la oficina. Me extrañó no verlo con Alejandra (últimamente no se despegaban). Se ve que prefirió venir solo.
Y la verdad es que disfruté la idea de que pudiéramos tener una conversación de "hombre a hombre".
Mientras caminábamos por la avenida, le pregunté dónde quería ir.
Previsiblemente, terminamos comiendo hamburguesas.
El tiempo se nos pasaba volando. Busqué la oportunidad para sacarle el tema del regalo, presintiendo lo que me esperaría la noche de su cumpleaños: la casa invadida por un ejército de adolescentes revoltosos. Algunos especímenes engominados de moñito y sobretodo hasta los tobillos. Otros, con pantalones de esos que parecen heredados de sus abuelos. Música de los años '50. Y mi secreta esperanza de que algún fusible saltara devolviéndonos la paz y el silencio. Ya me veía refugiándome con Susana, mi mujer, en la cocina, mientras los invasores se dedicaban a devorar como si jamás hubieran probado algo decente.
Nico me miraba como si sospechara algo.
De golpe le disparé la pregunta:
–¿Qué querés que te regale para tu cumpleaños?
Ya me imaginaba la respuesta: una moto, una tabla de surf, un equipo de audio.
No, nada de eso. Nico me sorprendió.
–Ya soy grande, pa –me dijo–. Pensándolo bien, me gustaría que me abrieras una Cuenta First. Así manejo yo mismo mis gastos y administro mi dinero sin depender de vos.
Durante diez interminables segundos me quedé mirando hacia adelante, sin ver nada ni poder decir nada. Cuando me recuperé del impacto, le contesté:
–¡Hecho!
Orgulloso estreché su mano de hombre.
No había más que hablar. Fuimos hasta la sucursal de Lloyds Bank, que nos quedaba muy cerca, donde nos atendió una chica bárbara del Centro de Servicios. Ella nos explicó todo sobre la Cuenta First, una Caja de Ahorros especial para gente joven.
Pero Nico ya estaba al tanto de todas sus ventajas y si se hizo el que no entendía, fue porque estaba "copadísimo".
Ahora, mi hijo se encarga de sus gastos, hace sus extracciones. Paga la cuota del gimnasio. Se compra los libros del colegio. Y con los intereses, ahorra para su famosa guitarra eléctrica y su viaje de egresados.
Ya no me pide más para sus salidas. Y si se va de vacaciones, me olvido de los giros urgentes. Porque con la tarjeta Banelco, Nico puede operar los 365 días del año, las 24 horas.
En fin: se ha convertido en un pequeño gran responsable. Con decir que hasta pagó las hamburguesas!

De hombre a hombre.

UN PURA SANGRE ENTRE LOS BANCOS.

131

first direct is a division of midland bank plc.

banking without branches. it's extraordinary.

first direct
0800 22 2000

132

For vigorous growth, plant your money with us.

W2124

130
Lloyds Bank
Argentina
Agency: Ayer Vazquez, Buenos Aires
A father recounts how he and his son Nico had a man-to-man talk over a hamburger on the eve of the boy's 16th birthday. Asked what he wanted as a present, Nico surprised his father by requesting a First Account at Lloyds. Headline 'Man to man'.

131
First Direct
United Kingdom
Agency: Howell Henry Chaldecott Lury, London
First Direct is a Midland Bank subsidiary, launched in late 1989, which establishes direct marketing links with customers by telephone and enables them to perform all their banking operations without visiting a branch. Much of the agency's advertising, both print and television, has gone in for apparently irrelevant images in an attempt to create interest even at the risk of puzzling the reader/viewer. Typical TV spots have had shots of three fish or two buckets. Agency partners Axel Chaldecott and Steve Henry are respectively art director and copywriter on the example shown here.

The rationale behind this sustained teasing is that, to entice the sceptical consumer, the ads need to be as different from other banks' ads as First Direct claims to be from other banks. Banal, rather than exciting, images are chosen to persuade people that the enterprise is free of hype. After six months new customers were said to be signing up in large numbers.

132
Legal & General insurance company
United Kingdom
Agency: Young & Rubicam, London
The company's familiar emblem of the multicoloured umbrella is used here to particularly clever effect.

133
Delta Dental insurance
USA
Agency: Zwiren Collins Karo Trusk & Ayer, Chicago
The picture, perhaps unfamiliar to some readers, is a close-up of part of a US dollar bill. Delta Dental, which specialises in dental care insurance, claims to save its customers money.

133

A dental plan should be designed to save more than teeth.

Delta Dental brings more smiles to more employers than any other plan. Not just in terms of how it affects employee morale. But in how it affects a company's bottom line. ☐ Unlike insurers who provide dental coverage as part of a package of benefits, Delta Dental is the only major company specializing in dental programs. *We invented them. Pioneered them. And perfected them.* ☐ Our unique three-point system of cost management features, plan design flexibility and 106,000 dentists in the nation's largest participating network enabled us, last year alone, to save our groups and subscribers over $100 million. ☐ It's a program only Delta Dental offers. That's why we now cover more than 20 million people in 23,000 groups and pay more than $2 billion a year for dental care. To learn more about how your group can benefit from Delta Dental, call 1-800-441-3434 today.

Delta Dental
America's Leader In Dental Health Plans.

SEVEN DECADES OF LEADERSHIP

For New India, growth has always been synonymous with service and innovation.

And that meant having to understand specific needs. Appreciate risks. And offer futuristic covers in tune with the changing times.

The first in the field

This credo soon found expression. In the type of insurance covers New India pioneered through the early years. Motor Insurance with the advent of the Ford Model T. Aviation Insurance with the historic Karachi - Bombay flight by J.R.D. Tata. Insurance for the first steel plant. The first textile mill. In fact, covers that reflected every new facet of India's development.

This leadership was consolidated soon after nationalisation in 1973. When New India expanded its activities to also cover rural India. Through much needed welfare-oriented insurance covers for the weaker sections of society.

70 years later

Service and innovation continue to find new expression. Through pioneering health insurance schemes (such as Cancer) where prevention is actually a part of the benefits. Plus a wide range of sophisticated covers. From Sea Food and Grape to every single satellite from the 'Aryabhatta' onwards. On to Himalayan Car Rallies. Even Test Match Weather.

No wonder New India's premium base exceeds Rs.725 crores. Serviced by over 1100 offices in 30 countries. Backed by a team of nearly 800 experts, including engineers and veterinary surgeons, offering specialised services.

New India. The giant, 20000-strong insurance company whose success lies on the solid foundation of service.

Service with a special personal touch.

For us, times change. Values endure.

BORN TO LEAD

A public sector enterprise with the entrepreneurial spirit.

134

134
New India Assurance
India
Agency: Contour Advertising, Bombay

The Ford Model T stands for car insurance, introduced by the New India company in the early 1920s. The Big C is cancer (in Latin the wordddd *cancer* means 'crab'). New India was the first Indian insurance company to offer cancer insurance.

135
Bain Clarkson insurance brokers
United Kingdom
Agency: Primary Contact, London

To read most of the copy you have to turn the ad upside down. Then you learn that 'an accident at your plant could turn the company upside down'. Bain Clarkson operates a scheme for chemical industry clients which includes disaster recovery services and public relations consultancy as well as insurance cover.

An accident at your plant could turn the company upside-down.

And if your contingency plans and insurance are not properly organised it could close you down.

The Bain Clarkson Chemical Industry Facility is designed to stop this from happening.

It includes a risk control programme, extended damage, interruption, liability, contamination and pollution covers, loss mitigation, disaster recovery services and a P.R. consultancy.

Our eighty years in depth experience dealing with both U.K. domestic and multinational chemical companies has taught us a great deal.

However, our clients aren't just with us because of our experience and resources, but because should the unthinkable happen we would have thought to insure against it.

Trust Bain Clarkson to provide a fresh point of view.

For further information contact your local Bain Clarkson office, or call Carol Merritt on (071) 481 3232.

Bain Clarkson would.

Some brokers wouldn't see the risks at this chemical plant.

135

Nogle gange er skrivebordet for langt fra virkeligheden

Som virksomhedsleder har De krav på, at Deres bank kan give Dem andet og mere end skrivebordsløsninger.

Et professionelt beslutningsgrundlag skal kunne kombinere de mange finansieringsmuligheder, der er til rådighed, på en sådan måde, at virksomhedens drifts- og investeringsplaner kan realiseres.

Derfor lægger vi i Den Danske Bank vægt på en løbende kontakt mellem virksomheden og bankens erhvervsrådgivere.

136

136
Danske Bank
Denmark
Agency: Young & Rubicam, Copenhagen

One of a series aimed at business customers, this is headed 'Sometimes the desk is too far from real life'. Copy says the bank believes in the importance of continuous contact between the client company and the bank consultant who looks after its account.

137
3i
United Kingdom
Agency: Howell Henry Chaldecott Lury, London

Darwin's head on a monkey. One of a series of press ads for the investment institution which invite people to read, literally, between the lines. Art director and copywriter are respectively agency partners Axel Chaldecott and Steve Henry.

138, 139
National Westminster Bank
United Kingdom
Agency: Collett Dickenson Pearce and Partners, London

The two ads are concerned with different specialised NatWest services, respectively stockbroking, including the Brokerline facility whereby customers can buy and sell shares by telephone, and house mortgages. The Flexible Mortgage scheme enables borrowers to reduce the burden of debt repayment for selected periods.

140, 141
Creditanstalt bank
Austria
Agency: Demner & Merlicek, Vienna

A touch of role reversal in these two magazine ads for 'CA, the bank for success'. The copy line accompanying the man holding his baby is 'It is never too early to provide a financial pillow for one's offspring'. The career woman with her yuppy phone is told the time is ripe to open a high-interest savings account.

137

138

HOW DO YOU TAKE THE GAMBLE OUT OF PLAYING THE STOCK MARKET?

139

HOWEVER YOU'RE FIXED, YOUR MORTGAGE PAYMENTS NEEDN'T BE.

140

141

142

143

144

142, 143
Eurocard
Iceland
Agency: Hvíta Húsið, Reykjavík
Brian Pilkington's funny illustrations are matched by the headlines. The one in the Noah's Ark ad says 'The right card makes all the difference'. The other is 'Will your card be welcome where your holidays take you?'

144
Iceland Insurance Company
Iceland
Agency: Hvíta Húsið, Reykjavík
From a series of press and TV ads depicting what life might be like without insurance, this one is headed 'There are simpler ways to arm yourself against accidents'.

145
American Express Optima card
United States
Agency: Ogilvy & Mather, New York
O&M has recently produced a number of strongly emotive mini-movies for Amex in the US, of which this is one of the most cunningly designed to tug at the heartstrings. The father–child relationship is exploited again in another Amex commercial, where a man loads his new video recorder with a cassette and tells his infant son the machine is eating it. Later the little boy tries feeding his breakfast into the slot. Result: when Daddy tries to use the machine, out drops a mass of porridge. He calls Amex and is reassured by a charming woman that purchases are protected when made with an Amex card and he will be reimbursed. In yet another film a couple about to return from a second honeymoon decide on the spur of the moment to miss their plane, abandoning their luggage, and spend more time on another holiday island. The wife buys new clothes, using the card which gives you 'everything you need when you need some time together'.

1. **Audio:** *Music up and under.*

2. **Boy:** *Yeah, Dad – it'll be fun. Me and you on a boat.*

3. **Audio:** *Music.*

4. *See? It'll be just us; just fishing.*

5. **Man:** *Marsha, do I have anything on next week's schedule that can't be postponed?*

6. **Woman:** *No, no . . .*
Man: *Good, then postpone it.*

7. **Audio:** *Music.*

8. **Audio:** *Children cheering.*

9. **Audio:** *Music.*

10. **Audio:** *Music.*

11. **Man:** *Hey, here's one fishing hat; one fishing vest complete with daredevil lures.*

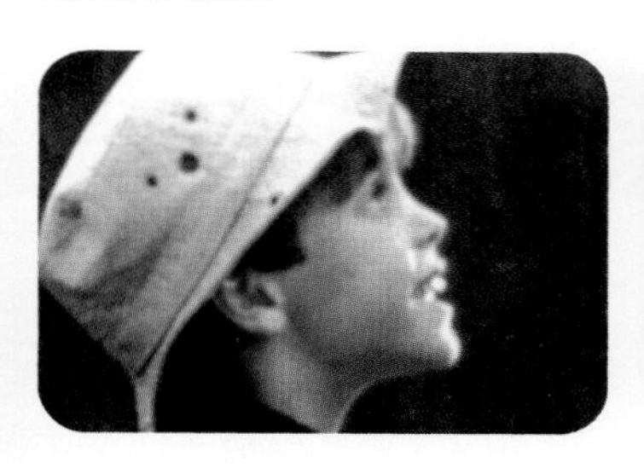

12. **Boy whispers:** *Whose is it?*

13. **Man:** *It's ours.*

14. **Boy:** *Did your Dad ever do anything like this?*

15. **Audio voice-over:** *You've got the option.*

16. *The Optima Card from American Express.*

146

147

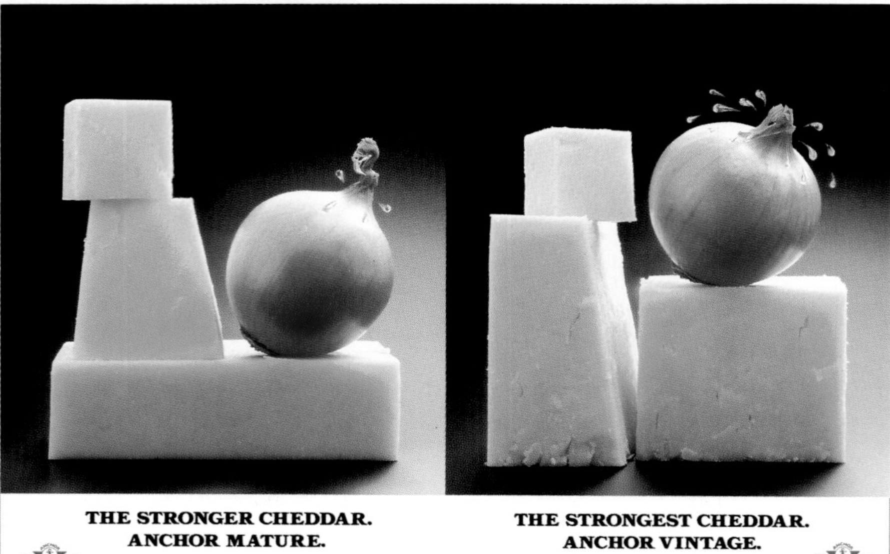

148

146
Apple juice
Sweden
Agency: Hall & Cederquist/Y&R, Stockholm
Copy asks the question: 'Eight apples weigh one kilo. How much do 16 apples weigh?' The ad supplies the answer: '255 grammes'. A neat way of saying how much fruit goes into one carton of apple juice sold by the Mejerierna (Swedish Dairies).

147
Colombian Coffee
United States
Agency: DDB Needham, New York
To some of us two o'clock might seem more like lunchtime than coffee break time. Never mind, this ad embodies a nice idea. Copy says: 'Colombian Coffee inspires people to do things they'd never do. Which is why it's no surprise over half of America is willing to pay a premium for the richest coffee in the world.'

148
Anchor cheddar cheese
United Kingdom
Agency: Saatchi & Saatchi, London
Anchor's Mature Cheddar is matured for a year longer than its standard brand, and Vintage for two years longer. The latter's strength makes the onion sweat even more.

149
Amul Ghee
India
Agency: ASP, Bombay
Ghee is clarified butter, the use of which in cooking appears to make all the difference to whether a dish is eaten or not. At least that's what the pictures say.

150
Rupp Käsle cheese
Austria
Agency: Demner & Merlicek, Vienna
The brand comes in squares and triangles. Hence the pictures and the headline 'From spotted to angular cattle farming'.

151, 152
Twix
United Kingdom
Agency: DMB&B, London
A smart way of giving eye appeal to the chocolate biscuit snacks made by Mars. Note the lock of hair coming out of the coffee pot.

149

VON DER FLECKVIEHZUCHT
ZUR ECKVIEHZUCHT.

Die Vorarlberger Kühe treiben es immer bunter. Nachdem sie schon in den letzten Monaten „s'beschte Eck vom Käs'" auf hochalpine Absatzpfade geführt haben, sind sie jetzt zur Produktion von viereckigen Käseecken in Form von Scheiben übergegangen – was man einzelnen Exemplaren schon von weitem ansieht.

RUPP KÄSLE
S'BESCHTE ECK VOM KAS.

Das Resultat kann sich im Kühlregal sehen lassen: Milde Toastscheiben für sanfte Genießer, Pikante Toastscheiben für phantasievolle Köche, Leichte Käsle Scheiben für modern Ernährte und klassische Enzian Käsle Scheiben für Traditionalisten. Bei so viel alemannischer Tüchtigkeit muß ja Ihr Eck-Umsatz Zinsen tragen.

150

151

152

153

154

153
Danone white cheese
Belgium
Agency: Young & Rubicam, Brussels

Two posters separated by time. The teaser with jumbled letters was replaced after one week with the one where the message is spelt out clearly: 'Danone cheese puts you together again'.

154
Sinalco soft drink
Switzerland
Agency: Advico Young & Rubicam, Zürich

'No, it does not make you pleasanter' says the first of the ad's two panels. 'But fresher' says the second. From a visually striking series which rings a few simple changes on the same basic theme.

155
Saratoga mineral water
United States
Agency: TBWA, New York

The product is different, the layout is different, the effect is different – but the basic idea is not too different from that of Y&R's Belgian ad for Danone cheese. There is probably no end to the visual uses to which good creatives can put words.

156, 157
Evian mineral water
United States
Agency: TBWA, New York

A couple of punchy one-liners with perfectly matched visuals.

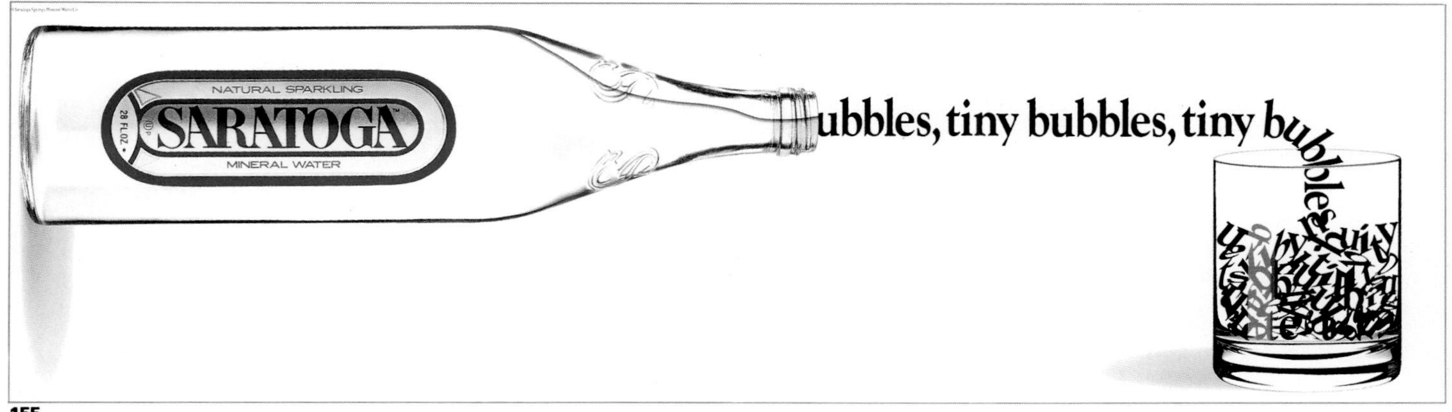
NATURAL SPARKLING
SARATOGA
28 FL.OZ.
MINERAL WATER
ubbles, tiny bubbles, tiny bubbles

155

© 1989 Evian Waters of France.
Our factory.
The balance.
evian
natural spring water from the French Alps

156

evian
natural spring water from the French Alps
evian. The balance.
It's never too early.

157

158

159

158, 159
Kit Kat
United Kingdom
Agency: J. Walter Thompson, London

JWT's advertising for Rowntree's Kit Kat chocolate bars – slogan 'Have a break, have a Kit Kat' – has built up a tradition of visual ingenuity. Here we have in one ad the grass at Wimbledon covered with the brand's emblem, while in the other the emblem appears among the graphic instructions for washing hair.

160, 161
Aqua Libra
United Kingdom
Agency: Ayer, London

Health is the message prettily conveyed here, though whether it would be healthy to have a load of flowers growing in your insides is another question. Exactly how a mixture of spring water, fruit and vegetable ingredients, tarragon and ginseng brings about physical wellbeing is also not explained.

162, 163
Sugar
Austria
Agency: Demner & Merlicek, Vienna

Art-directed by agency partner Franz Merlicek, these two ads emphasise respectively the purity and variety of sugar. The purity line is spun in the copy accompanying the picture of a sack in the form of a sugar beet and headlined 'From nature's horn of plenty'. Copy in the other ad, headed 'A picture of sugar', describes how an expensive restaurant will offer its customers many different kinds of sugar with their coffee.

160

161

162

163

164, 167
Milk
Netherlands
Agency: PPGH/J. Walter Thompson, Amsterdam
Two more ads from a campaign that has built a reputation over the years for visual wit. A previous example appeared on the front cover of the 1988 edition of this annual.

165
Eagle Snacks
Portugal
Agency: Ayer, Lisbon
The brand, made by the Anheuser-Busch group, is a newcomer to the Portuguese market, where the snacks are consumed as aperitifs with drinks. Hence the simple but effective device of presenting them in drinking glasses. Headline: 'Straight . . . or with a drink'.

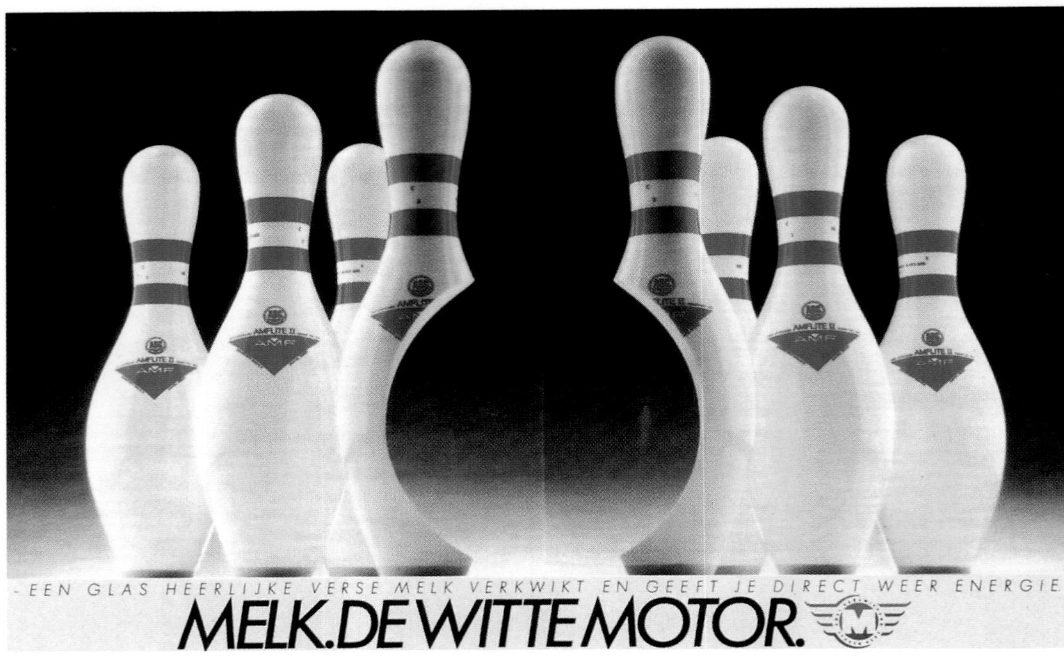

164

165

166

175
Vittel mineral water
France
Agency: Lintas, Paris
The message 'We all need Vittel' is spread across the three panels of this triptych. The pictures, in keeping with the marketing platform of the product, emphasise natural, open-air healthiness. But what is a latrine doing in the middle of open fields?

176
Lesieur olive oil
France
Agency: Saatchi & Saatchi, Paris
'Lesieur chooses the olives the sun has already chosen' is the copy line, backed up by the simple but engaging illustration of southern climes with sacks of olives in the foreground.

177
Sea fish
United Kingdom
Agency: BMP DDB Needham, London
The copy actually says not that fish can be cooked in a toaster but that cooking it is 'one step on from a slice of toast'. However, the image is eye-catching. The client is Britain's Sea Fish Authority.

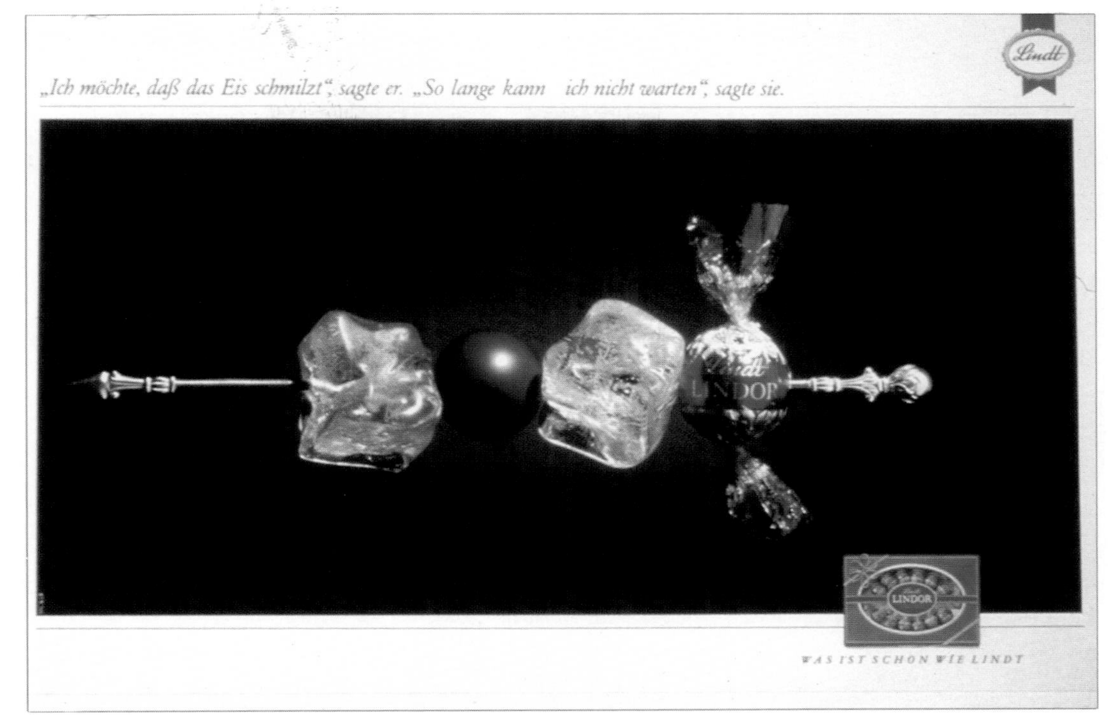

174

175

176

177

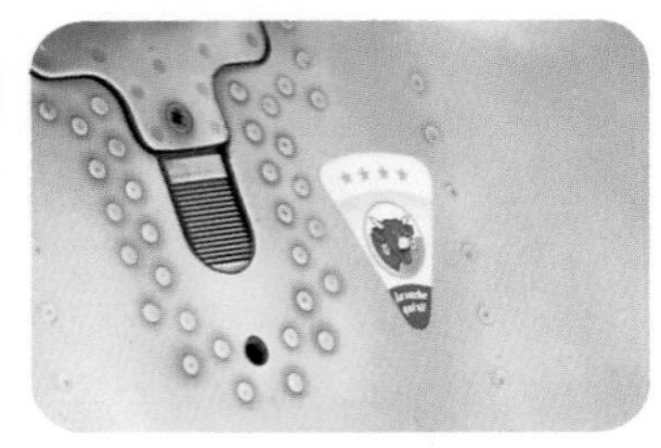

178

178
La Vache Qui Rit cheese
France
Agency: RSCG, Paris

A commercial fairy tale, devised to appeal to kids. The pilot who begs a chunk of cheese from a little boy and sticks the label on his plane makes up in watchability for what he lacks in credibility.

179
Mamie Nova chocolate mousse
France
Agency: CLM/BBDO, Paris

The brand name means 'Granny Nova', which supplies the cue for the ad campaign. In this commercial two elegant elderly ladies are seen conversing in an art gallery. Their exchange goes as follows.

Gisèle: My dear, I am a misunderstood artist.
Friend: You, Gisèle?
Gisèle: Yes, you know my granddaughter Angélique? Do you know what she had the nerve to say to me?
Friend: Tell me, tell me.
Gisèle: Granny, your chocolate mousse is lousy. You ought to buy Granny Nova's instead.
Friend: Tut, tut!
Voice-over: Granny Nova. Grannies don't thank her.

179

180
Nestlé Gold Blend
United Kingdom
Agency: McCann-Erickson, London

The faces of two of Britain's best known television actors – though most viewers may never have learned their names – as they appeared at the end of 1989 in the fifth episode of McCann's long running advertising soap opera for Gold Blend. What had made the couple's faces, if not their names, Sharon Maughan and Tony Head, famous was indeed the ad campaign, which had begun two years previously. In the first episode they became acquainted as residents of neighbouring apartments, with one borrowing a jar of Gold Blend from the other. Their increasingly flirtatious, coffee-based relationship developed slowly through subsequent commercials.

The ad-makers were in no hurry to move the story along, but after two years they clearly felt the need to inject some dramatic tension. So, in the fifth episode, when Tony knocks at Sharon's door he is disconcerted to find it opened by a handsome young male stranger, whom we have just seen talking to her and sipping coffee ('Gold Blend, I'm impressed') while she goes to change her clothes. The stranger, actor Philip Bretherton, tells Tony that the lady of the house is changing 'in the bedroom' (said with a sexy leer). Tony leaves with his tail between his legs. When Sharon re-emerges Philip reports her neighbour's visit and, questioned as to whether he disclosed his own identity, replies 'He didn't ask'.

Viewers were left to wonder whether the new man was intended to be lover, brother, colleague or whatever. The mystery earned the campaign the distinction of a double-page editorial spread in a mass-circulation daily newspaper, Rupert Murdoch's *Today*, which inquired of manufacturers Nestlé what the next step in the story was going to be. The company declined to give any hint. A spokesman said the commercial would run for about six months until the wear-out factor started to take effect. Viewers might or might not discover in a subsequent commercial who the mystery man was. In fact Sharon revealed in that subsequent film that he was her brother.

Whatever can be said for or against the campaign – and it is less popular with advertising professionals than with ordinary viewers – it is no mean achievement for McCann to have made Gold Blend's advertising an object of genuine public curiosity. The fact that in real life the sophisticates, or pseudo-sophisticates, depicted in the ads would be more likely to apologise for instant coffee than to boast about it is, by contrast, a matter of small importance.

180

181

181
Batchelors Mushy Peas
United Kingdom
Agency: BMP DDB Needham, London

If KMO's 'Food from Andalusia' film (no. 182) aspires to be – and succeeds in being – genuinely poetic, this very English spoof is merely mock-poetic. It goes down well in its own country.

Visual: A beautiful white plate in an empty white set. On the plate sits a solitary pea.

SUPER: Ode to a pea.

As the ode begins, we slowly track into the pea.

Audio: (MUSIC) – *Elgar cello concerto.*

Voice-over: *Oh pea.*

Oh perfect viridian orb.

Why dost thou taunt me with thy beauty?

What mighty table will one day thy splendour grace?

Friend to the fish. Brother to the banger. Chum to the chicken.

Oh pea.

How couldst one improve on one so perfect as thee?

By way of a reply, a fork enters the screen and squashes the pea.

Cut to the packshot: a tin of Batchelors Mushy Peas.

182
Food from Andalusia
Spain
Agency: KMO-Leo Burnett, Madrid
This is television advertising raised to the level of art – and very well done, too. Film director: Ricardo Albiñana.

182

1 **Visual:** A series of constantly changing images done in the style of Pablo Picasso*. ***Audio:*** *Music inspired by Manuel de Falla* and Garcia Lorca's* poem 'Verde que te quiero Verde'.*

2. **Visual:** A black-and-white silhouette of Andalusia turns into a face.

3. Then a number of typical Andalusian food products emerge from it . . .

4. . . . sardines . . .

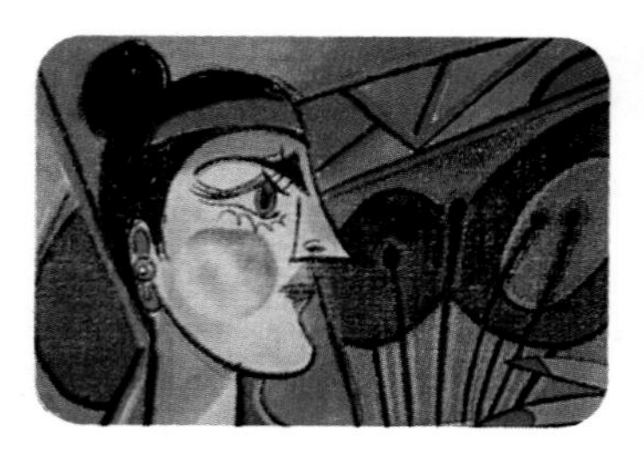

5. . . . the cheek on the woman's face becomes . . .

6. . . . a peach . .

7. . . . a painted bull on the plate turns into . . .

8. . . . a black olive.

9. At the centre of this still life is a jug of olive oil.

10. In another, a leg of boar . . .

11. . . . appears . . .

12. . . . and grapes . . .

13. . . . and finally, the sun, which contributes so much to food produce from this region.

14. Cut to super: Food from Andalusia. Green. How I love you green. ***Audio:*** *'Food from Andalusia. Green. How I love you green.'*

**All famous sons of Andalusia.*

183
Phileas Fogg snacks
United Kingdom
Agency: Bartle Bogle Hegarty, London

One of a series of very funny commercials satirising the brand's 'competitors' in other countries.

Visual: Open on the very stark interior of an army barracks.
We pan along a line of several huge, brutish, ugly legionnaires who are wearing non-identifiable fatigues (grubby white T-shirt, khaki trousers). One of them has a metal plate screwed onto his head. They are each fed a shovelful of baked beans from a cement mixer. ***Audio*** (MVO): *The men of the Desert Legion. Desperate men, ruined men, men who have something to forget.*

Cut to Jean Basteaux, a short moustachioed ex-chef. He's eating his beans in a very precise manner. *One such pitiful case is Jean Basteaux.* We match dissolve to a sequence of Jean Basteaux's former days of glory. We see him presenting a table of Parisian glitterati with a huge silver salver. He lifts the lid off to reveal a solitary but perfect garlic crouton. *Once the finest garlic crouton chef. His creations the envy of Paris. Le je ne sais quoi. Le weekend. La bohème. Le cul-de-sac. Le blob.*

183

We cut to him at an awards ceremony being presented with the 'Golden Crouton Award'. *Seven times winner of the coveted Crouton d'Or.* As he

leaves through the foyer, he becomes submerged in a melee of photographers. Suddenly, in his moment of triumph, a hand thrusts a packet of Phileas Fogg Mignons Morceaux towards him. He absent-mindedly takes one and eats it. *Until, at the height of his fame, from Medomsley Road, Consett, County Durham, came Mignons Morceaux, garlic croutons every bit as good.* Camera bulbs flash and we are taken back to the barracks. He pulls a corrugated sheet over him. The lights go out. *Now, he too is just another crouton floating on the bouillabaisse of life.*

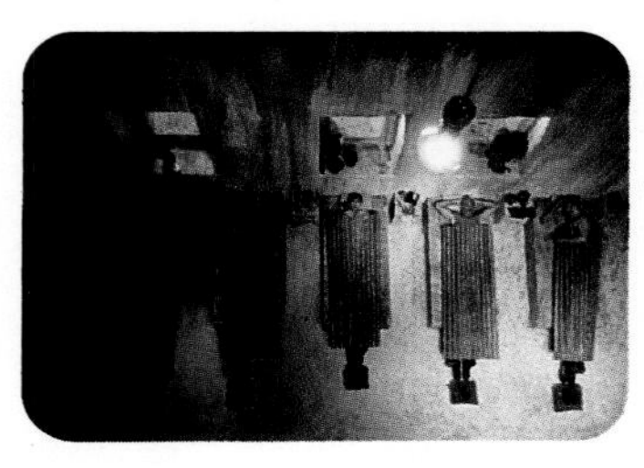

Cut to revolving globe, hand device and super. MVO: *Pay attention. Phileas Fogg Authentic Snacks, made in Medomsley Road, Consett.*

184
Hershey's Kisses
United States
Agency: Ogilvy & Mather, New York

In this animated commercial a voice-over asks 'Why do Hershey's Kisses come in great big bags?' A school bell is heard, and the Kisses – little chocolates – come running out of the bag to the sound of childish yells. The voice-over adds 'So they don't get lonely'. The film is one of a series targeted principally not at children but at women.

184

185

186

187

185, 186, 187
AEG household electrical appliances
United Kingdom
Agency: Young & Rubicam, London
Zoltan's quirky illustrations are what gives this campaign its originality. Y&R called in the artist precisely because it was thought his work would appeal to the upmarket young females at whom the campaign is aimed. Note that two of the three ads here have copy emphasising fashionable 'green' themes. AEG Lavamat washing machines have a valve that prevents undissolved detergents from being pumped out of the wastepipe, 'which means nothing nasty gets flushed into our ponds, rivers and streams'. The company has also cut by 50 per cent the environmentally harmful CFC content of its refrigerators. As for its cookers, they are 'less fattening' because of fat-absorbing filters.

188
La Foire du Ventilateur electric fans
Canada
Agency: Young & Rubicam, Montreal
'More than 400 other models in stock' says the ad. Presumably upside-down helicopters are not actually available for purposes of ventilation.

189
Levis paints
Belgium
Agency: Lowe Troost, Brussels
Paintbrushes as flowers. The picture, by photographer Daniel Jouanneau, is headed 'Gentle acrylic paints'.

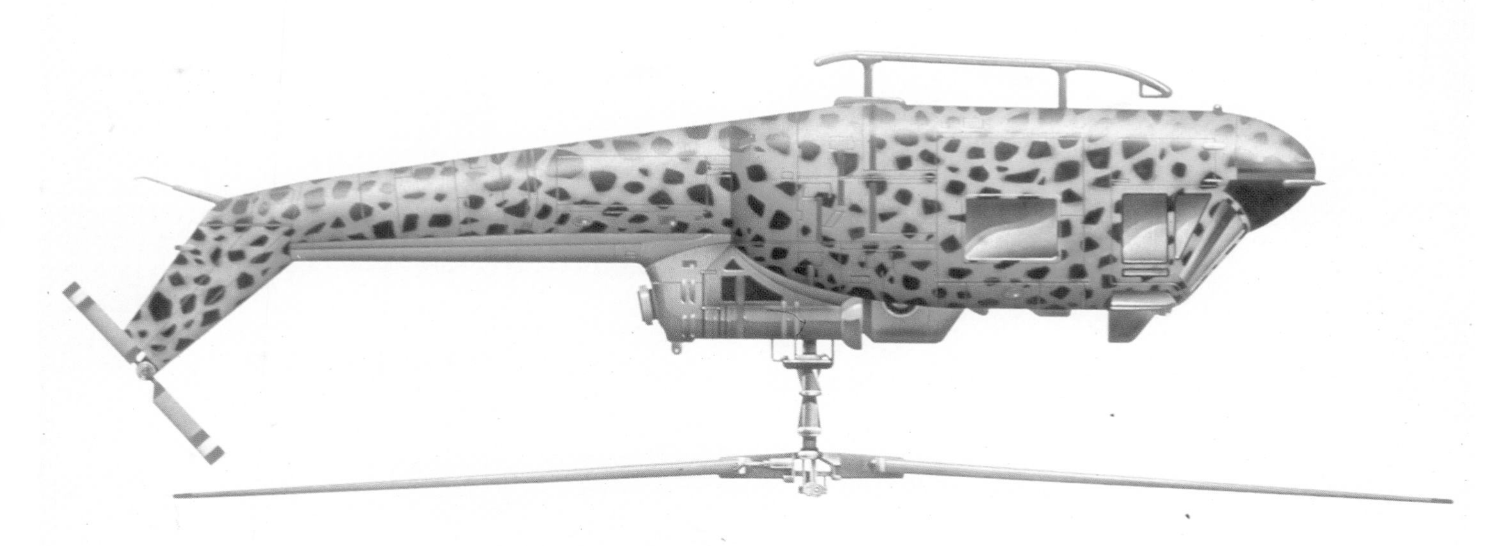

Plus de 400 autres modèles en magasin.

LA FOIRE
DU VENTILATEUR

188

189

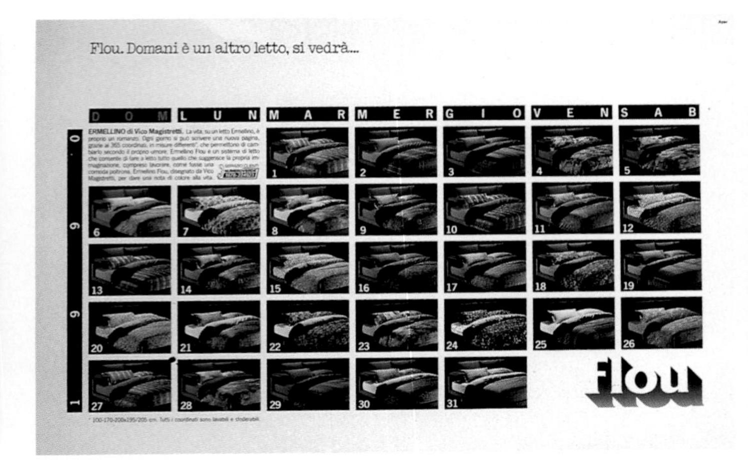

190

191

190
Flou beds
Italy
Agency: Ayer, Milan
This two-part ad aims to communicate Flou's main product benefit, namely that its beds come with such a great variety of fittings and accessories in different designs and colours that they can be made to look different every day of the year. The first double-page spread, showing the man typing in bed, is headed 'Wednesday 9th. I added a note of colour to the novel.' The following spread, headed 'Flou. Tomorrow is another bed', demonstrates what that actually means.

191
Claire Burke home fragrances
United States
Agency: Fallon McElligott, Minneapolis
One of a series in which different fragrances have a magical effect on their surroundings. The fragrance in this example is called Oh Christmas Tree.

192
Sandtex masonry paint
United Kingdom
Agency: Saatchi & Saatchi, London

Sandtex, made by Akzo, is the brand leader in a £20 million market. Before Saatchi won the account in 1988, the brand had made advertising use of both press and television. Saatchi decided to concentrate its efforts on outdoor on the grounds that people who painted the exteriors of their own houses were likely to be owner-occupiers living in certain definable locations.

This hypothesis was confirmed by market research supplied by several sources, particularly the Pinpoint Analysis firm. The latter breaks 23 million British addresses into small clusters of homes which are allotted to 60 different geo-demographic categories. The two groups most likely to use masonry paint were found to be suburban commuters and unmodernised private dwellings, and this determined the choice of locations for the 48-sheet posters of the campaign.

Creatively the objective was, apart from reinforcing awareness of the brand, to emphasise its main advantage, namely that the paint lasts for 15 years, longer than any competing product. Since exterior painting is a difficult job that nobody wants to repeat in a hurry, this is seen as a key benefit. The creative solution, simple but elegant, was to contrast the pristine freshness of the painted word Sandtex with the sadly dilapidated state of a word painted with a competing 'Brand X'.

Art direction is by the agency's creative director, Paul Arden. The campaign is credited with some responsibility for a 16 per cent increase in the brand's market share.

192

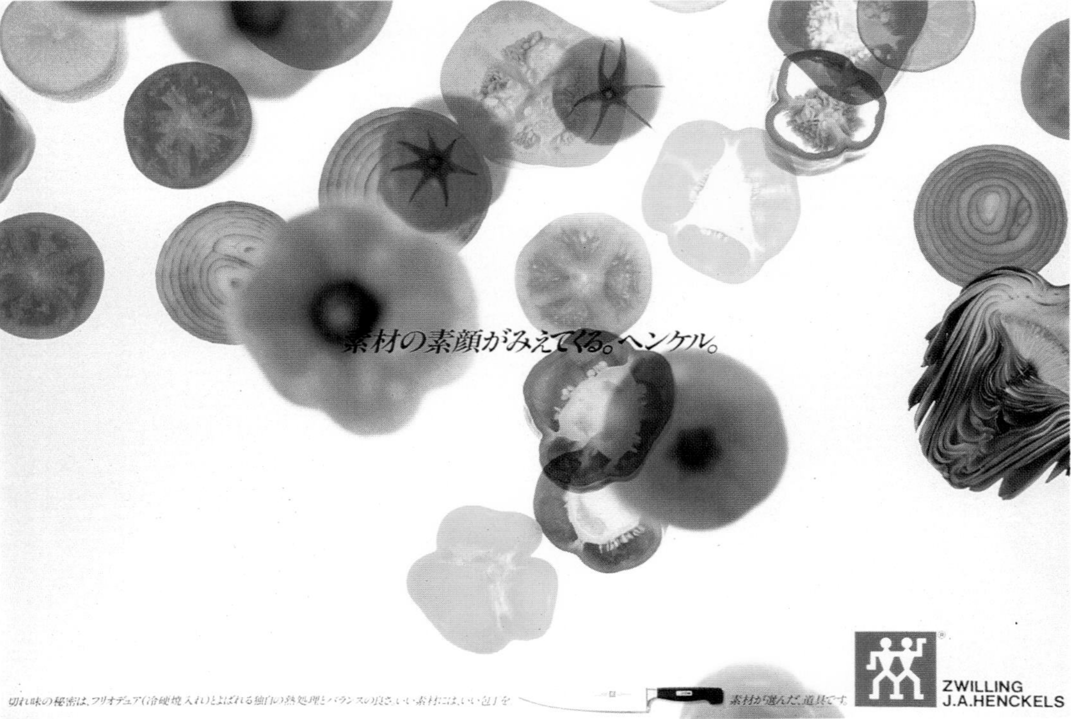

193

193
Zwilling J. A. Henckels kitchen knife
Japan
Agency: Dentsu, Osaka

Artistic photography by Nob Fukuda is the main point of interest here.

194

195

194
3M Safest Stripper
United States
Agency: Martin/Williams, Minneapolis

The claim is that the product allows paint and varnish to be removed without the need for protective gloves or special ventilation, since it gives off no unpleasant odours or harmful fumes. The alleged dangers of competitive brands are graphically depicted.

195
Louis de Poortere carpets
Belgium
Agency: Young & Rubicam, Brussels

The intriguing photograph of the chameleon's shadow on the carpet, in the absence of any visible chameleon on the twig, backs up the headline 'It's the finest achievement of my career'. Copy enthuses about the colour nuances of the Chameleon carpet. Pay-off line: 'The carpet that creates a whole world'.

196, 197
Le Creuset kitchenware
United Kingdom
Agency: Saatchi & Saatchi, London

Exceedingly distinctive advertising for cooking pots is based on the analogy between traditional French cooking in pots and traditional French cooking of pots, as still carried on in the Le Creuset factory at Fresnoy-le-Grand. The aim of the campaign is to identify Le Creuset with the best French country cooking.

198
Laufen bathroom ceramics
Austria
Agency: Demner & Merlicek, Vienna

'Three years of a person's life are spent in the bathroom' says copy on the left of the ad. On the right, over the picture of Laufen's new range, comes the punch line: 'Seen this way, that's a pleasure'. Art director: agency partner Franz Merlicek.

199, 200
Dulux Woodtones and Woodsheen
United Kingdom
Agency: WCRS Mathews Marcantonio, London

Puns provide the hooks on which to hang strong clean photographs, by Graham Ford, demonstrating the products' capabilities.

196

197

198

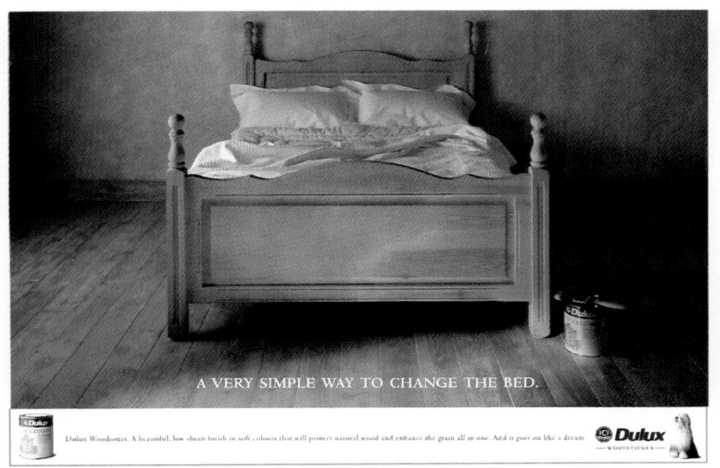

199

200

201
National washing machine
Japan
Agency: Dentsu, Tokyo

Two cymbals-players are contrasted in this film. One produces a loud sound, but the other can hardly be heard. The quiet cymbals are made of special vibration-reducing steel – no good for an orchestra but just right for a washing machine. A television voice-over says: 'Using this material, we've created a quieter washing machine with less vibration. The debut of the quiet, quiet National washing machine. Choose it by its sound.'

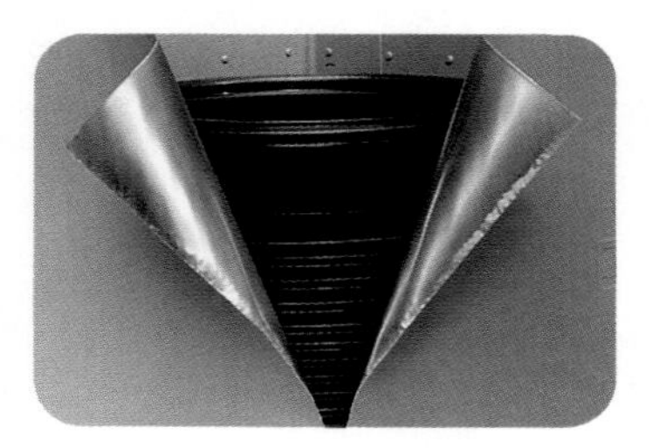

201

202
Axion 2 washing powder
France
Agency: Young & Rubicam, Paris

The point of this TV commercial for Colgate Palmolive's Axion 2 is that it cleans white garments so thoroughly that, against a white background, they can no longer be seen. We start with a man clearly visible in dirty white clothes. He takes them off, puts them in the washing machine and goes away. When he comes back and dresses again, only his face, hands and feet can still be seen. Voice-over: 'Axion 2. White has never been so white.'

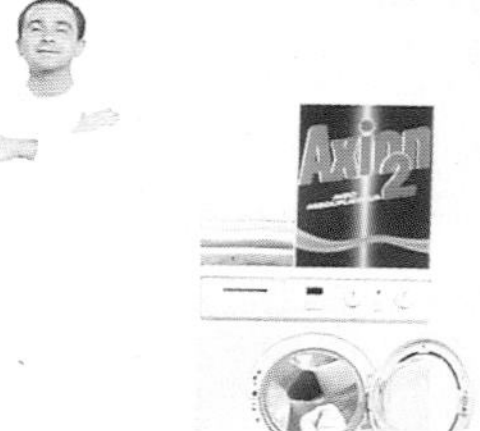

202

203
Woodlife wood preservative
United States
Agency: Zwiren Collins Karo Trusk & Ayer, Chicago

A touch of the horror movie about the humorous anthropomorphism of this effective commercial for DAP's Woodlife.

1. **Visual:** Open on two dummies seated side-by-side on a deck. ***Voice-over:*** *Meet Woody and Tommy.*
We see Woodlife Premium being applied to Woody. *We treated Woody with Woodlife Premium Wood Preservative.*

A competitive brand is being applied to Tommy. *And Tommy with a leading water repellant.*

It begins to rain. *Both brands repel water.*

203

But wood also needs protection from things that cause premature ageing and decay. As well as from mildew. And the sun. Beams of sunlight burst through. Tommy ages. He slumps, warps, turns grey and gets cracks. *Only Woodlife Premium Wood Preservative can do all that. Oh. There's one more thing Woodlife protects against. Termites.*
Both dummies suddenly sit bolt-upright, visibly alarmed by this news. They look at each other in surprise.
DUMMIES: *Termites!!!*

Buzzsaw to represent swarm of termites on the attack. Suddenly, Tommy dissolves into a heap of clothes and sawdust.

Woody, visibly shaken, quickly lifts can of Woodlife to camera. SUPER: DAP. For the jobs you only want to do once.
WOODY: *Please use Woodlife!*

Dealer names.

204
Ambi-Pur room freshener
Spain
Agency: RCP/Saatchi & Saatchi, Barcelona

In this simple but engaging little film the dog walks out on the child on the chamber pot, obviously driven away by the smell. The answer: Ambi-Pur, of course.

204

205, 206
Jeyes Hygiene Services
United Kingdom
Agency: Arc International Advertising, London

Working in an industrial cleaning market dominated by bigger competitors of Jeyes, Arc's objective is to demonstrate its client's dedication to customer service and understanding of customers' budget pressures. The service angle is emphasised in the ad with the man strapped to the can. There is a play on the word 'buff', meaning both a cleaning leather and an expert. Copy says 'every one of the Jeyes Hygiene team is a buff, an expert in every aspect of cleaning'. The other ad shows graphically how 'you can clean more for the same money'.

205

206

207
ICI chemical products
United Kingdom
Agency: Alliance International, London

ICI has developed a product, Avocet, that converts methanol, a cleaner alternative to diesel, to a fuel capable of being used by conventional diesel engines. That is what the ad is all about. Charles Settrington's disturbing photograph, however, focuses on the harm diesel does to the human body.

208
Dual herbicide
United States
Agency: Martin/Williams, Minneapolis

This Ciba-Geigy product is safe for use with both soybean and corn crops, explains the copy. Hence the brand name and hence the claimed advantage over other weed-killers that, having been applied to a soya crop, linger in the earth and damage next year's corn. But the sharks' fins say the same thing much more powerfully.

Your body may be like an engine. But can it run on diesel?

An engine run on dirty fuel will soon choke and may cease to function.

Our bodies, forced to breathe excessively polluted air, will do the same.

The diesel emissions we breathe on city streets carry 30-100 times more dirt than those from ordinary petrol engines (leaded or unleaded). So, with the use of diesel engines increasing (because it's cheap), things are looking black.

Exhaust from fleets of buses, taxis, lorries and vans reduces visibility and blackens the outside of our buildings. Inside it leaves a film of dirt.

The same dense, sooty diesel smuts leave people dirtier outside too. Clothes, skin and hair all need to be washed more frequently. Inside the damage is less easy to repair.

Diesel particulates penetrate deep into our lungs. Worryingly, long-term health effects aren't yet documented, but it clearly leaves us more open to ailments such as bronchitis and lung cancer.

There is a cleaner alternative to diesel fuel. Methanol. But Methanol can't be used alone. Not without a radical re-design of engines that would negate all the economic benefits that are making diesel so popular in the first place.

The conundrum is enough to leave most people in a fog.

But not ICI Chemical Products. We stepped in to clear the air.

For several years a specialist team had been working on modifying, not the engines, but the Methanol fuel itself. To provide an additive, a 'chemical spark plug' that would allow it to burn cleanly and efficiently in conventional diesel engines.

After exhaustive research, they developed 'Avocet.' Just a small amount converts Methanol (or Ethanol) to a diesel fuel which burns in conventional engines more cleanly, more quietly and with greater power output than regular diesel. Tests in New York, Vancouver and Tours in France have already proved 'Avocet' will be a major help in ensuring that urban air comes clean. It will soon be on trial in Los Angeles.

True, the Methanol/'Avocet' mix won't be quite as cheap as ordinary diesel. But judging by the interest shown by government bodies all over the world, the extra is a small price to pay for the health and cleanliness of our cities.

Now there's a breath of fresh air.

If you need a problem solved or want more information, contact Edna Moore, ICI Chemicals and Polymers, Wilton Centre, P.O. Box 90, Middlesbrough, Cleveland TS6 8JE. Tel: (0642) 432852.

ICI Chemical Products is a business within ICI Chemicals and Polymers.

CHEMICAL PRODUCTS *we'll make it happen*

207

208

209

210

209
Ford New Holland farm machinery
United Kingdom
Agency: Butler Borg, London

No, not a joke but a completely straightforward comparison. The same idea that lies behind the pivoting head razor has also, says the ad, given rise to 'the Lateral Float Header – designed to give your fields a closer shave'. It follows ground contours and keeps the cutter bar of a combine at an even height, 'ensuring that you pick up more of the crop'.

210
Laing Design and Construct service
United Kingdom
Agency: Cronin Morgan Stokes, Watford

This campaign is credited with having helped to move John Laing Construction from the number two spot to leadership of the UK market for combined design and construction of buildings. The visual device of the pencil-cum-pickaxe became something of a talking point.

211
Rockwool roofing board
United Kingdom
Agency: McCann-Erickson Wales, Penarth

A clever visual to press home the claim that Rockwool's new Hardrock roofing board is strong enough to stand up to current building practices. Nowadays the roof is often the first part of a building to be completed; roofing boards, though their prime purpose is insulation, must be able to take heavy roof traffic as plumbing and electrical work proceed.

212, 213
H. & R. Johnson tiles
United Kingdom
Agency: The Buchanan Company, Manchester

This campaign represents an attempt to put some pep into the client company's previously somewhat staid image. Enter the with-it young character Johnson, who in the 'show us your colours' ad is said to have 'surprised a lot of people in the business'. The other ad draws attention to a new range of highly durable floor tiles. Note that the ads, created for the architectural and interior design press, are written in the first person as if by not the advertiser but a customer.

Our new roofing product is as tough as old boots.

You simply can't put a foot wrong with Hardrock.

Our new production techniques provide a roofing board with the high density and rigidity to cope with the inevitable roof traffic and on-site handling.

Even heavy equipment dropped on Hardrock won't have the shattering effect it might have on some of our rivals' roofing boards.

Hardrock also has a unique glass-tissue facing which radically reduces bitumen uptake to guarantee an excellent bond between it and the first layer of felt.

And, being fire-safe, it is dimensionally stable even at a temperature of 700°C. It won't need a vapour escape sheet either, saving both time and money.

Environmentally speaking, Hardrock is, of course, another natural product from Rockwool.

During the lifetime of a building the use of Rockwool can save up to 1048 times the atmospheric pollution its manufacture creates.

So, if you're about to take the next step and specify flat roof insulation, put your foot down and insist on Hardrock.

Rockwool
We're in insulation. Nothing but.

Rockwool Limited, Pencoed, Bridgend, Mid Glamorgan, CF35 6NY. Tel: (0656) 862621. Telex: 497346 R-WOOL G

211

"WE'RE GOING TO WALK ALL OVER YOU JOHNSON.

I've been meaning to put you down for a long time, Johnson. And this new 'Summit' collection of fully vitrified floor tiles has presented the perfect opportunity. Highly durable, resistant to frost and chemical attack and suitable for use indoors or out, this is a range that bears the Johnson stamp of quality through and through. I note no less than 16 plain and mingled colourways, available in smooth or slip-resistant finishes. And co-ordinating possibilities that link directly into your 'Plains' wall tile range with its unbeatable palette of 80 fashionable colours. Nice to see the prestigious textured and embossed options in your 'Glazed Range' of floor and cladding tiles, too.

All in all, a perfect marriage of creative flair and down to earth practicality. You've made a great impression, Johnson."

Full details of the 'Summit' range and other collections from the Johnson portfolio are now available.

Please write or telephone for your free information pack to: The Contract Office, H & R Johnson Tiles Limited, Highgate Tile Works, Tunstall, Stoke-on-Trent ST6 4JX. Telephone: 0782 575575 (Head Office) 01-863 9444 (London Office)

H & R JOHNSON

212

"SHOW US YOUR COLOURS, JOHNSON.

You've surprised me, Johnson. Off the record, you've surprised a lot of people in the business. You've shown us your true colours. The fashionable plain and decorative wall tiles in your 'Mix 'n' Match' collection, for instance, show a feel for contemporary design that puts many continental offerings in the shade. Creative potential? The variety of colourways, combined with the directly co-ordinating field and border tiles, offers a palette of startling design scope. And that's not to mention the choice of 80 colours available in your new 'Plains' range, with its gloss brights, powder pastels, midtones, neutrals, deeps and satin finish options.

Yes, I can honestly say that you've never looked better. Nice work, Johnson."

Full details of the 'Mix 'n' Match' concept and other collections from the Johnson portfolio are now available. Please write or telephone for your free information pack to: The Contract Office, H & R Johnson Tiles Ltd., Highgate Tile Works, Tunstall, Stoke-on-Trent ST6 4JX. Telephone: 0782 575575 (Head Office) 01-863 9444 (London Office)

H & R JOHNSON

213

We've been making filters longer.

Filtrona have been manufacturing specialist filters for the tobacco industry a great deal longer than anyone else.

So when it comes to finding the perfect filter — at the best price — for your product, we can often suggest simple short-cuts to the ideal solution.

As number one in the filter world, we spend more money than anyone else developing new filters.

Whatever you're looking for … a long cool draw, a smoother smoke, a richer, more novel flavour, make sure you talk to our technical people in the early stages.

Because the long and short of it is, we believe we've got all the answers you're looking for.

FILTRONA

The technology to draw on.

Filtrona International Limited, Filtrona Court, Arden Grove, Harpenden, Hertfordshire, AL 5 4SJ. England. Telephone: (0582) 763171, Facsimile: (0582) 766599/765798. Telex: 826370.

214

Russe beweist es. Hunderte Ärzte ohne Visum in Moskau. Kurzsichtigkeit ist heilbar. Professor Swatoslaw Fjodorow beweist es seinen Kollegen in aller Welt.
Eine Utopie, die sich mit einer Großanlage von Schrack schon heute realisieren ließe: die Operation per Telefon vorzuführen. Durch eine weltweite Vernetzung könnten die Kongreßteilnehmer rund um den Erdball den Eingriff in Moskau miterleben. Gleichzeitig. Per Fernsehtelefon. Verbunden durch Glasfasertelefonleitungen. Mittels Konferenzschaltung könnten sie Bilder, Sprache und Daten kommunizieren. Digital. In beide Richtungen. Utopie oder Vision? Einzige Voraussetzung: internationale Satelliten- und Glasfaservernetzung. Die Schrack Großanlagen sind heute schon bereit. Wer an Utopien nicht glaubt, muß sie realisieren.

SCHRACK
TELECOM

215

214
Filtrona cigarette filters
United Kingdom, United States, Europe
Agency: Cronin Morgan Stokes, Watford

Unlike the Ford New Holland visual, this one is intended as a joke. Filtrona, a subsidiary of Bunzl and a world leader in its field, has been making filters not of greater length but for a longer time than others. Copy emphasises ways in which Filtrona can help tobacco manufacturers.

215
Schrack telecommunication systems
Austria
Agency: Young & Rubicam, Vienna

This striking picture of an eye undergoing surgery relates to the work of the Russian Professor Fyodorov, who has devised a simple operation to cure myopia. Copy begins 'The Russians know it. There are hundreds of Western doctors in Moscow without visas.' It goes on to explain how foreign specialists were enabled to watch such operations via a Schrack system using fibre-optic cables and a communications satellite. 'A conference switch lets you communicate with pictures, words and data.'

224

225

226

227

224, 225, 226, 227
Zeon watches and clocks
United Kingdom
Agency: Coplan Advertising, London

A sequence, published as such in the trade press, of four ads covering a range of different watches in different situations. Very few people outside the trade would ever have seen any of them if the 'fashion watches' one, featuring the semi-nude beauty, had not been used in the survey (already referred to in the commentary on Hennes in this book's Clothing section) commissioned by the Advertising Standards Authority into sex in advertising. It was among a dozen ads shown to a sample of about 2,000 people who were asked to comment on them specifically as well as to give their general views. The Zeon example was classified by 7 per cent of them as being in bad taste, while 3 per cent called it offensive. One per cent said it should not be allowed.

While this reaction was less adverse than in the case of some other examples shown to the survey sample, it was enough to get a reproduction of the Zeon ad prominently featured in at least one national newspaper article about the ASA survey. Instead of revelling in this unexpected publicity, Terry Scott of Coplan complained that the ad had been taken out of context and that only one person had ever objected to its appearance in the publications for which it was intended.

228

229

228, 229
Diamond International Awards
United States
Agency: Ayer, New York
Innovative diamond jewellery designed by winners of the 1990 International Awards justifies the 'shatters all the rules' line. These ads are, needless to say, aimed at upscale women.

230
Pulsar watches
Netherlands
Agency: Campaign Company, Amsterdam
It is the copy line – 'First a Pulsar, then the rest' – which gives a point to the picture of the watch-clad tailor's dummy.

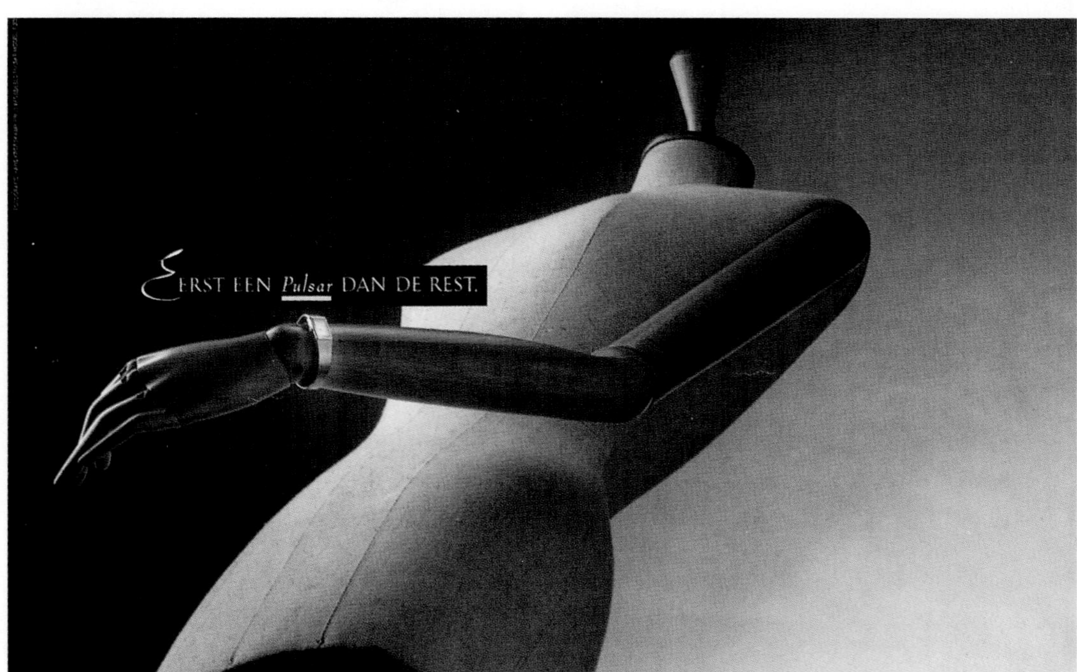

230

231

231
Diamonds of Distinction
United States
Agency: Ayer, New York

The headline is a play on words (ice cream = I scream), but that's of no great importance. This is one of 12 monthly selections of new American diamond jewellery designs. Each selection is given a seasonal theme; hence the ice cream.

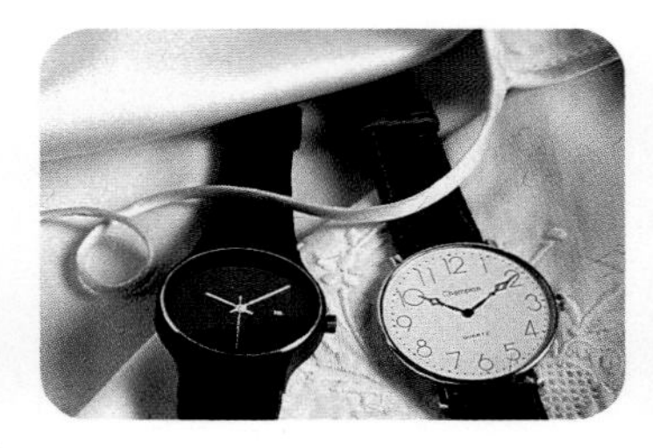

232

232
Champion watches
Brazil
Agency: Guimaraes e Giacometti, São Paulo

This erotic little number is from a series in which people are congratulated for being 'champions' (in line with the watches' brand name) for putting up for more than a minute with, for example, a mother-in-law or a brother. Here the girl in bed is on the line to her boyfriend, who bores her so much that she takes the receiver away from her ear and holds it over her shoulder. Voice-over: 'If you can tolerate your boyfriend for more than one minute, then you are a Champion'. But wait, who is this other man in bed with her? Clearly not the boring boyfriend. One wonders what respondents to the British survey on sex in advertising, prompted to pass judgement, would have said.

BLAÐ SEM VARPAR NÝJU LJÓSI Á KYNLÍF

Loksins gefst tækifæri til að kynnast hinum ýmsu hliðum kynlífs í skemmtilegu og fordómalausu blaði.
Bleikt og blátt er nýtt tímarit sem fjallar um heilbrigt og ánægjulegt kynlíf og tekur tillit til ólíkra viðhorfa.

Bleikt og blátt á erindi til allra – líka þín.
Fæst á næsta blaðsölustað
eða í áskriftarsíma 68 17 20.

233
Bleikt & Blatt, magazine
Iceland
Agency: Hvíta Húsið, Reykjavík
The visual key is the tiny white dot in the middle of the black rectangle. Headline: 'A magazine that sheds new light on sexual matters'. Caption, next to the magazine's pictured front page: 'Ignorance, misunderstanding and prejudice thrive on darkness'.

234
Time magazine
United Kingdom
Agency: Saatchi & Saatchi, London
'Advertising is news when it's in *Time*', says copy. 'After just one appearance in a *Time* editorial feature, this man was a celebrity.' It is no accident at all that the image chosen by agency Saatchi & Saatchi to make this point in the advertising trade press comes from another of its own ads. The pregnant man, who figured in a Health Education Council poster done by the agency when it was still quite small in the early 1970s, is still perhaps the most famous single piece of work to have come out of it. The poster was supposed to persuade young men to use contraceptive measures. There's no evidence it had much effect on sexual behaviour; on the other hand it has done wonders over the years for the promotion of Saatchi & Saatchi itself.

235
VTM television news
Belgium
Agency: Young & Rubicam, Brussels
VTM makes a strong point of its political independence as compared with the State-owned channel BRT, which is accused of reporting news only from Parliament. The caption is: 'Why sit in the Chamber when the message on the streets is clear?'

234

Wat politici onder elkaar beslissen kan soms verregaande gevolgen hebben voor de man in de straat.

Dus gaan onze reporters niet in de Wetstraat op een verklaring staan wachten als verderop zonder omwegen over de feiten wordt gesproken.

VTM kiest voor heldere taal. Omdat u als kijker recht hebt op duidelijke informatie.

Waarom in de Kame r zitten als op straat klare taal ges proken wordt?

235

236

deVolkskrant
HET MEEST INFORMATIEVE OCHTENDBLAD VAN NEDERLAND

deVolkskrant
HET MEEST INFORMATIEVE OCHTENDBLAD VAN NEDERLAND

237

238

236, 237
de Volkskrant, newspaper
Netherlands
Agency: PPGH/J. Walter Thompson, Amsterdam
Two from a series in which clever games are played with the nib of an old-fashioned pen, representing journalism. In the examples here we see the journalist's pen in its roles as investigative probe and alarm bell. (These days most journalists use word processors, but they would hardly fit the same pictures.) The copy line is 'The best informed morning newspaper in the Netherlands'. Photographer: Hans Kroeskamp.

238
Kurier leisure supplement
Austria
Agency: Demner & Merlicek, Vienna
Freizeit Woche (Leisure Time Weekly) is a new Saturday supplement to the daily *Kurier*. Headline: 'Long live leisure'.

239
Cash, financial weekly
Switzerland
Agency: Advico Young & Rubicam, Zürich
Like Howell Henry's British ads for 3i (see Financial section), this campaign is based on the idea of reading, literally, between the lines. Copy at the foot of the ad declares that *Cash* never simply swallows the official line. The paragraph in the middle of the page says: 'The Nestlé company has maintained profitability despite expensive acquisitions and is offering shareholders increased dividends'. Between the lines in bold type is printed: 'We write clearly and intelligibly what the press releases leave to be read between the lines'.

If advertiser and agency had had the courage of their convictions, they ought surely to have printed between the lines a sentence telling us what Nestlé was really up to.

Abopreise

52 Wochen CASH, 112.-
plus 8x gratis
26 Wochen CASH, 59.-
plus 4x gratis
13 Wochen CASH, 20.-
Tel. 062/50 30 50

CASH

Die Wirtschaftszeitung der Schweiz

Fr. 2.40

Ab Donnerstag 16.00 liegt CASH auf der Strasse und am Kiosk. Am Freitagmorgen haben Sie CASH im Briefkasten oder auf dem Pult.

Der Nestlé-Konzern hat trotz
Wir schreiben klar und
kostspieliger Akquisitionen die
deutlich, was bei den Pres-
Ertragskraft verteidigt und offe-
secommuniqués zwischen
riert den Aktionären höhere
den Zeilen steht.
Dividenden.

Was an Pressekonferenzen gesagt wird, nimmt CASH nicht einfach als bare Münze. CASH zeigt Hintergründe und Zusammenhänge und zieht manchmal die inoffizielle Version der offiziellen vor. Wer in der Wirtschaft mitreden will, braucht CASH. CASH, die Wirtschaftszeitung der Schweiz, schreibt direkt und verständlich und informiert fundiert. Auf eigenwillige, unabhängige Art. So wird Wirtschaft nicht zur Pflichtlektüre, sondern jede Woche zum Geld- und Geist-reichen Lesevergnügen. Deshalb wollen alle nur das eine, wenn sie einmal CASH haben: mehr CASH.
Unter der Nummer 062/50 30 50 kommen Sie zu einem Schnupperabo – 13 Wochen für 20 Franken. CASH. Das neue Wirtschaftswunder.

239

240

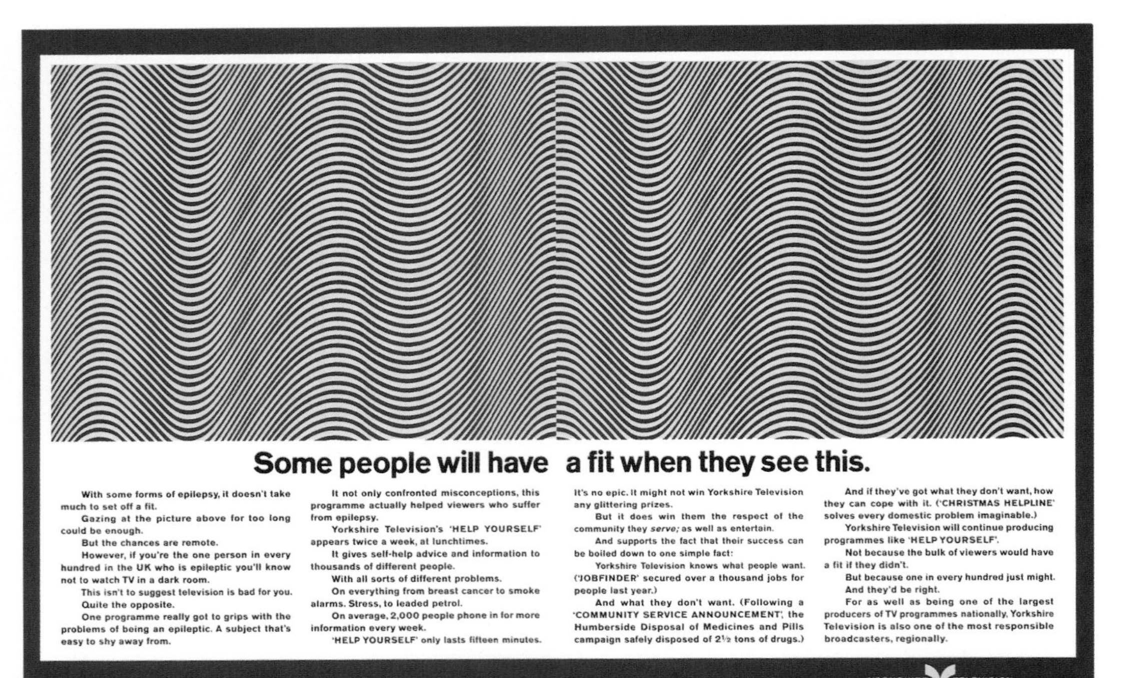

241

241
Yorkshire TV
United Kingdom
Agency: Young & Rubicam, London
To publicise Yorkshire TV's public service activities this ad focused on its twice-weekly programme *Help Yourself*, which gives advice to people with all sorts of problems. Specific reference was made to one edition that dealt with epilepsy. As stated in the copy, written by agency creative director Neil Patterson, the picture shown could set off an epileptic fit if looked at too long by certain individuals. A noteworthy idea, but the ad was attacked as irresponsible and was withdrawn. The incident was unrelated to Patterson's subsequent decision to leave and start his own agency.

240
Sonntagsblick, Sunday newspaper
Switzerland
Agency: Advico Young & Rubicam, Zürich
'We wish everyone a nice Sunday', says the caption. The headline seen on the newspaper being read by the boy says 'Survey shows young people are reading more and more'.

242
ITV Association
United Kingdom
Agency: J. Walter Thompson, London
A knocking ad directed against Britain's new satellite television stations, Sky and BSB, by the established independent TV companies. It majors on the cost to the viewer of taking the new services. Hence the headline pun, playing on the expressions 'soap opera' and 'money for old rope' (i.e. money easily earned).

A satellite dish – £200.

A satellite dish capable of receiving a signal from Mr Murdoch's Sky Channel costs around £200. Having it installed will cost you a further £70.

If you'd like to watch Sky movies and Disney channel, you'll have to subscribe to them. That's another £12 a month.

Then you'll need a decoder; they could be priced at anything up to £150.

And if you'd like to record one channel while you're watching another, you'll need a

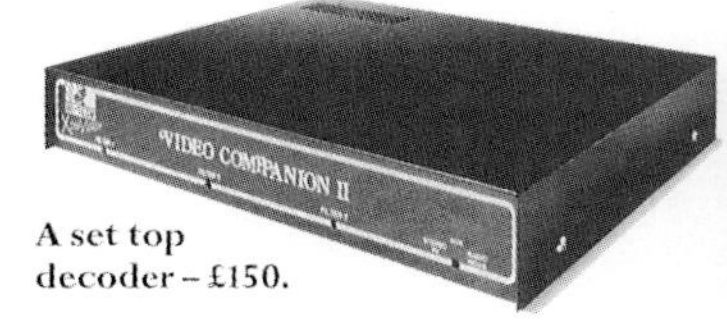

A set top decoder – £150.

second receiver. They're not available yet, but they certainly won't be free.

In October BSB launch their Satellite channels. BSB's package will cost around £250. Again installation is extra.

BSB are planning to run movies free of charge during the day, but throughout the evening the signal will be scrambled. To de-scramble their signal BSB will charge you £9·99 a month.

And if you want both Sky and BSB you'll also have to spend some time applying to the council for planning permission so you can erect two dishes.

Then there is cable television, which carries a signal directly to your home. Cable will cost approximately £30 to install.

But cable services will not be available quickly. In fact, it is predicted that there will never be a national network, owing to the prohibitive cost of laying cables to the more remote parts of the country.

And hooking up to a local network will mean weeks of inconvenience, while your pavement and garden are dug up in order to lay the necessary wires.

So does microwave television offer a ray of hope for millions of cost-conscious consumers? Hardly.

Microwave channels will require a de-scrambler unit costing around £200, as well as a separate aerial.

And if you have an old (i.e. 4 channel) TV, but don't wish to give up one of the existing channels in order to obtain a new one, you'll need an up-to-date set. Another £400.

Microwave television is also susceptible to fade. If your aerial isn't in direct line of sight with the transmitter, picture quality can

Money for old soap.

be affected by rain, snow, trees or even buses.

So what sort of programmes can you expect to see, assuming you can afford the necessary hardware?

On average ITV drama costs £400,000 an hour to produce.

By contrast Sky Channel is thought to be allocating £4,000 an hour for its drama. One hundredth of what ITV spends.

Draw your own conclusions.

A new generation TV set – £400.

Cable TV installation – £30.

Even when it comes to popular studio-based programmes like game shows and soaps we outspend them.

Sky is said to be spending approximately £5,000 an hour on this kind of programme. ITV currently spends £50,000 an hour on the same type of show.

So what are the chances of Satellite TV treating everyone to in-depth documentaries or serious drama?

Satellite TV subscription – £12 p.m.

Not as good, it seems, as the chance of being treated to 'I Love Lucy' (1956) or 'The Young Doctors' (1976) which have already been scheduled.

Not what you'd expect perhaps from Britain's newest broadcaster.

ITV on the other hand, have been producing an enormous breadth of quality entertainment for thirty-three years, all of it free of charge.

And all achieved without turning Acacia Avenue into a cross between Cheltenham's GCHQ and Jodrell Bank.

The best advice available to viewers is do not adjust your set.

243

Pleitiers sagt man vieles nach.

Was sagt der trend?

Firmenlegenden werden in Jahrzehnten gewoben, die Fama der Pleite dagegen braucht manchmal nur Stunden. Um zwischen Dichtung und Wahrheit unterscheiden zu können, brauchen Sie nur einmal im Monat den trend. Das große österreichische Wirtschafts-Magazin.

trend

244

245

243
Exchange & Mart
United Kingdom
Agency: Howell Henry Chaldecott Lury, London
Exchange & Mart is the British weekly newspaper devoted to classified advertising, much of it by private sellers. The idea, expressed in this campaign through a series of smiles and scowls, is that you can always buy more cheaply via the paper.

244
Trend, monthly business magazine
Austria
Agency: Demner & Merlicek, Vienna
The witty and disturbing picture is headed 'Much is said about the bankrupt'. Copy continues at the foot of the ad: 'What does *Trend* say? Company reputations take decades to build up, whereas the rumour of bankruptcy needs only hours. To distinguish between fact and fiction you need *Trend*.'

245
ARD and ZDF, State TV and radio stations
West Germany
Agency: Young & Rubicam, Frankfurt
The picture, surprisingly headlined 'Our man in Washington', is of Chief Taoula, who acts as a news stringer on the Polynesian island of Washington. Copy goes on to speak of ARD-ZDF's network of more than 100 professional foreign correspondents. Tag line: 'With ARD and ZDF you are sitting in the front row'.

246
KTCZ-FM, radio station
United States
Agency: The Edison Group, Minneapolis
The nuclear mushroom cloud issuing from the saxophone is inspired by the word 'fusion' as in the 'contemporary jazz fusion' claimed to be a feature of the station's output. An eye-catching image, though perhaps too disturbing for the subject advertised.

CITIES' JAZZ HOUR. Weeknights at 10 p.m. you'll hear the best in contemporary jazz fusion on The Cities' 97. And throughout the rest of the week you'll hear a surprising mix of music from jazz to new age, rock classics to breaking artists. If you like to experiment with different kinds of music, turn to 97.1, KTCZ-FM.

246

247
El Mundo, newspaper
Spain
Agency: TAPSA/Ayer, Madrid
Both TV and print versions of the launch advertising for the paper used the same graphic device of representing key topics bursting through the front page.

247

248
WXRT, radio station
United States
Agency: Young & Rubicam, Chicago
One of several short TV spots aimed at people aged between 18 and 35 with the message that WXRT is 'cool' in the American slang sense of 'fashionable', 'desirable'. The lizard is, of course, looking for coolness in a different sense. The spots are accompanied by music of the kind the radio station broadcasts.

248

249
Ekonomik Panorama, weekly magazine
Turkey
Agency: Young & Rubicam/ Reklamevi, Istanbul
The graph line of economic change is transformed into the magazine's title. The voice-over says: 'It falls into depression – stagnates – grows – shrinks. Economics one has to follow. Each week, with your magazine *Ekonomik Panorama*, you keep the pulse of the economy in your hand. Read it.'

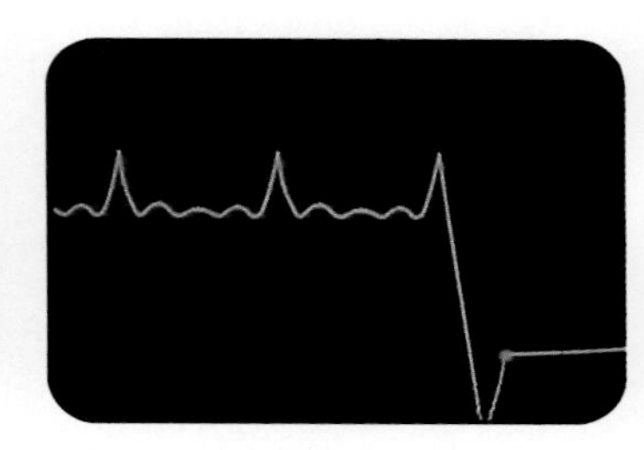

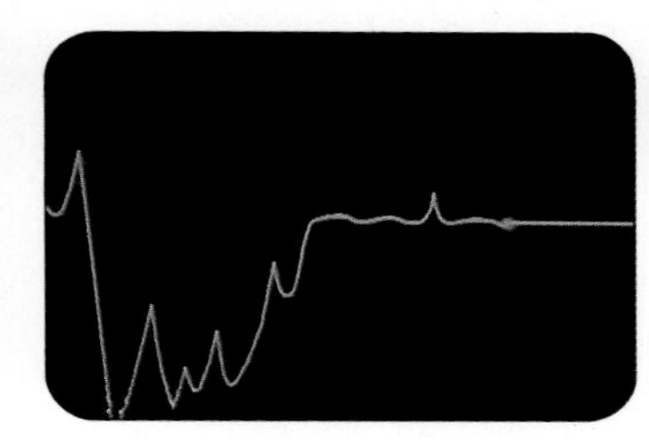

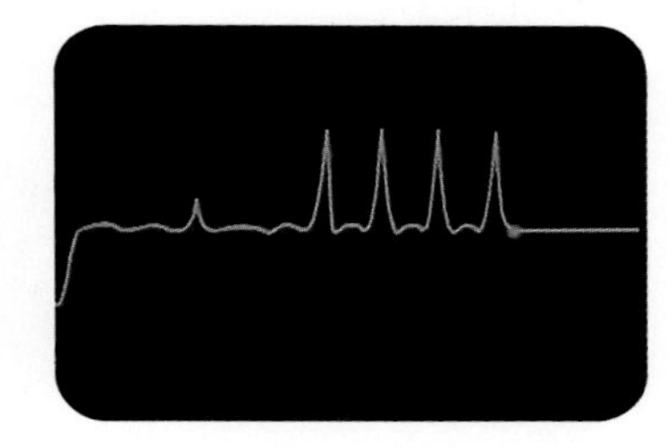

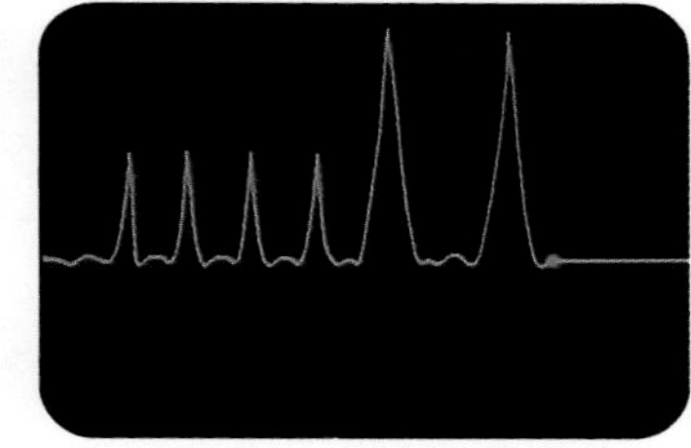

249

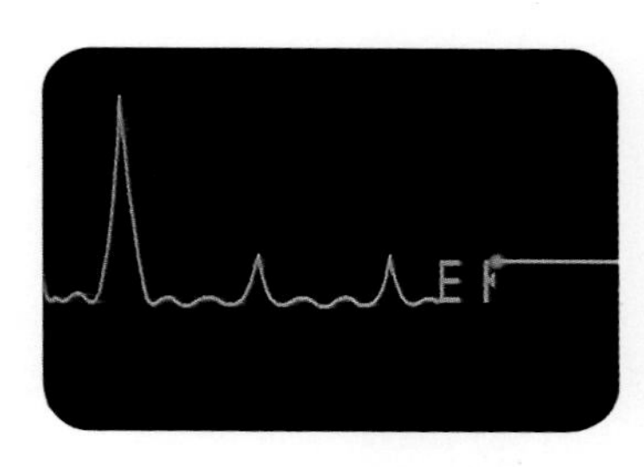

250

250
Mitsubishi pencils
Japan
Agency: Dentsu, Tokyo
The pencils are arranged in the shape of a loudspeaker not merely to amuse the eye but to back up the statement, in copy, that 'Mitsubishi Pencil's carbon technology . . . has begun to play an important role outside the field of writing implements. Speakers are one example. The technology of pencil leads is well adapted to the carbon cones of speakers.' Now it is clear why the ad is headed 'A pencil with a nice sound'.

251
3M Image Graphics
United States
Agency: Martin/Williams, Minneapolis
The bull has leapt out of the trademark to show how 'alive' are the effects to be obtained with the product.

251

252
Cross writing instruments
United Arab Emirates
Agency: Inca Tanvir Advertising, Sharjah
It's the way the ad is laid out on the page (from the English-language *Gulf News*) that catches the eye.

253
Kodansha paperback novels
Japan
Agency: Dentsu, Tokyo
A sequence of three posters which together outline the story of a detective novel: 1. the investigation; 2. the evidence; 3. the criminal.

252

253

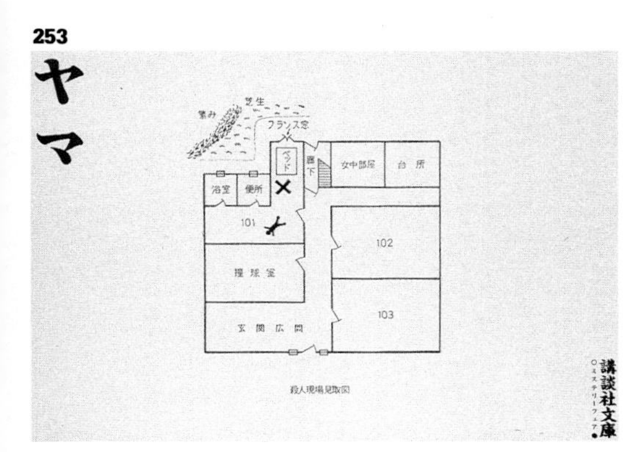

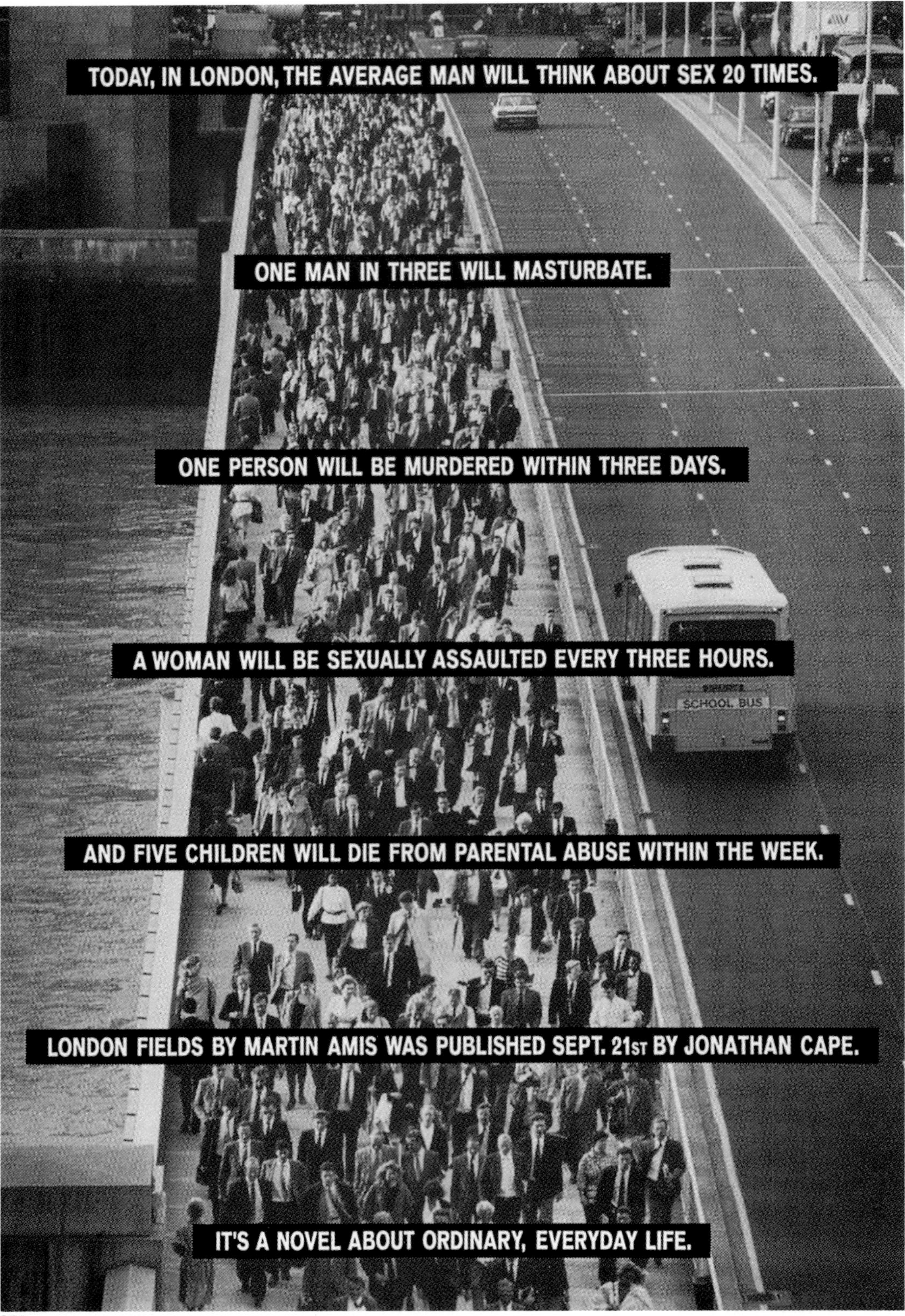

254

254
London Fields, novel by Martin Amis
United Kingdom
Agency: Bartle Bogle Hegarty, London

Amis's novel contains a great deal of sordid material. The ad sets out to match the book's effect.

255
Estoffi eyewear
Singapore
Agency: Ketchum Advertising, Singapore
Sepia tones are intended to give a European feel to this campaign to introduce an Italian brand to Singapore.

256, 257
Robert La Roche
International
Agency: Robert La Roche (in-house), Vienna
The photographs, by Gerhard Heller, are calculated to make you look twice.

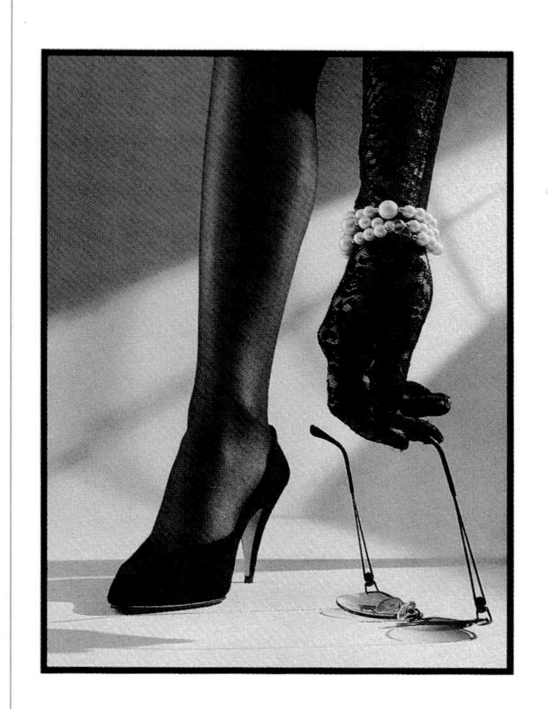

Estoffi. Italian.
Sunglasses and frames. Dramatic.
Famous. Fabulous.
Smooth. Savvy.
From affordable to expensive.

SkyBright Optical 100 Beach Road, #22-01 Shaw Towers, Singapore 0718. Tel: 2945879. Telex: RS 37809 SKYBTC. Fax: 2971631. Available at all leading opticians

255

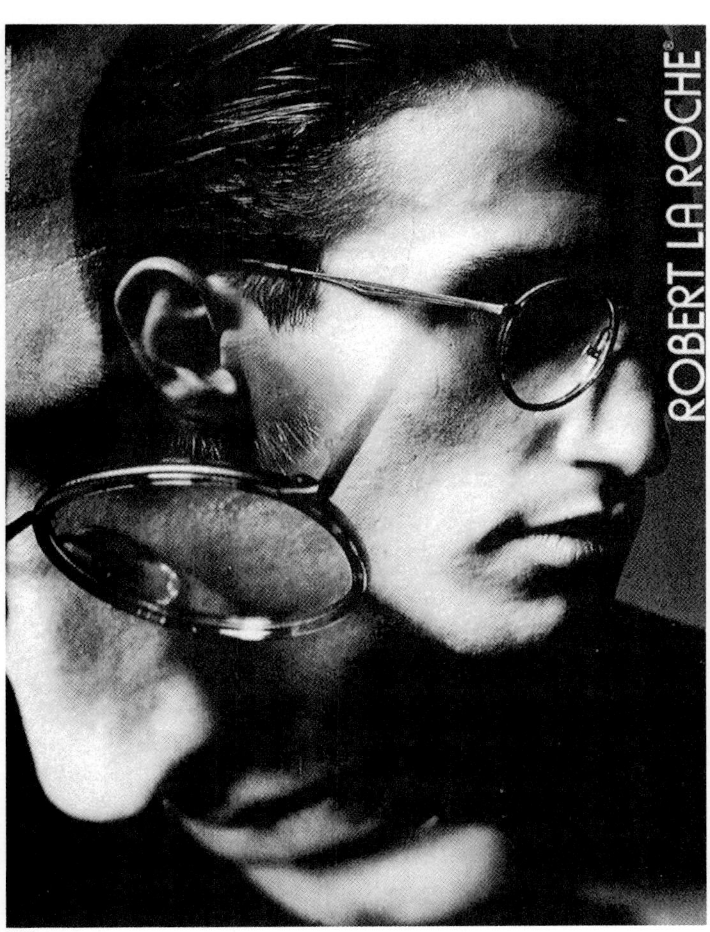

256

257

258

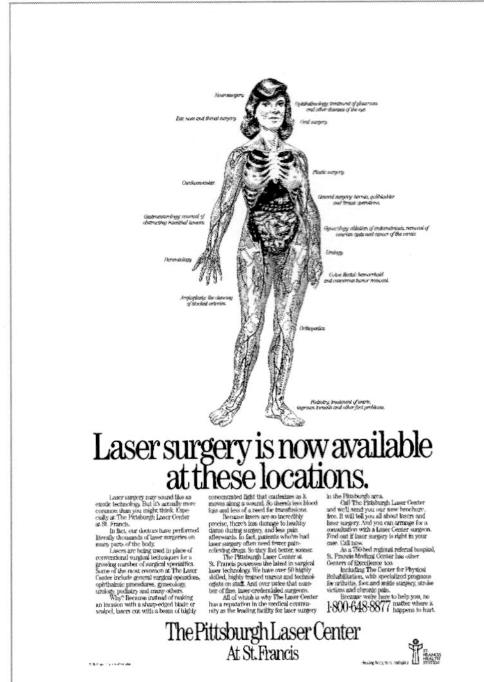

259

258
Ophthalmic treatment
Spain
Agency: TAPSA/Ayer, Madrid

'If you can read this, go to the ophthalmologist' says the headline. The paradox is explained in further copy, according to which there are many eye problems apart from short sight. To be sure of preventing them one should have one's eyes inspected at least once a year. The advertiser is the Spanish Ophthalmology Association. The copywriter is Manuel Olano, the agency's creative director. Art direction is by associate creative director Juan Ignacio Beltran.

259
Pittsburgh Laser Center
United States
Agency: The Edison Group, Minneapolis

Despite the punning headline, the ad is concerned with only one geographical location. Medical treatment is, it should be remembered, big business in the US, and the full range of marketing skills is used to sell it.

HE SWEARS HE'S GIVEN UP BURGLARY. BUT IS THIS A PICTURE OF INNOCENCE?

Yet another London house is burgled and antique objects worth thousands of pounds stolen. A "reliable source" says Mr X was involved. But Mr X claims that he has been totally straight since leaving prison two years ago. Is he telling the truth? Study the picture carefully, then use your powers of observation and deduction to decide. **Photograph by Don McCullin**

LET'S START with an admission. There are many important things this picture can't tell you. Like whether Mr X's body language – his posture, gestures and his voice – indicate that he may be lying. But can you spot a more obvious clue?

As a detective you are trained to notice tiny details that the majority of people would miss. And to make connections that would escape most.

"It is the little things," said that most famous of detectives, Sherlock Holmes, "which are infinitely the most important."

So before you read on, take a good long look at the man, the room and everything in it. Then take another look.

Still puzzled?

Well, let's see how the great Mr Holmes himself might have tackled the problem. (Luckily we have Watson's account to hand.)

"Cast your eye about the room, Watson," said Holmes. "Does nothing strike you as odd?"

"Why, frankly, no!" I returned. "There are no signs of any antique objects at all."

"Precisely," said Holmes. "The owner of these rooms has not the slightest interest in antiques."

He stooped and picked up a volume from the pile that lay on the table.

"Why then does he possess a copy of Miller's Antique Guide, a work which gives the value of every conceivable sort of antique object? What better for determining the value of stolen property?"

"He may have had it for years," I said.

Holmes smiled gently. "As you will observe Watson, it is the latest edition."

If you noticed all those things and drew the logical conclusion, congratulate yourself. You were observant and your deduction was good. But don't imagine the case is solved.

The clue of the book is, by itself, of little value. It might be a gift for his Aunty Emily.

In a real case, you would not confront your suspect until you had enough evidence to charge him.

So the first thing you would consider, after receiving the tip-off, would be whether a surveillance operation is justified.

It might mean weeks of patient and, frankly, boring work. Long days and nights spent sitting in a parked car, or a nearby flat, watching him come and go.

With luck, this surveillance will uncover hard evidence that ties him to the crime.

You want to know who he mixes with. Possibly he will lead you to other members of the burglary gang. Or to where the stolen property is hidden, or to the 'fence' through whom it will be disposed.

Meanwhile, other detectives will be following different leads.

Sightings. Was he seen in the area of the burglary at the relevant times? Was his car spotted?

A sandwich wrapper was found at the scene of the crime. Where were the sandwiches bought? If at a service

Let's see how the great Mr Holmes himself might have tackled the problem.

station, does the assistant remember anything about the man who bought them? Or his car?

Has someone else who has admitted complicity in the crime given sworn evidence that Mr X was involved?

Here's another thing. Your man has previous convictions for burglary.

Did he have a recognisable 'modus operandi'? For instance, did he always use a car jack to jemmy open windows? Or have a distinctive way of taping glass before breaking it?

You must check. But his previous convictions must not cloud your judgement. Never, during the investigation, must you ever assume that he is guilty. That's not your job. There is only one purpose for your enquiries and that is to establish the truth – demonstrable facts that will stand up in court.

Let's now suppose that weeks of patient work have yielded several bits of evidence linking Mr X to the burglary.

You go to his flat armed with a search warrant. (This is also when, more than likely, you will arrest him.)

It goes without saying that you'd spot the antique guide, but what you

You are trained to notice tiny details that the majority of people would miss.

really want is evidence that admits of no doubt. The stolen property itself.

So you'd look under the floorboards, in water tanks and lavatory cisterns. You'd check for false partitions.

You'd also have a forensic science team looking for evidence that links the suspect to the scene of the crime. Suppose some blue fibres were found in the burgled house? Do they match fibres from his clothing? Are the grease traces on the jemmied window frame the same grease as on his car jack?

These days, it is much more likely to be forensic evidence that snares a criminal, rather than individual flashes of Holmesian brilliance.

However we don't want to disappoint you completely. There are always instances where an eagle eye and a quick deduction crack the case.

Recently, police were called to a flat where a young woman had been immolated. Doused in petrol and set alight. There were no obvious clues, until a keen eyed detective spotted a return tube ticket to Heathrow.

A call to the police at the airport quickly unearthed a jittery man with burned hands and clothes that reeked of petrol.

He subsequently went to prison for the killing.

Want to be a detective? Not so fast! You'll start with twenty weeks of basic training at Hendon. Then, while your training continues, still in uniform, it's out on the streets for two years to learn what only experience can teach you.

If during this period you show an aptitude for detective work, you can ask to be assigned to the local Crime Squad, which works alongside the CID. They don't have to take you. Competition is tough, but once you're in you'll start to acquire the skills and experience you'll need as a detective. The final step comes with the intensive training you receive at our Detective Training School.

Interested?

Thrillers and TV programmes often give the impression that detective work is all glamour and excitement. It is not without its moments but mostly it is steady, painstaking attention to detail that gets results.

Still interested?

Please fill and post the coupon below. You should be fit, aged between 18 and 45, at least 172cms (5ft 8in) tall if you are a man, 162cms (5ft 4in) if you are a woman. We would especially like to see more candidates from ethnic minorities. Of all the qualifications you may bring to the job, by far the most important are your personal qualities and potential.

Please telephone: 01-725 4492 (Ansaphone: 01-725 4575) or fill in the coupon or write to: The Recruiting Officer, The Metropolitan Police Selection Centre, Department MD104, Freepost, London W2 1BR.

Name
Address
Postcode Age

METROPOLITAN POLICE

260

260
Metropolitan Police recruitment
United Kingdom
Agency: Collett Dickenson Pearce & Partners, London
Long copy, by Indra Sinha, borrows from a Sherlock Holmes story to point out the suspiciousness of a room devoid of antiques having in it an up-to-date copy of *Miller's Antiques Guide*. Unusually for an ad of any kind, the photographer, Don McCullin, famous for his war pictures, gets a prominently printed credit.

261, 262
Royal Air Force recruitment
United Kingdom
Agency: J. Walter Thompson, London
JWT has caught the interest of several recruitment clients with a presentation on the problem of the 'demographic trough', the reduction in the number of young people coming on to the UK jobs market. It is estimated that by 1994 the youth labour pool will have shrunk by 25 per cent compared with ten years previously, and there will be hot competition between employers to hire the likeliest lads and lasses. The RAF is one employer which, in anticipation of the trend, has already intensified its recruitment efforts. These two ads are aimed at persuading youngsters to become respectively pilots and nursing officers.

YOU DON'T HAVE TO BE ABLE TO FLY TO BECOME A PILOT.

Contrary to popular mythology, you don't need to have come from the planet Krypton to make it as a pilot in the Royal Air Force. (U.K. citizenship will suffice.)

You don't need to possess X-ray vision. (Though regrettably you'll never get beyond the first hurdle if your eyesight is less than perfect.)

Leaping tall buildings in a single bound may not come naturally to you. (But a healthy interest in sport can be a distinct advantage on your c.v.)

Perhaps you haven't dedicated your life to fighting for Truth, Justice and the American Way. (However, we *are* looking for people who think first before opening their mouths, who know what's going on in the world, and who understand that they may indeed be called to fight for Queen and Country.)

In other words, the only qualities we're after in would-be pilots are human ones: fitness, confidence, aptitude, maturity.

These are the building blocks from which we will train you. The Right Stuff.

At the moment, no-one – not us, not you – can tell if you've got what it takes to pilot a jet fighter that really *does* fly faster than a speeding bullet. But that is exactly what you could be doing in three years' time.

How? Because – unlike Superman – super pilots are trained, not born.

For more information ring 0345 300 100 any time for the cost of a local call
or post this coupon to Gp Capt. Peter Canning, Freepost 4335, Bristol BS1 3YX
Mr, Mrs, Miss
Address
Postcode
Date of birth
Present or intended qualifications

ROYAL AIR FORCE OFFICER

Race Relations – We offer equal opportunities

261

WOULD YOU WELCOME THE PRESSURE OF RUNNING A WARD AT 30,000 FEET?

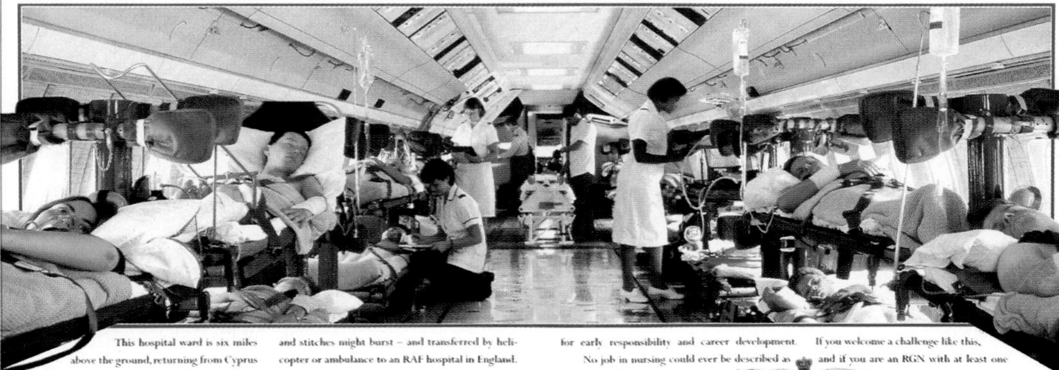

This hospital ward is six miles above the ground, returning from Cyprus to England. It's inside a VC-10 aircraft that has been specially modified for the journey.

In charge of the patients is a Nursing Officer from Princess Mary's Royal Air Force Nursing Service, and her team. It is their responsibility that the patients are safely loaded in Cyprus, made comfortable during cabin pressure changes on the flight – when limbs can swell in plaster casts and stitches might burst – and transferred by helicopter or ambulance to an RAF hospital in England.

Aeromedical evacuations like this are just one of the highly specialist areas in which PMRAFNS nurses operate. Few jobs in nursing offer such a wide variety of environments in which to practise your skills – from the UK to Germany, from Hong Kong to Belize. Few hospitals have such a high ratio of nurses to patients. And few nurses will ever encounter such excellent opportunities for early responsibility and career development.

No job in nursing could ever be described as nine to five, but as a Nursing Officer in PMRAFNS, you have all the extra responsibilities that the word 'Officer' implies – caring not just for your patients but also for the men and women under your command.

If you welcome a challenge like this, and if you are an RGN with at least one year's experience and a second professional qualification, please fill in the coupon or telephone and we'll send you further details about commissions as an Officer in Princess Mary's Royal Air Force Nursing Service.

For more information ring 0345 300 100 any time for the cost of a local call
or post this coupon to Gp Capt. Peter Canning, Freepost 4335, Bristol BS1 3YX
Mr, Mrs, Miss
Address
Postcode
Date of birth
Present or intended qualifications
XXXXX XX/XX

ROYAL AIR FORCE OFFICER

Race Relations – We offer equal opportunities

262

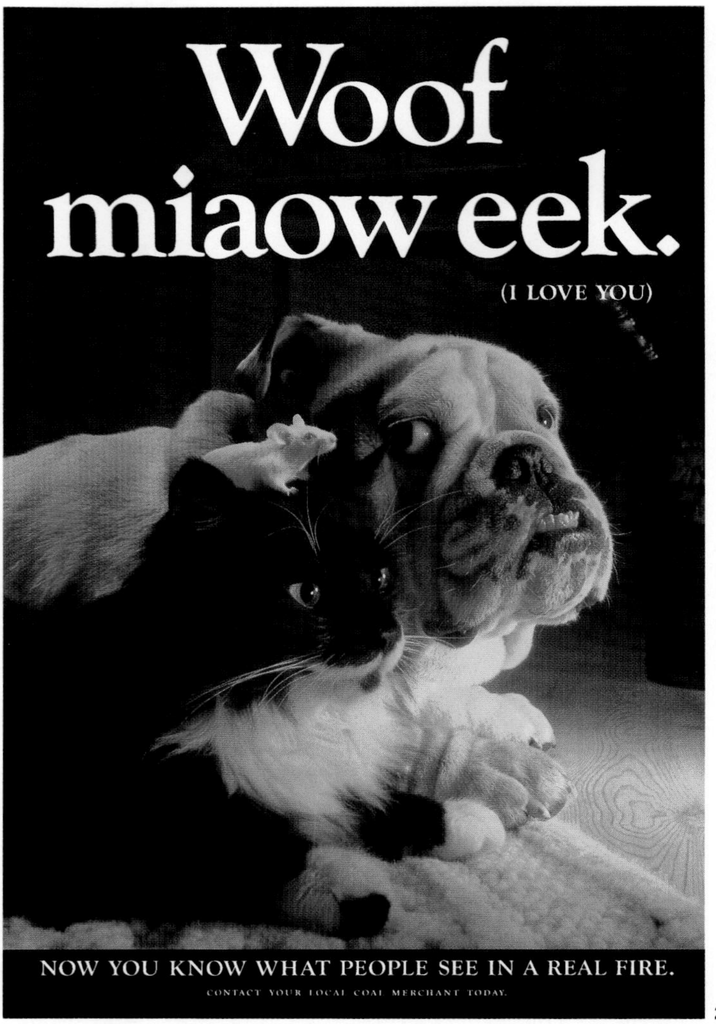

263

263
Coal fires
United Kingdom
Agency: Saatchi & Saatchi, London
The press version of a much admired TV commercial, directed by Tony Kaye, showing the loving relationship between these three unlikely friends. The advertiser is the Solid Fuel Advisory Service.

264
Federal Express
Europe
Agency: KHBB, London
From a pan-European campaign that had the task of establishing America's and the world's leading parcel delivery service in a region where it was almost unknown. Research indicated that sending a parcel is an emotional subject for the business executive, who is more interested in the reliability of a delivery service than in statistics about its size. KHBB, a Saatchi group subsidiary, decided accordingly on a humorous, human interest approach, based on the line 'Guess who didn't send it by Federal Express'. The campaign is claimed to have doubled awareness of Fedex from 19 to 38 per cent in its first five weeks.

264

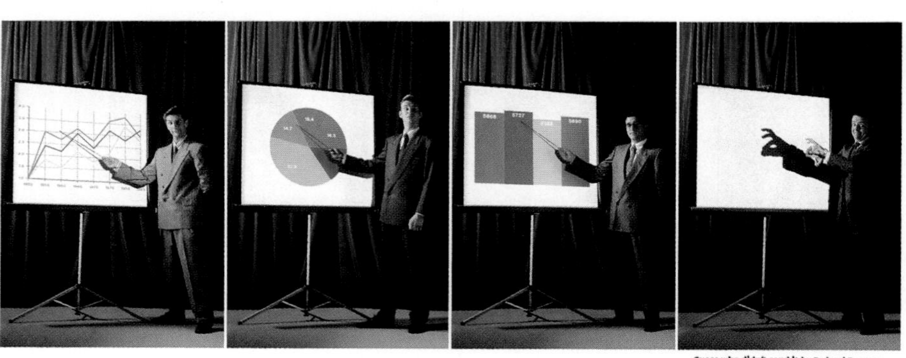

265
Vidal Sassoon salons
Scotland
Agency: DMB&B, London
The thistle is, of course, the national emblem of Scotland.

266, 267
Luncheon Vouchers
United Kingdom
Agency: Simons Palmer Denton Clemmon & Johnson, London
From a series of witty and well-executed ads by a new agency with a cumbersome name.

265

266

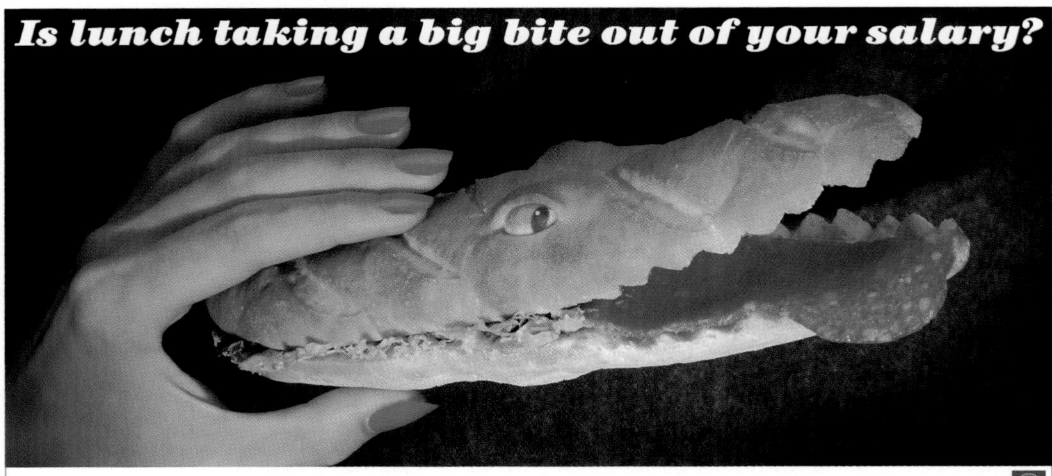

267

268
British Telecom
United Kingdom
Agency: J. Walter Thompson, London

A little gem from one of Britain's best loved TV advertising campaigns of recent years. The campaign's origins go back to late 1987, when the newly privatised British Telecom was struggling with an image problem aggravated by an engineers' strike and the poor state of its public call boxes. BT's brief to the agency included the instruction 'to encourage people to understand the value of a phone call in an inter-family relationship ... e.g. phone your mother'.

Copywriter Richard Phillips, who also directed the film illustrated here, recalls: 'Here I was, a nice Jewish boy of nearly 40 years' experience, being asked to write a commercial about phoning your mother. Talk about the right man for the job! Without question, I was one of the world's greatest living authorities on the subject of phoning your mother ... it was but a minuscule leap for me to think of using the character of a Jewish mother in a commercial.' These words come from a book written by Phillips and Maureen Lipman, the actress who stars as the Beattie character in all the commercials. Called *You Got an Ology?* (after a line in one of the earliest films), the book, published by Robson Books, London, at £8.95, consists mainly of 20 film scripts with accompanying black and white photographs. The fact that it was aimed at, and bought by, the general public is no small tribute to the effectiveness of the campaign.

It was not immediately apparent back in 1987 that the campaign would become such a success. Pre-publication testing by a research company of the first films, using focus groups of ordinary viewers, gave the campaign the thumbs-down. Bravely the client decided to go ahead regardless. The decision was vindicated by a tracking study that showed public approval of BT advertising rising remarkably, with more than 60 per cent of people interviewed describing the commercials as enjoyable. BT also reports that, in weeks when the campaign is running, the number of phone calls increases.

Visual: Open on late evening in Beattie's and Harry's bedroom. Harry is in bed and has already fallen asleep over his book. Beattie is sitting in bed, talking on the phone. ***Audio:*** *½ second silence.* BEATTIE: *Hello, Rose? It's me, Beattie.*

Cut to the other side of the world and a beautiful view of Sydney Harbour. Rose is lying asleep on a sunlounger out of frame. Cut to closeup of Rose, as she sits up startled. ROSE: *Beattie? (Rising alarm) What's happened?*

Cut back to Beattie. BEATTIE: *Nothing's happened.*

Cut back to Rose, she is sitting on her sunlounger in her garden, with her husband Sydney (bearing a remarkable resemblance to Harry) lying asleep on his sunlounger next to her. His hat covers his face from the sun. ROSE: *You can't fool me. It's Harry isn't it?* Cut to closeup of Beattie. ROSE: *I may be 12,000 miles away but I'm still your sister. What is it: another woman?* Cut to closeup of Harry, snoring and not looking a pretty sight. Cut to closeup of Beattie. BEATTIE: *Don't be ridiculous Rose.*

Cut back to Rose, she peels the nose shield from her nose. ROSE: *So it's Melvyn? Melvyn's left Bernice? Oh,*

Cut back to Beattie who is beginning to lose patience. BEATTIE: *Melvyn and Bernice are fine.* Cut back to Rose, still talking as she looks to her husband. ROSE: *So it's Elaine. Elaine's left Raymond. I can't say I'm surprised. You know, your daughter.* Cut to Beattie who is now exasperated. BEATTIE: *Harry is with me, Melvyn is with Bernice. Elaine is with Raymond. There's no special reason for phoning. I just thought it would be nice to have a gossip.*

MVO: *These days calling overseas doesn't have to be a big event.*

ROSE: *So Harry is still with you, Melvyn is still with Bernice, Elaine is still with Raymond.* Cut to Rose talking to herself. *This she calls gossip?*

Cut to B.T. Logo.

MVO: *British Telecom. It's you we answer to.*

Cut to Beattie and Harry in bed, Beattie is still on the phone, Harry rolls over in his sleep. HARRY: *Oh, Beryl.*

Cut to Beattie. BEATTIE: *Who's Beryl?*

Cut to closeup of Rose looking puzzled.... *Do you know a Beryl?* Cut to closeup of Beattie looking anxious, she glances towards Harry.... *He's rolled over in his sleep and said 'Beryl', I didn't know he had it in him.*

268

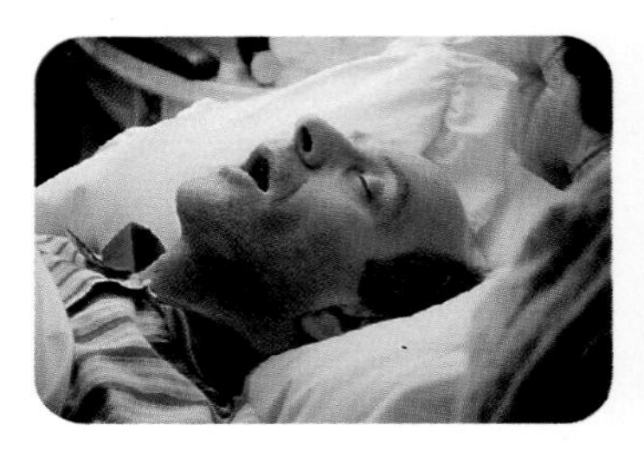

269
Pedo diapers
Turkey
Agency: Young & Rubicam/ Reklamevi, Istanbul

This commercial launched a new line of coloured diapers. The idea for the product came from the agency, as did that of presenting it through a fashion show.

Visual: 1. Audience clapping. ***Audio:*** PRESENTER: *Ladies and gentlemen!* . . . 2–3. Kids coming out to the podium. Audience continues clapping. *Here's the fashion event of the year!* . . . 4–5. They keep coming to the podium. *Dry, free and coloured Pedo!* 6–7–8. Kids walking around podium. *No leaks, no rashes and it comes in four fabulous colours . . . pink, blue, green and white . . .* 9. Pack-shot. (VO): *Pedo. Latest fashion in diapers.* 10. One kid still on the podium staring at the spots. PRESENTER: *Bravo!*

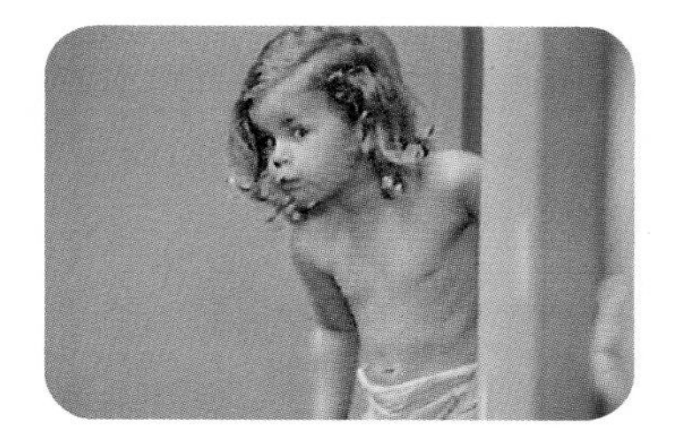

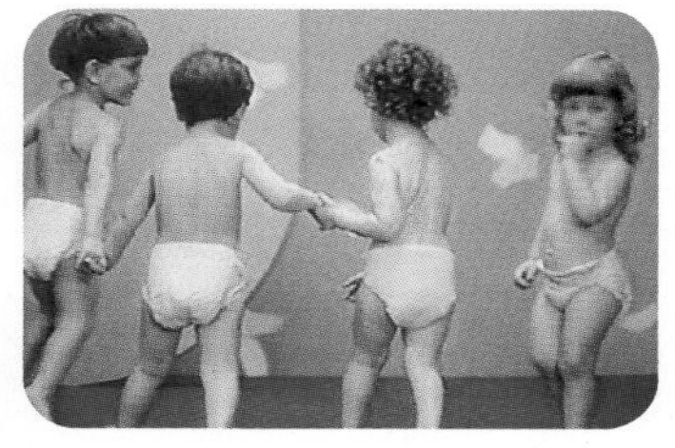

270

Olympus introduce the first camera to cure red-eye.

It's a common enough complaint.

A perfectly healthy-looking roll of film comes back with fully developed conjunctivitis.

Eyes that seemed green through the view-finder have turned red quicker than a set of traffic lights.

So what causes these unsightly spots, you ask?

The answer is, of course, the flash.

In low light your pupils dilate, so when the flash fires, light bounces off the retina causing red-eye.

That is, until Olympus developed the AZ-200 Superzoom.

Simply switch the camera to Auto-S mode and the flash emits a series of soft, pulsing pre-flashes causing the pupils of your subjects' eyes to contract. So when the flash fires, red-eye virtually disappears.

But we don't just take care of eyes.

If the person you're looking at is on the gloomy side, the auto flash will brighten them up again, while the unique variable strength flash (which gives more power the further away the subject is) stops them looking washed out.

To ensure that their features aren't fuzzy there is an auto focus system that takes readings from three separate spots, ensuring scalpel sharp pictures.

Furthermore, it has a built-in power zoom that goes right in to 80mm or pulls back to a wide-angle 38mm so that your subjects are always perfectly composed.

And should you finally want to see how you're looking the camera includes a small, detachable remote control unit that lets you operate the shutter from up to five metres away.

The Olympus AZ-200 Superzoom.

Available, without prescription, at most good stockists.

OLYMPUS AZ-200 SUPERZOOM

271

272

270
Olympus AZ-200
United Kingdom
Agency: Collett Dickenson Pearce & Partners, London
The extraordinary visual is justified by copy that explains that flash-lit portraits are commonly spoiled because 'In low light your pupils dilate, so when the flash fires, light bounces off the retina causing red-eye'. However, the AZ-200 'emits a series of soft, pulsing pre-flashes causing the pupils of your subjects' eyes to contract. So when the flash fires, red-eye virtually disappears.'

271, 272
Kodacolor Gold film
Denmark
Agency: Young & Rubicam, Copenhagen
The caption in both ads is 'Colour, too good to be true'.

273, 274, 275, 276
Kodacolor Gold film
Switzerland
Agency: Advico Young & Rubicam, Zürich
Hans Feurer's photographs give full force to the 'painted by . . .' theme. Art director: Roland Scotoni.

273

274

275

276

277

277
Kodak disposable cameras
France
Agency: Young & Rubicam, Paris
Y&R's French advertising for Kodak has firmly established the device of the mischievous little 'colour thieves', who drain the high colour from real objects into their photographs. Here, one of the colour thieves, 'swimming deliriously', helps to launch Kodak's 'completely throwaway' cameras.

278
Kodak Ektachrome
Germany, Austria, Switzerland, Japan
Agency: Young & Rubicam, Frankfurt
One of a series of picturesque real-life scenes framed in giant slide-holders.

278

279

279
Kodak
France
Agency: Young & Rubicam, Paris
A spoof 'wanted' notice announcing heavy penalties for colour theft. Anyone with information about the three colour thieves is asked to contact Y&R or, 'if nobody is there, the Minister of the Interior'.

280
Kodacolor Gold film
France
Agency: Young & Rubicam, Paris
Once one has seen this 'colour thieves' commercial, Kodak's French press advertising makes a lot more sense.

280

1. **Visual:** A young woman in a bright red dress is walking down the street. ***Audio:*** *Collage of music and sound effects (street noises, police sirens, etc.) that punctuate the extremely quick cuts of the spot.*

2. **Visual:** (Cut) Little 'colour thieves' from Kodak rush up . . .

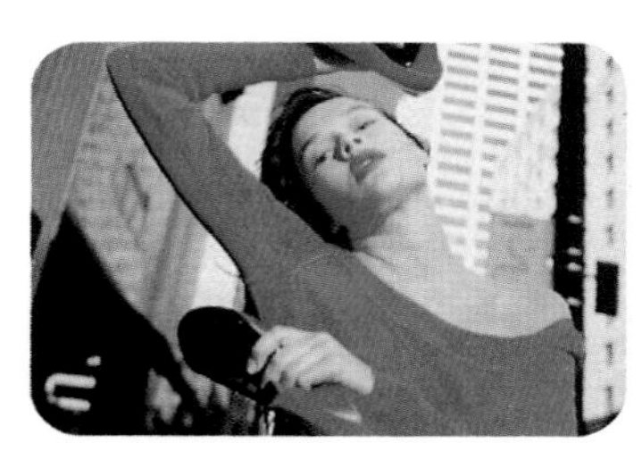

3. (Cut) . . . and take a picture of the young woman.

4. At once, all colour disappears from her dress and her shoes.

5. (Cut) Next, they storm into an ice cream parlour and photograph the speciality of the house.

6. The customer promptly loses his appetite.

7. (Cut) Their next victim – a man with a bunch of flowers . . .

8. (Cut) . . . which, after they are through, look like a funeral arrangement.

9. (Cut) A police car in hot pursuit of the 'colour thieves'.

10. (Cut) Finally caught, they are confronted with the evidence of their deeds – the beautiful colour photos they've taken.

11. (Cut) They stand lined up with their knees shaking.

12. (Cut) But when the police officer turns the spotlight on them . . .

13. . . . they almost collapse with laughter.

14. Cut to Kodak film. SUPER: Kodak. Always a click ahead. ***Audio*** (MVO): *Kodacolor Gold. The colour thief.*

281

281
Polaroid high definition film
France, United Kingdom
Agency: BDDP, Paris

A man, seen in silhouette, gets hold of a photo and, startled by what he sees, falls forward on to the floor. Voice-over: 'This man was not prepared to see a non-instant high definition photo. Polaroid launches its first non-instant, high definition film.' Another man enters from the other side of the screen and does the same thing, except that he falls backwards. The announcement is repeated. Finally, two men move towards each other, stare together at a photo, knock their heads together and fall over. Voice-over: 'These two men were not prepared . . . etc.' A zany but memorable way of getting the message across.

WHY SHOULD YOU WORRY? FUTURE GENERATIONS WILL ADAPT TO THE GREENHOUSE EFFECT.

Let's continue pumping out gases that destroy the ozone layer. Who cares if carbon dioxide traps heat in the atmosphere, or the forests are burnt?

Sure, the planet's getting warmer - can't be all bad.

Why worry about skin cancers, cataracts and crop failures? About the collapse of the food chain? About droughts, hurricanes and rising sea levels?

So what if everyone has to protect their eyes with sunglasses? Even in the dark.

After all, it's not our problem. Is it?

Now get in touch with the Friends of the Earth. They don't see it that way. **FRIENDS OF THE EARTH**

FRIENDS OF THE EARTH TRUST, 26-28 UNDERWOOD STREET, LONDON N1 7JQ. TELEPHONE: 01-253 3553.

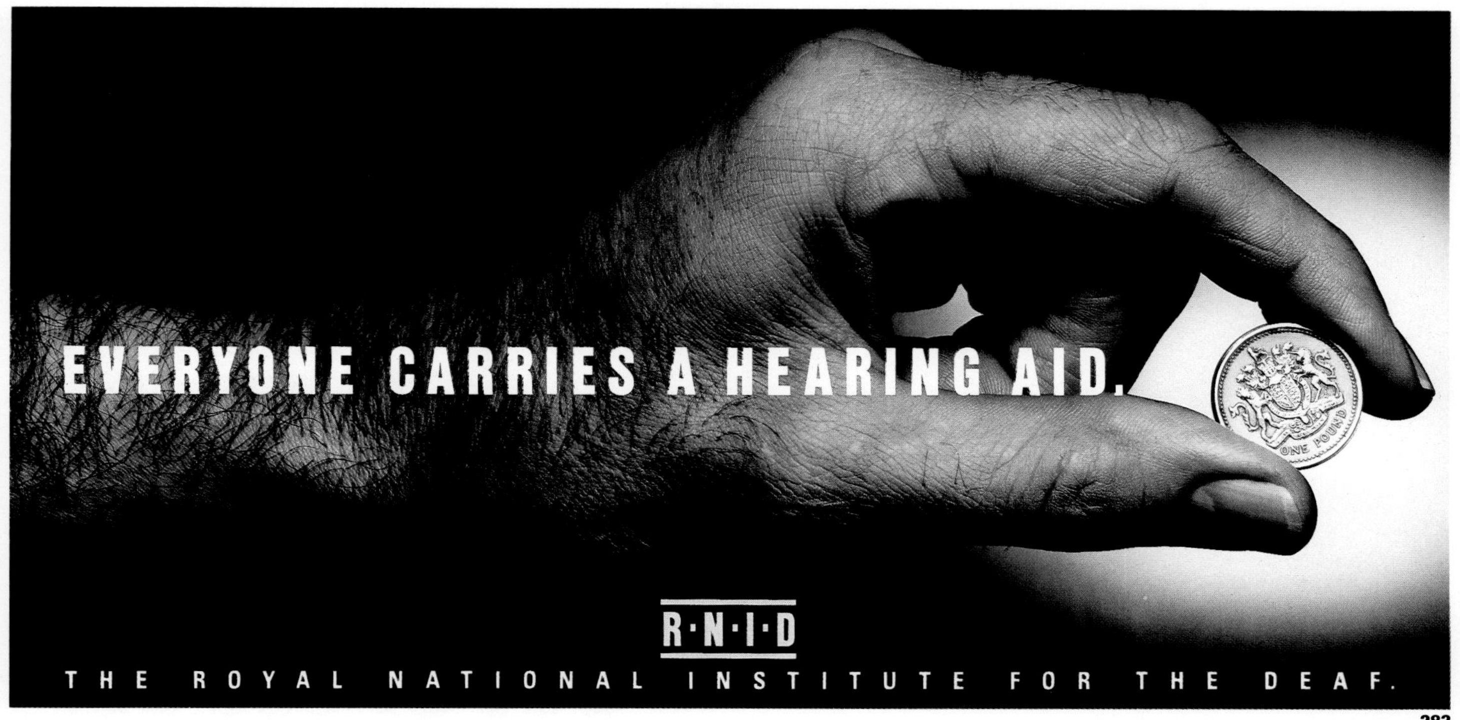

283

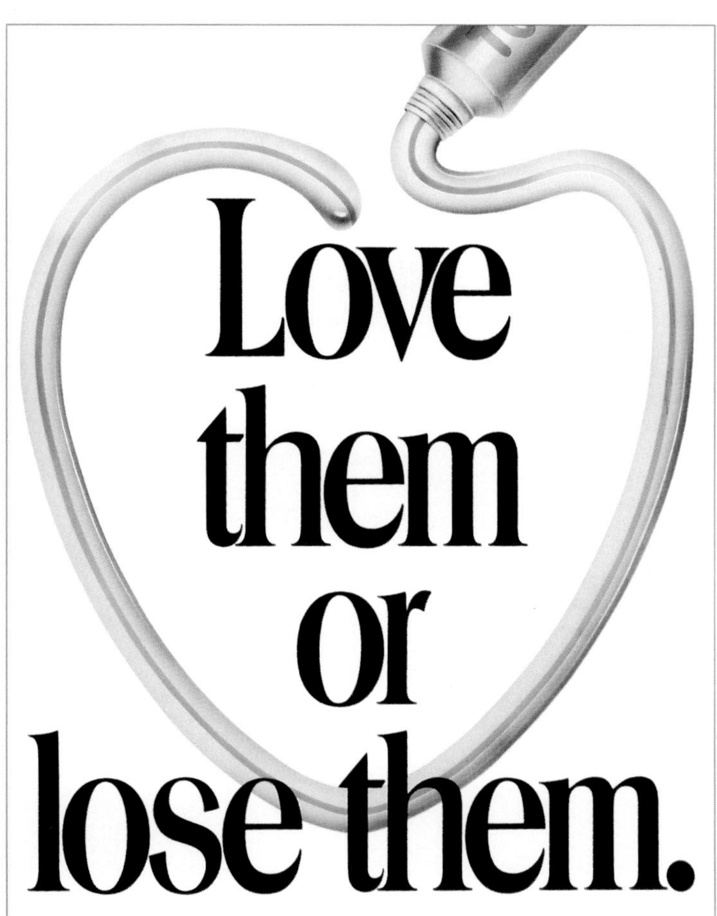

284

282
Friends of the Earth
United Kingdom
Agency: Burkitt Weinreich Bryant, London
The image is witty, but that does not prevent it from being frightening too.

283
Royal National Institute for the Deaf
United Kingdom
Agency: Ogilvy & Mather, London
The pound coin is a hearing aid if donated to the RNID. A masterpiece of compression, with words and picture perfectly integrated. Pete Bradly and Marc Hatfield share both copywriting and art direction credits.

284
Dental health education
Singapore
Agency: Ketchum Advertising, Singapore
An attempt to coax people, rather than frighten them, into taking proper care of their teeth. The copywriter is the agency's creative director, Jim Aitchinson.

285

285
River Po Protection Association
Italy
Agency: Armando Testa, Turin

This poster plays games with both words and shapes. The emblematic banks of the river are composed of the letters forming its name. The caption, taking advantage of the double meaning of the word, means either 'A little of everyone, a little for everyone' or 'Everyone's Po, a Po for everyone'. Art direction is by Armando Testa in person, whose signature can be seen on the poster.

286

286
Red Cross
Belgium
Agency: Young & Rubicam, Brussels

The crudely executed visual is sufficient to strengthen the appeal for blood donors.

287
Anti-smoking
United States
Agency: Martin/Williams, Minneapolis

An original image to press home an old message.

If You Smoke, You Might As Well Start The Day With A Mouthful Of This.

Minnesota Department of Health

© 1989, MDH

IF YOU HAVEN'T GOT THE TIME TO READ THIS, YOU'RE JUST THE PERSON WE'RE LOOKING FOR.

You may well be at the helm of the company you started.

So giving up any time to things that do not directly involve your company's growth and profitability gets scant attention.

Recognise yourself so far?

If you have, Business in the Community (BiC for short) would like to suggest you carry on reading.

It could be time well spent.

20 SECONDS.

Your community should be important to you.

After all it's where you live, where you work, where most of your employees probably live and work.

Neglect of a community not only imposes a high cost on the people who live and work in it.

But it's not so good for your business either.

Now, you might well feel that you're already 'doing your bit' for the community.

After all you're paying local taxes and local rates. You employ many local people. You try to help school leavers. Isn't this enough?

The short answer is, no.

45 SECONDS.

What is needed from you is your flair and your skills.

Those very qualities that have made your business a success could be put to further use in your community.

You wouldn't be alone, either.

There are scores of businessmen like yourself whom BiC is bringing together in a partnership that can make an extremely powerful force.

A force that can work with the local authorities, and voluntary organisations across the community.

A force that can help things happen.

1 MINUTE, 5 SECONDS.

By now, if you're half the businessman we think you are, you'll want the answer to one simple question: "What's in it for me?"

Clearly, an improvement in your local community can only do you good. A thriving, prosperous area, where the streets are safe, will do your business no harm at all.

It creates opportunities for start-ups, which may well become your future customers or suppliers. And who knows how big they might become?

Naturally, the more you help, the more people will notice your help. And there's nothing like a good piece of PR for boosting company morale and improving staff relations.

In other words, the happier your company, the happier people will be to work there.

1 MINUTE, 40 SECONDS.

So, how easy is it to get involved?

Basically, it's as easy as you want to make it. You may already have ideas of what you can do.

Things like trading with your local suppliers, for instance.

You might get involved in job training schemes, possibly forge links with local schools. Even offer work-space to the self-employed.

Those are the sort of initiatives your company can make without too much effort.

Other ideas might include lending some of your staff to help advise small businesses on start-ups.

Or, on a broader scale, you might

get involved in the regeneration of run-down neighbourhoods.

No matter how much you help, every little helps.

2 MINUTES, 5 SECONDS.

So far, we've taken very little of your time.

The next step will take a little more because it involves filling in the coupon and sending it to BiC.

We will then get in touch with you to answer any further questions you might have, and to discuss with you exactly how you can help your community.

You'd be surprised how much you can put in. And how much you can get out.

Please send me more information about how my business can get involved in my local community. Return to: Business in the Community. Freepost BS 3333 BS1 6GZ. Or phone free 0800 500 236 (24 hours).

NAME ____

COMPANY ____

POSITION ____

ADDRESS ____

____ POSTCODE ____

NATURE OF BUSINESS ____

NUMBER OF EMPLOYEES ____

TELEPHONE ____

BUSINESS IN THE COMMUNITY

SPACE DONATED BY GRAND METROPOLITAN – STILL A SMALL COMPANY AT HEART.

289

290

288
Business in the Community
United Kingdom
Agency: Young & Rubicam, London
On the face of it, a negative appeal. In reality the ad is flattering the egos of the businessmen at whom it is aimed.

289
'Work less' campaign
Japan
Agency: McCann-Erickson Hakuhodo, Tokyo
'If we take on any more work, we won't have time left to play', says the ant. From a campaign designed to make the Japanese less workaholic.

290
Anti-drugs campaign
India
Agency: Rediffusion, Bombay
The skull in the eye, the head burning low – perhaps the ad would be even more of a shocker if it made do with only one sinister image instead of two.

291
Anti-smoking
New Zealand
Agency: Adventure, Wellington
The unusual illustration by the unusually named Fane Flaws makes this ad stand out.

292
Women's Counselling Service
West Germany
Agency: Grey, Düsseldorf
It is the contrast between the happy family group and the woman's black eye that compels attention. Headline: 'Every year four million women are beaten in our country'. Body copy says that 'when women are abused it is almost always by their own husbands or partners. . . . Violence towards women is irrespective of class and education.' Victims are advised to contact the Women's Counselling Service.

293
Environmental protection
Japan
Studio: Takayuki Itoh Design Office, Tokyo
Acid rain turns the litmus paper pink.

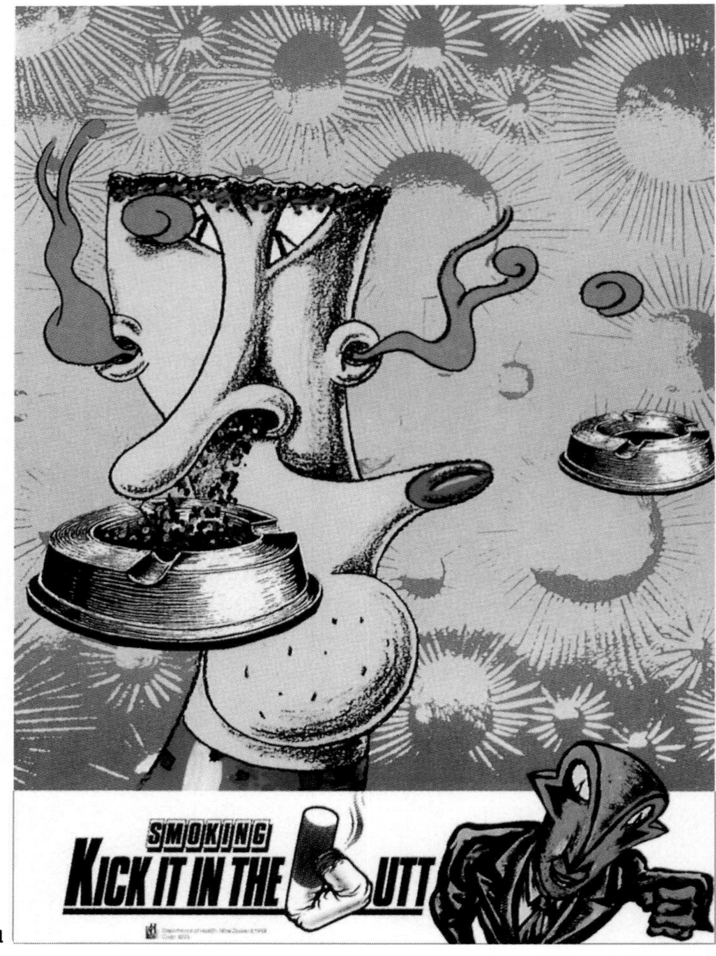

291

Jedes Jahr

werden bei uns

4 Millionen Frauen*

mißhandelt.

Fast immer sind es die eigenen Ehemänner oder Lebensgefährten, die Frauen mißhandeln. Körperlich mißhandeln – oft mit alltäglichen Gebrauchsgegenständen und so, daß die Umwelt nichts davon merkt. Seelisch mißhandeln – in vielen Fällen mit ganz bewußt eingesetztem Psychoterror. Gewalt gegen Frauen ist unabhängig vom Bildungs- und Gesellschaftsniveau. Und es ist schwer, die Ausmaße dieser Gewalt zu erfassen. Denn es dauert manchmal viele Jahre, bevor eine mißhandelte Frau über ihre Verletzungen spricht. Hilfe sucht. Gegenmaßnahmen ergreift. Wenn Sie betroffen sind, lassen Sie es nicht so weit kommen. Sprechen Sie mit einer Frauenberatungsstelle in Ihrer Nähe. Oder – rufen Sie uns an. Wir helfen Ihnen.

Frauenberatungsstelle Düsseldorf 0211/686854.

292

C L E A N E R   R A I N

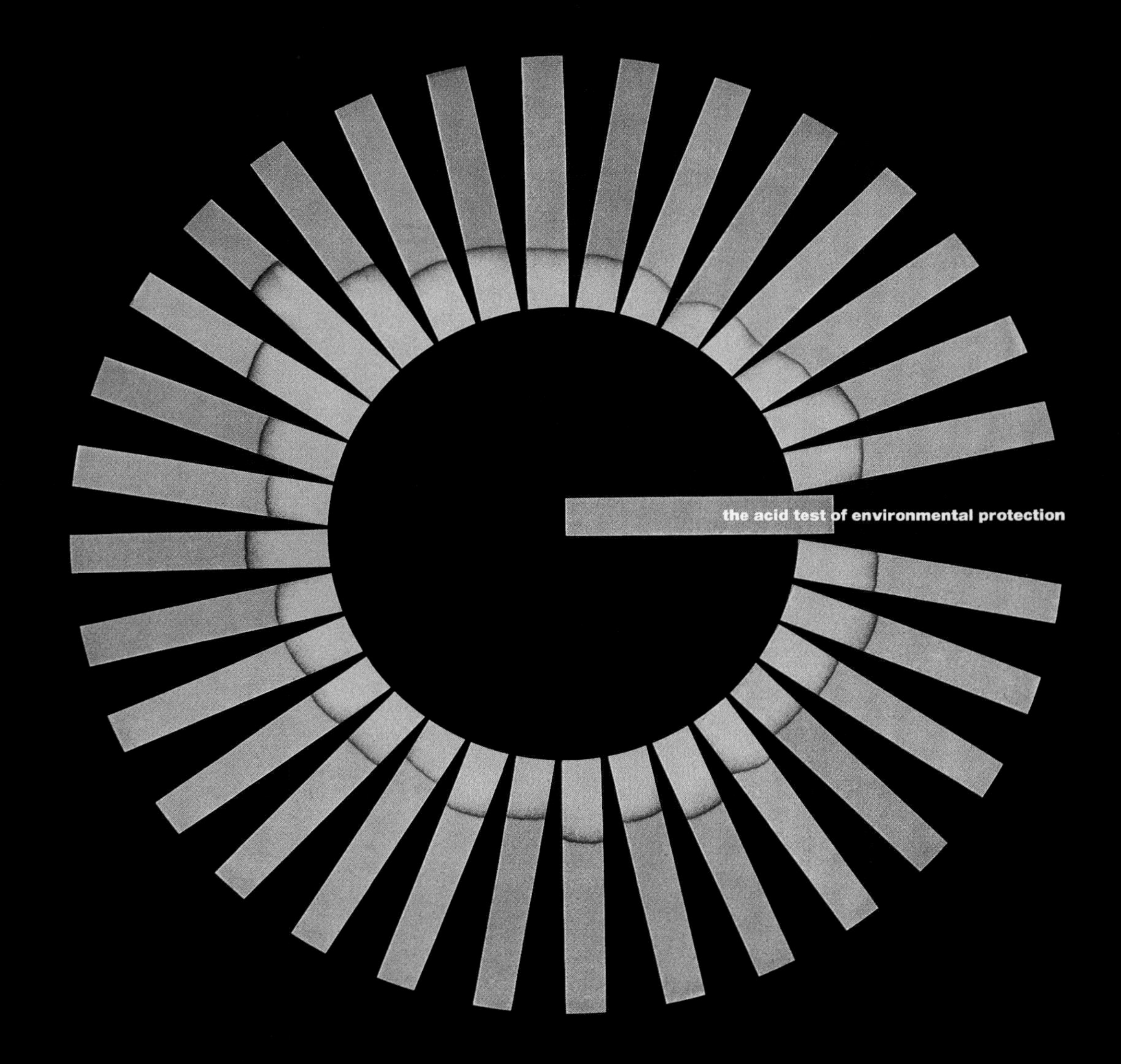

If we don't keep the air clean,
acid rain is going to destroy
all our trees and forests

294
Anti-vivisection
United Kingdom
Agency: BMP DDB Needham, London

The film, made for the British Union for the Abolition of Vivisection, ingeniously transfers the suffering of animals to the face of the model. As she applies make-up, her face becomes raw and bloody, her lips swell and crack, her eyes weep. Voice-over: 'Every year thousands of other animals suffer this ugly pain in the name of beauty. Please use cosmetics that are cruelty-free.'

294

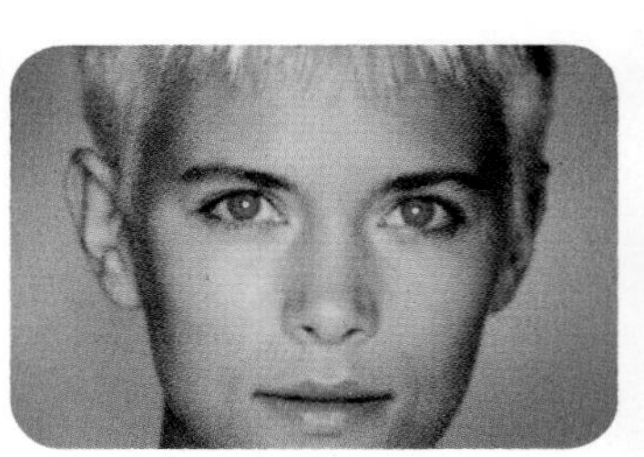

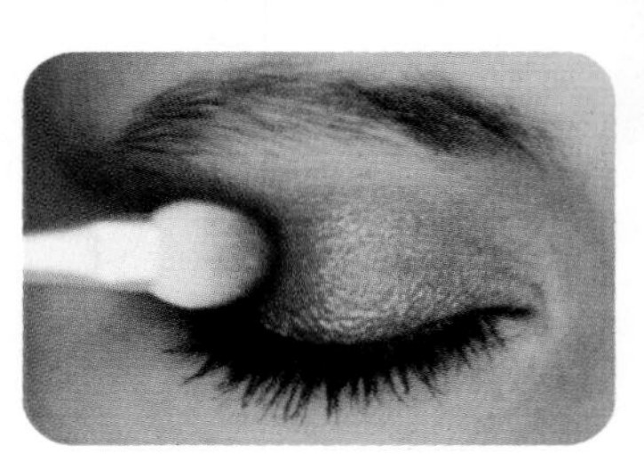

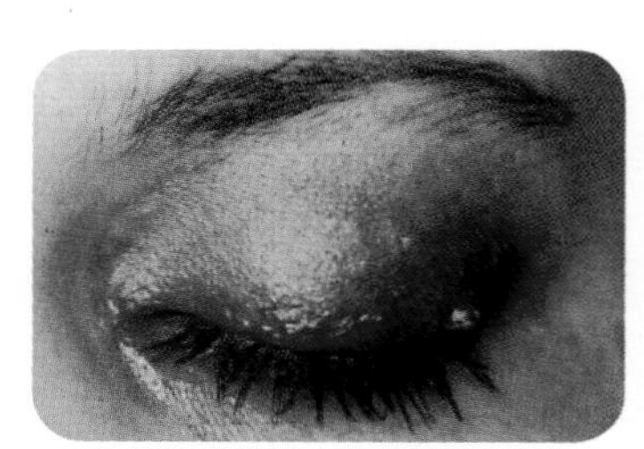

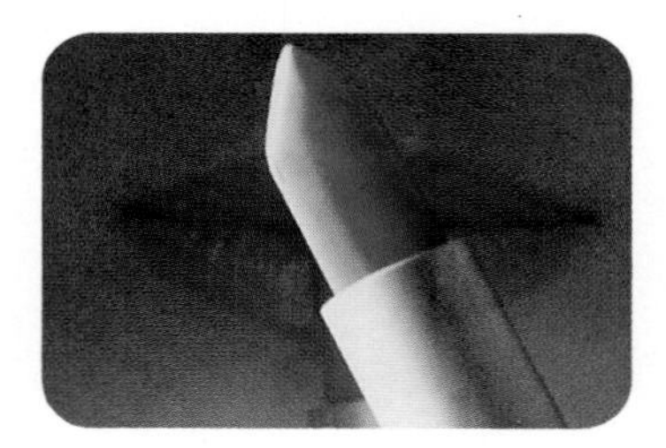

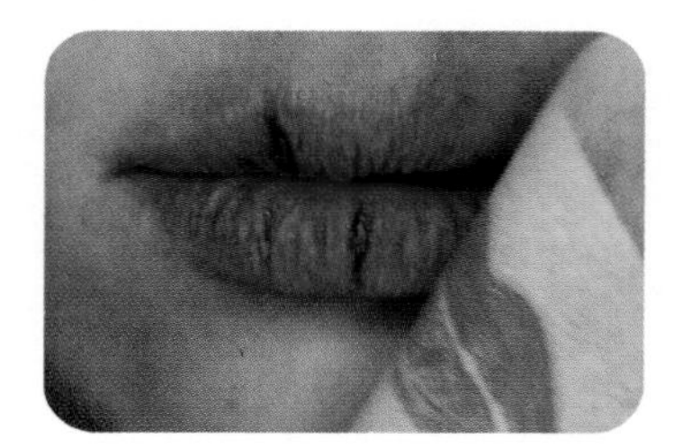

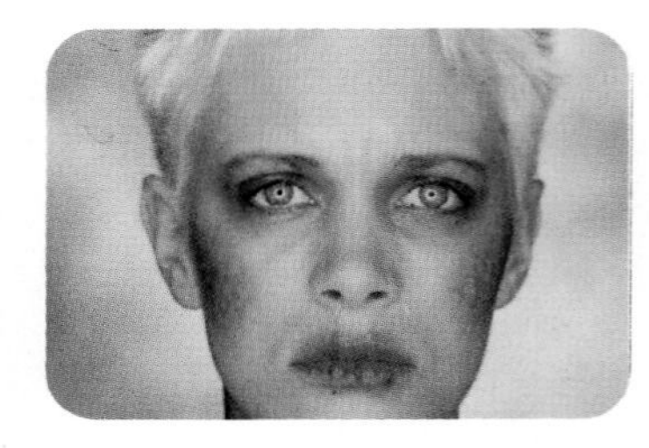

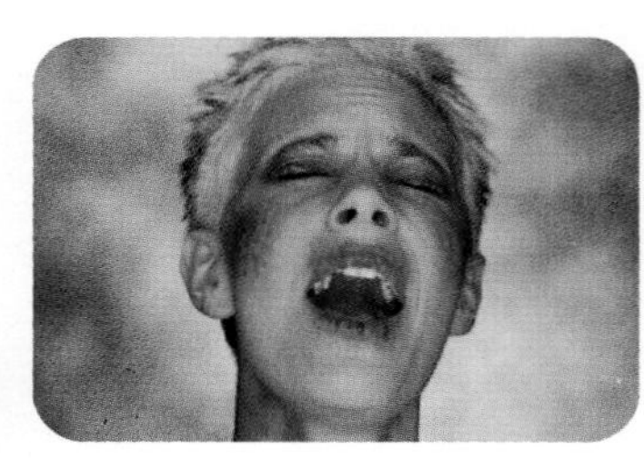

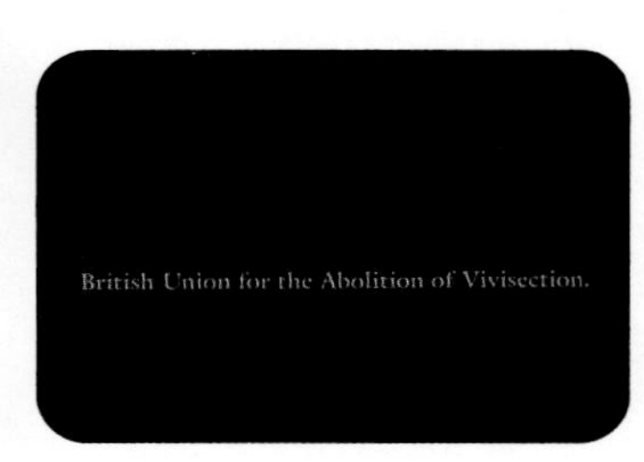

295
Campaign against drunk driving
Spain
Agency: Bassat, Ogilvy & Mather, Barcelona

'Mixing alcohol and petrol kills' warns this commercial. Petrol is seen being pumped into a glass of booze, which then turns out to be used as a flower vase in a cemetery.

295

296
Environmental protection
Brazil
Agency: MPM, Rio de Janeiro

This film, urging the protection of the Amazonian rain forest, begins by showing many species of animals and birds living there. A man appears with a mechanical saw to cut down the trees. When he starts the motor the animals and birds flee. Blood runs from a wounded tree trunk.

297

297
Monoprix
France
Agency: CLM/BBDO, Paris
'Our free range chickens arrive straight from the South-West.' And a fine, healthy-looking chicken it is.

298
Forum des Halles
France
Agency: CLM/BBDO, Paris
The headline makes brilliant sense of the visual muddle: 'Typical route followed by a Forum des Halles customer who liked everything, hesitated a lot and will return tomorrow with his wife'. Tag line: 'One could resist the Forum des Halles if one wished'.

298

309
McDonald's
France
Agency: BDDP, Paris

Two children take their grandfather to McDonald's for the first time. He discovers a world new to him where you can eat with your fingers. The gentle sentimentality of this film is in sharp contrast to the more aggressive approaches seen in those, from the US and New Zealand respectively, for Burger King and Kentucky Fried Chicken.

309

310
Burger King
United States
Agency: Saatchi & Saatchi, New York

A macho quality to this spot in which airmen return from their mission and collect their 'orders'.

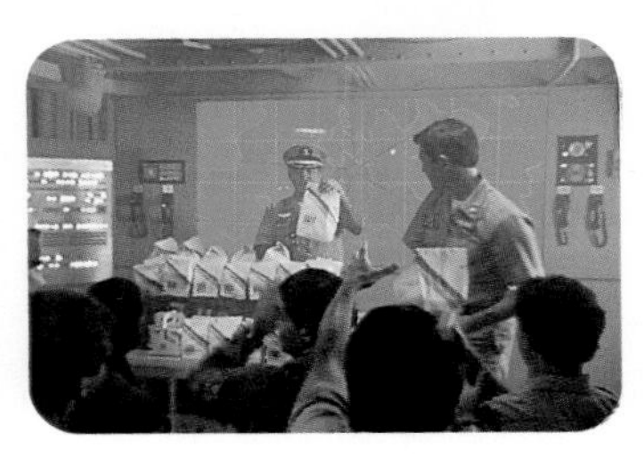

310

311

311
Fortuna cigarettes
Spain
Agency: TAPSA/Ayer, Madrid
The nicest touch in this ad is the red piano key.

312, 313, 314, 315
Dames cigarettes
Austria
Agency: Young & Rubicam, Vienna
In 1960 the London ad agency S. H. Benson, now defunct, brought out a television campaign for a new cigarette brand called Strand. The slogan was 'You're never alone with a Strand', and commercials showed a lonely and rather dejected young man puffing a cigarette to keep his spirits up. The campaign achieved instant notoriety, but the brand flopped.

Now, 30 years later, here are manufacturers Austria Tabak and agency Y&R using exactly the same slogan for Dames. However, the young man in these press ads seems a lot more cheerful, despite the scrapes he gets into, than did the star of the Strand commercials.

312

313

314

315

316

317

316, 317
Benson & Hedges Special Filter cigarettes
United Kingdom
Agency: Collett Dickenson Pearce & Partners, London
This classic campaign maintains its usual high standard of visual inventiveness.

LOW TAR As defined by H.M. Government
Warning: MORE THAN 30,000 PEOPLE DIE EACH YEAR IN THE UK FROM LUNG CANCER
Health Departments' Chief Medical Officers

318

LOW TAR As defined by H.M. Government
Warning: SMOKING CAN CAUSE LUNG CANCER, BRONCHITIS AND OTHER CHEST DISEASES
Health Departments' Chief Medical Officers

319

318, 319
Silk Cut cigarettes
United Kingdom
Agency: Saatchi & Saatchi, London

Saatchi's Silk Cut work is coming to rival CDP's B&H as a benchmark of cigarette advertising in an age when in many countries cigarette advertisers are no longer allowed to sing their products' praises.

320

When You
Know
What You're
Smoking
You Roll

STOPPING SMOKING REDUCES THE RISK OF SERIOUS DISEASES
Health Departments' Chief Medical Officers

321

320, 321, 322, 323, 324
Old Holborn tobacco
United Kingdom
Agency: J. Walter Thompson, London

Amusing pictures. Of course, if you were to pay proper attention to the Government health warning printed at the bottom, you might conclude

Warning: SMOKING C
Health Departments

322

that you'd be better off smoking old rope, a mackerel, a flower, a bone or a tea strainer.

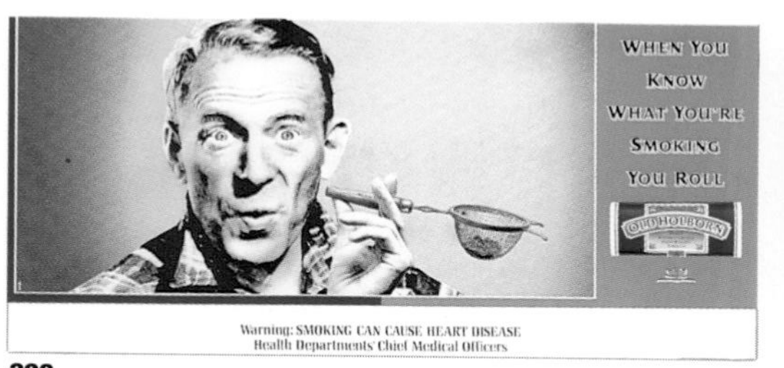

323

324

WHEN YOU
KNOW
WHAT YOU'RE
SMOKING
YOU ROLL

AUSE FATAL DISEASES
ef Medical Officers

325

325
Respons shampoo
Denmark, Sweden, Norway
Agency: Young & Rubicam, Copenhagen
One of a series showing how different hairstyles can change the personality. Headline: 'Be good to your hair. It's part of your personality.' Body copy continues: 'Once in a while you feel like a change, to renew yourself. An easy way to change type is to try a new hairstyle.' Whatever the style, however, it needs the 'loving care' of Respons.

326, 327
Revlon cosmetics
United Kingdom
Agency: The Leagas Delaney Partnership, London
The distinctive feature of this campaign is big close-ups of different parts of the face. The copywriter on this ad is agency partner Tim Delaney.

326

L H

A E

S S

BOWING TO PUBLIC OPINION, REVLON BRINGS BACK THE LASH.

The lash is back. Thick and curled, groomed and luscious. No more the caked mascara brush. Not for you the clogged and matted eyelash. Now Revlon introduces mascaras with unique hollow fibre brushes, a remarkable breakthrough that allows the mascara to be distributed equally across the brush. The result? The delicate job of applying your mascara is now more controlled, your lashes covered more evenly and more quickly. Available in Big Brush Waterproof Mascara containing lanolin to condition lashes; Big Brush Gentle Thickening Mascara with resin to thicken and lengthen; and Micropure Mascara which is hypoallergenic and fragrance-free for sensitive eyes.

REVLON
Mascaras with hollow fibre brushes.

P D

O E

W R

IS THIS THE END OF THE POWDERED NOSE?

The powdered nose. Has it always been thus? Why not the unpowdered nose? Introducing Revlon's New Complexion Loose Powder. Its exclusive formula contains tiny porous spheres allowing the powder to glide smoothly onto your skin without resistance. The effect is a natural, silky finish which never appears dry or powdery. And being porous, it doesn't block your pores, instead, it enables your skin to breathe. New Complexion Loose Powder also contains special colour pigments to ensure that the colours remain true throughout the day, a gentle sunscreen to provide protection against skin damage caused by sunlight and is fragrance and irritant free. In three translucent shades. All with their own unique brush-in-the-pot.

REVLON
New Complexion Loose Powder.

327

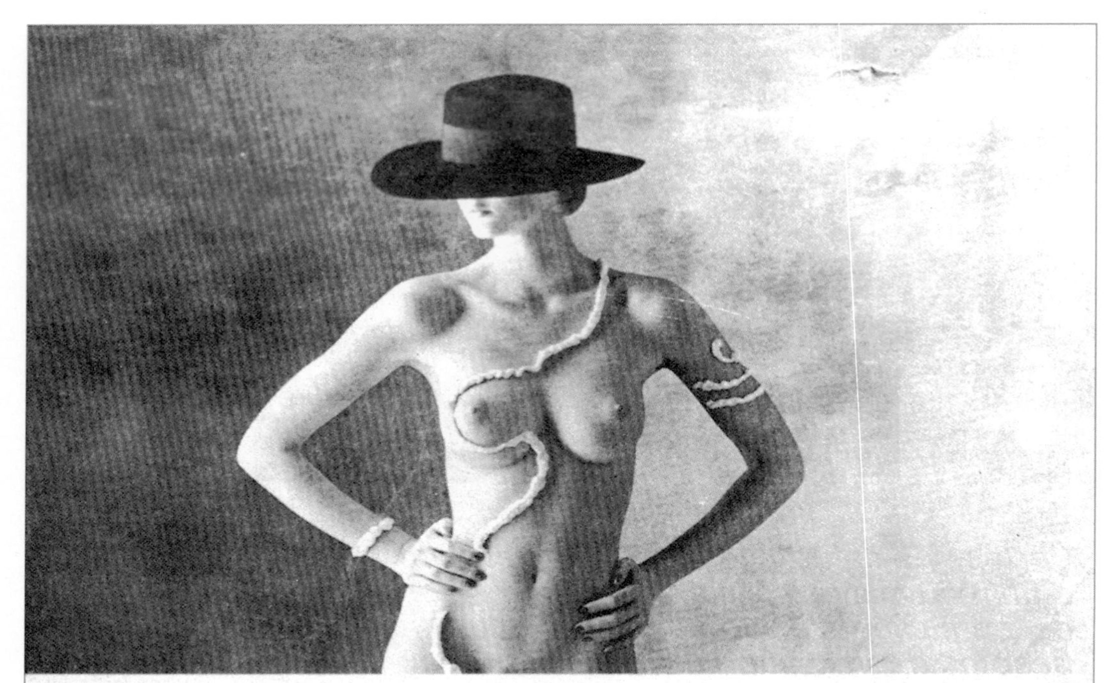

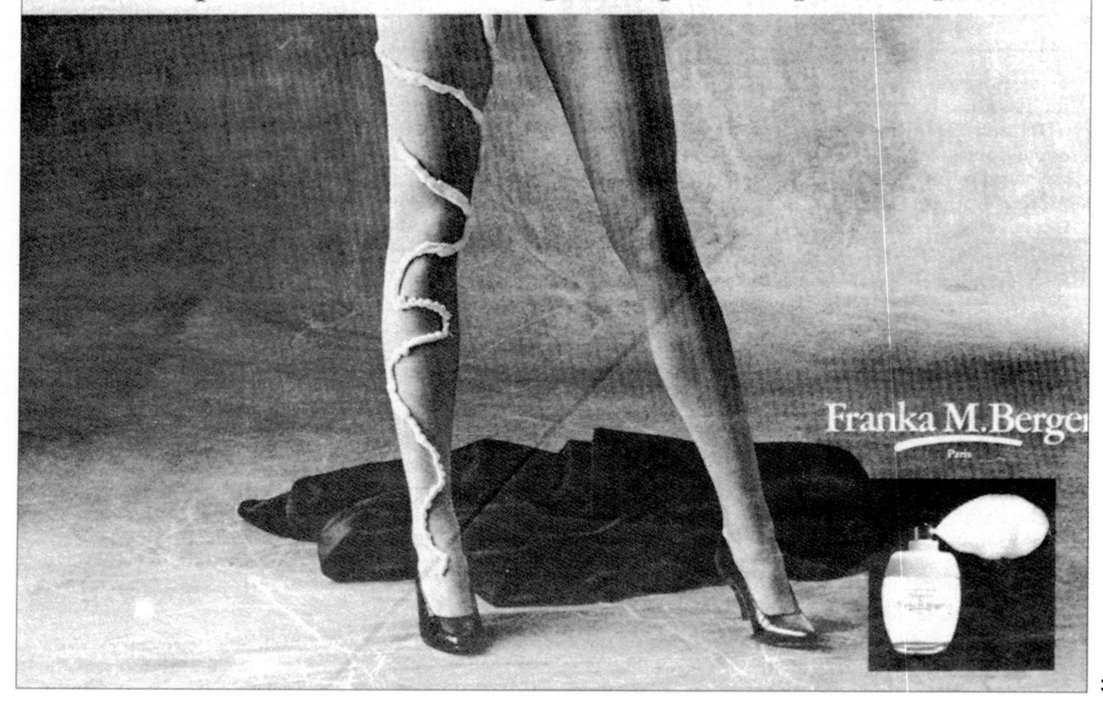

328

328
Franka M. Berger perfume foam
France
Agency: Saatchi & Saatchi, Paris
The copy line says 'The first perfume to get dressed in'. Strange that the model is almost entirely undressed. The eye-catching ad ran in daily newspapers.

329
Eurax
United Kingdom
Agency: Woollams Moira Gaskin O'Malley, London

Unlike Saatchi's French ad for Franka Berger perfume, to which it bears a slight and coincidental resemblance, this is not for a cosmetic but for a pharmaceutical product. Eurax anti-itching cream, though widely prescribed by doctors, was not previously advertised to consumers. The market would appear to be ripe for such advertising; according to research, about half the women in Britain suffer from itches. Women, especially in the prime target age group, 35 to 44, are largely ignorant of the existence of special creams for an ailment they consider not serious enough to require medical attention.

How to escape from scratching.

You itch, so you scratch. You scratch, so you itch. It's a vicious circle. The way to break it is with Eurax Cream.

Eurax contains a unique ingredient, Crotamiton, widely prescribed by doctors.

Available only from pharmacists.

It rapidly relieves all kinds of itches, from a mild rash to an allergic reaction, on any part of the body.

And, of course, if you don't itch, you don't scratch.

329

330, 331, 332, 333
Tri-Ac
United Kingdom
Agency: Woollams Moira Gaskin O'Malley, London

Teenage girls are the prime target for this product, claimed to be particularly efficacious against spots. The style of the campaign reflects the age of its targets.

If you don't want to look like a join the dots competition use Tri-Ac Medicated Cleanser. Tri-Ac is anti bacterial and antiseptic too. So it kills more of the nasties that cause spots in the first place. There's also Tri-Ac Facewash. It removes dirt and grease without making your skin dry. And keeps on working all day. Check them out, because spots can't show you up if you stop them showing up. For more information write to:- Tri-Ac Advisory Service, Ciba, Freepost, Horsham, West Sussex, RH13 5ZB.

TRI-AC
STOPS
SPOTS
RAISING THEIR
UGLY HEADS

ANTIBACTERIAL. ANTISEPTIC. ANTISPOTS.

330

331

REDUCES REDNESS IN

'ARRRRRGHH! A massive spot has erupted on my puny chest.' Yes, viewers, we've all made that plaintive cry at some point. But don't bang your head against a wall. (At least not any more than you usually do.) Bang some Tri-Ac Treatment Gel on the offender. Its active ingredients reduce the redness that makes spots so noticeable. In tests most people found they noticed the difference the following day. You can get Tri-Ac Cleanser and Facewash too. They're anti-bacterial, which means they help stop you getting spots in the first place. There. That's one problem off your chest. For more information please write to:- Tri-Ac Advisory Service, Ciba, Freepost, Horsham, W.Sussex, RH13 5ZB.

TRI-AC
BITES
THE HEADS
OFF
SPOTS

TWENTY FOUR HOURS

332

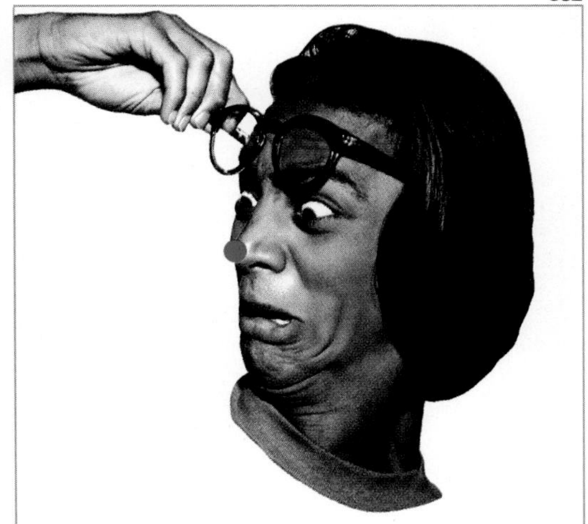

The embarrassing thi ng about spots is that they go red. Noisy, nas ty, look-at-me-i'm-a-zit-factory red. But to spare your blushes th ere's Tri-Ac Treatment Gel. Its active ingred ients reduce the red ness that makes spots so obvious. In tests mo st people noticed the difference the following day. You can get Tri-Ac Cleanser and Face wash too. They're anti-bacterial, which means they help stop you get ting spots in the fir st place. You will find they hit the problem right on the nose. For more information wr ite to:- Tri-Ac Advis ory S ervice, Ciba, Freepost, Horsham, West Sussex, RH13 5ZB.

TRI-AC MAKES SPOTS HARDER TO SPOT

REDUCES REDNESS IN

Not "when you are 21." Not "when you are a bit older." Not even "some time nex t week." Tri-Ac makes spots harder to spot to morrow. Its active in gredients reduce the red ness that makes spots so obvious. In tests most people noticed the diff erence the following da y. You can get Tri-Ac Cl eanser and Facewash too.

TRI-AC SPOT THE DIFFERENCE IN 24 HOURS

They are anti-bacterial, which means they help stop you getting spots in the first place. So n ow when you get a spot you needn't just take it on the chin. For more in fo write to:- Tri-Ac Ad visory Serv ice, Ciba, Freepost, Horsham, W. Sussex, RH13 5ZB.

TRI-AC Gel

TWENTY FOUR HOURS.

333

334

334
Lux toilet soap
United Kingdom
Agency: J. Walter Thompson, London

Both copy, hooked to the double meaning of the word 'bar', and picture evoke the movie *Casablanca*. It's a more subtle way of glamorising the product than the old film star endorsements.

335
Hawaiian Tropic sun tan lotion
United Kingdom
Agency: J. Walter Thompson, London

Such broad humour is unusual for this type of product.

336
Right Guard deodorant
United Kingdom
Agency: Saatchi & Saatchi, London

With the endangered environment such a fashionable concern, it is not surprising that punsters are drawing inspiration from it.

335

Nose zone friendly.

RIGHT GUARD

OZONE FRIENDLY

336

337
Clinica Lion toothpaste
Japan
Agency: Dentsu, Tokyo

Here's one Japanese joke a Westerner can appreciate. The father keeps telling his little boy not to be afraid of the dentist, but it turns out that it is the man, not the child, who is having his tooth fixed. In Japan more than 80 per cent of adults have dental cavities, and this campaign uses that fact as its starting point for a humorous attempt to persuade people to think about brushing their own teeth as well as their children's.

337

Audio: FATHER: *Don't worry. It'll be over quickly.* SON: . . .

FATHER: *See, if you don't brush your teeth properly, you'll get cavities.*

FATHER: *If you're afraid, just do this and you'll show how brave you are.*

WOMAN: *Hey, where are you going?* FATHER: *Oh, we're just going over to the dentist.* WOMAN: *Oh, it won't hurt a bit. Your father will be right there with you.*

FATHER: *They're going to grind the tooth, so it might hurt a little.*

DENTIST: *Mr Hosoda!* FATHER: *Yes!*

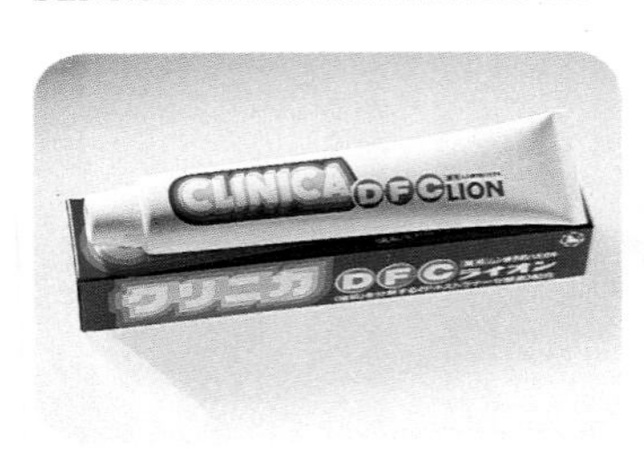

VO: *Dental problems among adults are currently on the increase. Clinica Lion with enzymes prevents tooth decay and helps promote good dental health.* SON: *It didn't hurt much, did it?*

338, 339
Margaret Astor cosmetics
West Germany
Agency: Michael Conrad & Leo Burnett, Frankfurt

The aim of the campaign is to dramatise the latest colours in the Astor range. One film, for Fire Red lipstick, has a woman applying the stuff, then breathing fire that envelopes the screen. In the other commercial, for Bang Red nail varnish, a woman with long, red nails takes a pistol from her bag and fires. Nail varnish runs down the screen.

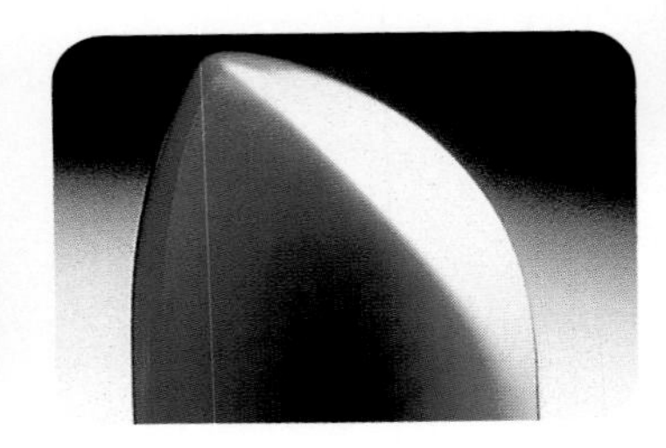

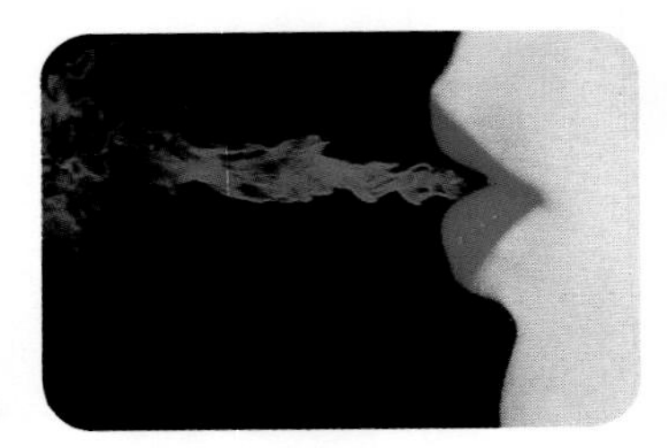

338

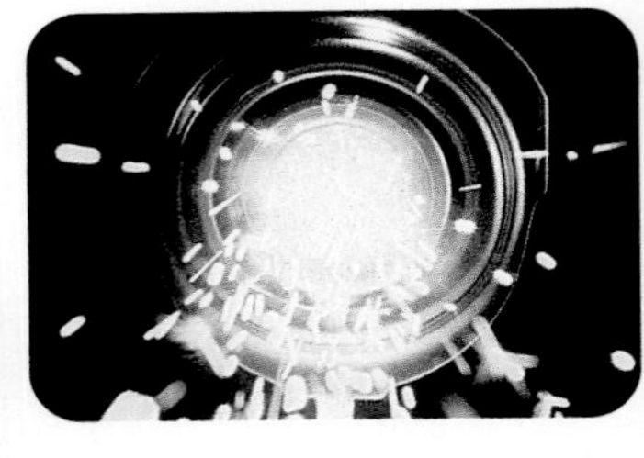

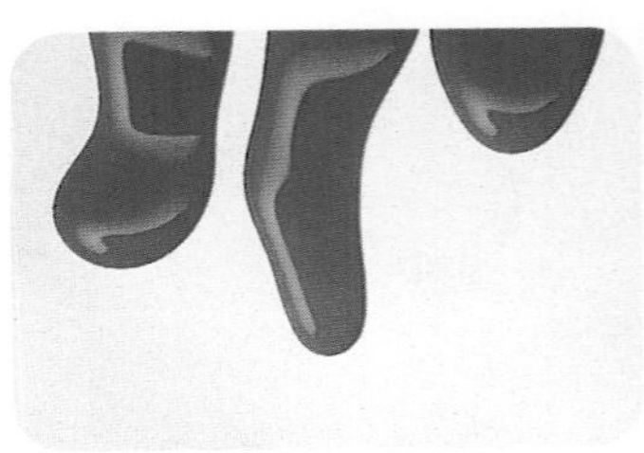

339

340
Cutex Strong Nail varnish
United States
Agency: Ogilvy & Mather, New York
This short film manages to be both funny and romantic at the same time.

340

Audio: (WOMAN VO) *I love him . . .*

I love him not. (SFX: *Click*)

(VO) *Only one nail strengthener has Knox Gelatine.*

Cutex Strong Nail.

It protects. Strengthens. Lasts.

WOMAN VO: *I love him.*
(VO) *Cutex Strong Nail.*

341

341
Northern Territory Tourist Commission
Australia
Agency: Saatchi & Saatchi, Sydney
An ad in Aboriginal style to draw tourists to one of the most unspoiled parts of Australia.

342
All Nippon Airways
Japan
Agency: Dentsu, Tokyo
This advertises the airline's flights to the Caribbean, Europe and Australia. The strong colours are supposed to give a Caribbean feeling to the ad, which urges readers to take holidays in winter as well as summer.

342

343, 344
Singapore Airlines/NTTC
United Kingdom
Agency: Edwards Martin Thornton, London

Both ads were aimed at travel agents and were jointly funded by the airline and Australia's Northern Territory Tourist Commission. The Rock pictured in one ad is the famous beauty spot Ayers Rock. The other ad, like Saatchi's Australian ad for the NTTC, draws inspiration from Aboriginal art.

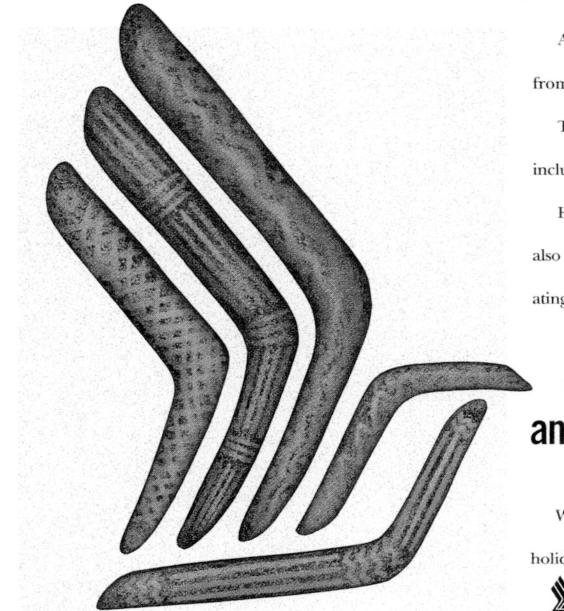

A 3-hour Singapore Airlines flight whizzes non-stop every week from Singapore to Darwin – gateway to the Northern Territory.

This hauntingly beautiful part of Australia is full of attractions including Ayers Rock, Kakadu National Park and Katherine Gorge.

Host to an enormous variety of exotic wildlife, the outback also holds ancestral grounds of the Aboriginal people – a fascinating culture described in ancient rock carvings and paintings.

Book them Singapore-Darwin and they won't want to come back.

When you throw your clients the choice of an exciting outback holiday, book Singapore Airlines with their legendary in-flight service and they're bound to come back.

Australia's
Northern
Territory

343

Book Singapore Airlines to Darwin and win tickets to a Rock show.

SINGAPORE
AIRLINES

Book a client on the SIN-DRW flight (or return) and for each sector booked you'll get an entry into our prize draw to win a holiday in Australia's Northern Territory. Ten lucky agents will earn a ten day trip in October 1990 flying from the U.K. via Singapore to Darwin, staying in top Sheraton Hotels.

The outback holds many attractions including Ayers Rock, Kakadu National Park and Aboriginal ancestral grounds. And there's the added attraction of flying Singapore Airlines with its superb in-flight service both ways.

Australia's
Northern
Territory

Please send completed coupon to: Auriol Gardner, NTTC, 393 Strand, London WC2R 0LT.

NAME ______
TRAVEL AGENCY ______
ADDRESS ______
______ PNR Number ______

When you book SIN-DRW or DRW-SIN on SIA just complete the coupon or send details on a postcard to the address above. All entries received by 31st August 1990 will go into a draw and the ten winners will be notified by post.

344

See where you can surf in winter too.
When going on a vacation in winter, go to where winter is at home: to the land of the downhill wedlers, snowboard riders, hot doggers, paragliders and ice skaters. You will meet lots of sports and fun. And you will be met with a friendly "Servus". Find out more at your nearest Austrian National Tourist Office or at Austrian Airlines.
Servus in Austria

345

Skyscrapers since 1433.
Our special skyscrapers may be a thousand years old: the towers and turrets of castles atop lofty crags, the spires of cathedrals in pulsing cities or of massive hilltop abbeys in the country, the domes crowning palaces and churches. In style, they may be Romanesque, Gothic, Renaissance, Baroque, Rococo. In beauty, they are unsurpassed. Find out about Austria's high-level treasures from the Austrian National Tourist Office – (212) 944-6880 in New York – or your nearest Austrian Airlines office.
Servus in Austria

346

On a long flight whose cabin staff would you rather be with?
A Breath of Fresh Air
Air Canada

347

349

348

345, 346, 348
Austrian National Tourist Office
Europe
Agency: Demner & Merlicek, Vienna
The witty 'skyscrapers' headline is accompanied by a photo shot at an angle that lends novelty to a very old building. *Servus* is the Austrian dialect word for 'welcome'. The other ads show respectively a Vienna art gallery's Gustav Klimt painting and a snowscape to cheer the hearts of skiers.

347
Air Canada
United Kingdom
Agency: Young & Rubicam, London
The maple leaf emblem is cleverly used in this unusual campaign.

349
British Airways Super Shuttle
United Kingdom
Agency: Saatchi & Saatchi, London
Copy says BA planes have equipment enabling them to land in foggy conditions with visibility down to 75 metres, 'shortest distance of any airline'. A 'pea souper' is, of course, a fog.

350, 351, 352, 353
Air France
United Kingdom
Agency: Ayer, London
The agency's stated twin goals were to produce stylish, modern images and to communicate specific consumer benefits. It could, of course, be argued that surrealism, as in the 'legs' and 'Magritte man' ads, while still stylish, is no longer very modern. The 'routes' ad is reminiscent of Y&R's epilepsy motif for Yorkshire TV in the Media section. 'Traffic jam' has been given a suitable French twist. Illustrators are respectively Warren Madill, Richard Prideaux, Jean Larcher and Ziggy.

WITH OUR LEG ROOM AIR FRANCE CAN TURN THE SHORT HAUL INTO A LONG STRETCH.

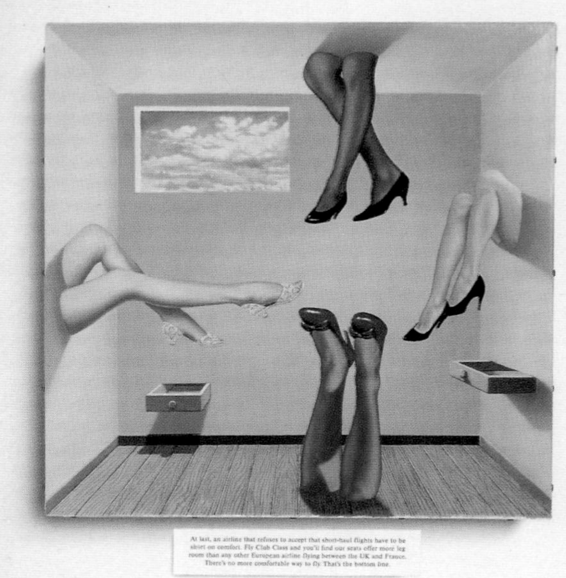

350

FLYING FROM MORE REGIONAL AIRPORTS GETS YOU OFF THE GROUND QUICKER.

351

WHEN YOU PUT ALL OUR ROUTES TOGETHER IT'S ENOUGH TO MAKE YOUR EYES WATER.

Which is hardly surprising when you consider we fly to more destinations in Europe than any other airline. So wherever you want to go in Europe, chances are we're already flying there. Now, how's that for an eye opener?

352

TO AIR FRANCE, JAM IS SOMETHING YOU PUT ON A CROISSANT.

Nothing is more tedious than being stuck in traffic. A fact Air France fully appreciate. This is why we fly from a choice of four London airports. That way you get to beat the queues. Because when you're trying to earn a crust, the last thing you need is to be stuck in a jam.

353

Die Wohnung, die Sie mit Ihrer Freundin teilen, ist Ihnen zu eng. Das Großraumbüro geht Ihnen auf den Nerv. Sie fliegen mit Condor. Und plötzlich macht es Ihnen überhaupt nichts aus, Ihr schmales Handtuch zu teilen.

354, 355, 356, 357
Condor charter flights
West Germany
Agency: Michael Conrad & Leo Burnett, Frankfurt

Condor, a Lufthansa subsidiary, wants to stimulate the desire to fly off on holiday. The ads are charming excursions into fantasy land. The one showing a woman and a penguin is captioned: 'The flat you're sharing with your friend is too small. You're fed up with the open-plan office. You fly Condor. And suddenly you don't mind sharing your narrow towel at all.' Copy on the mermaid ad says: ' "Male, single, in his late twenties, wants attractive female who likes holidays, diving and swimming." We recommend you take a Condor holiday flight and keep your eyes open.'

In the giant spatula ad the words read: 'The sun lamp is too cold, the sauna too full and the solarium always booked up. You don't care? Then you've been keeping a ticket for a Condor flight to Florida in your pocket.' The remaining ad is captioned: 'Building bricks, nappies, carrot purée. What more does the world have to offer? The best thing is to pack the brat in a Condor to Grand Canary and let him find out for himself.'

355

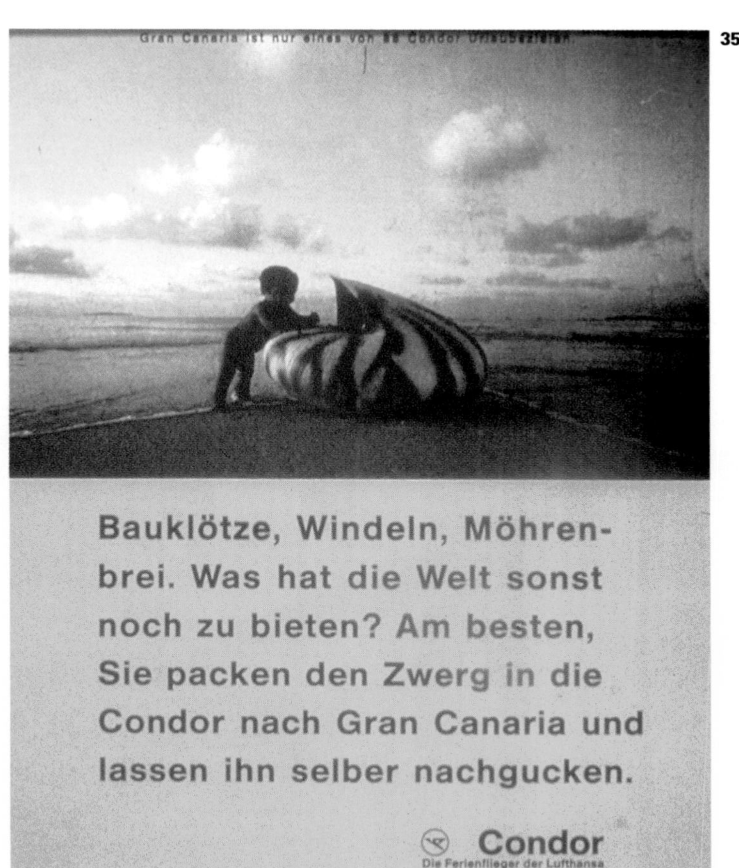

356

357

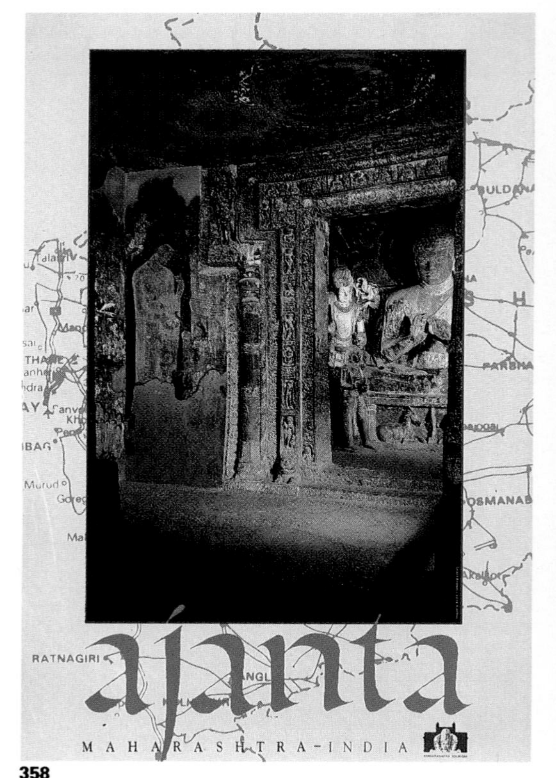
ajanta
MAHARASHTRA-INDIA
RATNAGIRI
358

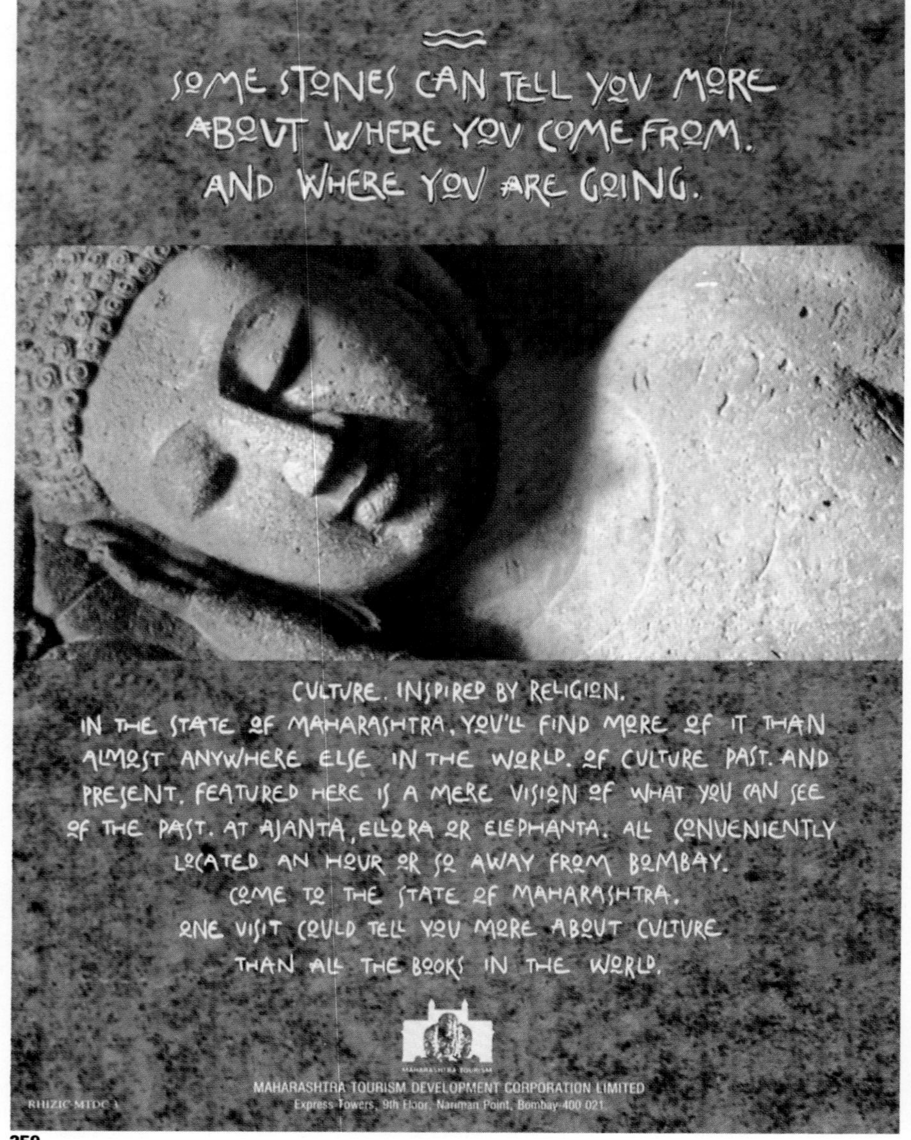
SOME STONES CAN TELL YOU MORE
ABOUT WHERE YOU COME FROM.
AND WHERE YOU ARE GOING.
CULTURE. INSPIRED BY RELIGION.
IN THE STATE OF MAHARASHTRA, YOU'LL FIND MORE OF IT THAN
ALMOST ANYWHERE ELSE IN THE WORLD. OF CULTURE PAST. AND
PRESENT. FEATURED HERE IS A MERE VISION OF WHAT YOU CAN SEE
OF THE PAST. AT AJANTA, ELLORA OR ELEPHANTA. ALL CONVENIENTLY
LOCATED AN HOUR OR SO AWAY FROM BOMBAY.
COME TO THE STATE OF MAHARASHTRA.
ONE VISIT COULD TELL YOU MORE ABOUT CULTURE
THAN ALL THE BOOKS IN THE WORLD.
MAHARASHTRA TOURISM DEVELOPMENT CORPORATION LIMITED
Express Towers, 9th Floor, Nariman Point, Bombay 400 021.
359

358, 359
Maharashtra Tourism Development Corporation
India
Agency: Rhizic, Bombay
The pictures are of the tourist attractions accessible from Bombay. Copy is by the agency founder, Rumi Mistry.

360, 361
Lauda Tours
Austria
Agency: Young & Rubicam, Vienna
'Disappointment free of charge' is the surprising heading on the attractive picture of the woman. Body copy explains that that 'is what you'll get when you book a holiday to Jamaica or the Dominican Republic if it's places of historic or cultural interest you're looking for'. But if lively people, lively music and lively parties are what is wanted, the firm promises to supply them. The other ad, showing giraffes in Kenya, is captioned 'Mountain dream'. Lauda Tours takes its name from the Austrian racing driver, Nikki Lauda.

360

361

362

Save money with a Young Persons Railcard. (Keep trying Gary).

If you're 16-23, a Young Persons Railcard costs £15 and gets you ⅓ off most rail fares for a whole year, so the more you travel, the more you save. You'll soon find it pays for itself. Pick up a leaflet at main BR Stations or Rail Appointed Travel Agents for full details.

362
Young Persons Railcard
United Kingdom
Agency: Saatchi & Saatchi, London
The card enables young people to travel at a discount on British Rail trains. The face in the ad is that of pop star Gary Glitter, known for trying to look younger than he is.

363
Trans World Airlines
United Kingdom
Agency: Young & Rubicam, London
The image and play on words, involving the American slang sense of 'cool' as an adjective of approval, are calculated to appeal to a certain type of Americanophile Briton.

364
Four Corners
United Kingdom
Agency: The Leagas Delaney Partnership, London
The client company is a subsidiary of British Airways. The risqué headline could perhaps have done with some slightly more titillating visuals.

363

TWA

It's 80°. But everyone's cool.

TWA now flies to the Golden State seven days a week throughout the summer.

Direct to the City of the Angels. And with our domestic network TWA flights reach eight other cities in California.

Our Getaway tours programme offers complete holiday packages, too.

Holidays which are supported this month by a TV and poster campaign in the London area.

And don't forget that every single booking you make will earn you extra points in our Passport incentive scheme.

So fly your clients TWA. It's a pretty cool way of booking your own ticket.

TWA
For the *best* of America.

TWA

364

After you get married, kiss your wife in places she's never been kissed before.

Iguassu Falls, Brazil.

Fatehpur Sikri, India.

Penang, Malaysia.

Half Moon Bay, Antigua.

Tsavo East, Kenya.

If you're planning a honeymoon, we've got some proposals you may find hard to turn down.

Such as a fortnight at the renowned Peponi Hotel in Lamu, Kenya. A week cruising up the Nile on an elegant river boat. Or three weeks spent island hopping in the Caribbean.

It's a difficult decision.

So before you say 'I do', call into Four Corners, Britain's newest travel company. We'll give you informed advice on these and many other equally exotic and fascinating places to honeymoon.

Antigua, one of the Leeward Islands, for instance, where you can lie back and not think of England on any of 365 white sandy beaches.

Or stroll around the colourful capital of St Johns and enjoy grilled Snapper fish and iced Rum Swizzles with the locals.

After which you can make your way back to one of Antigua's many delightful hotels.

Among our favourites is the Blue Waters in Soldier Bay, a peaceful hotel nestling in the northern tip of the island. Here you can relax by the pool or snooze in a hammock strung between two palm trees in the lush tropical gardens.

Should you wish to stay somewhere further removed from civilisation, we might recommend Bird Island in the Seychelles.

On this tiny coral island (just 1½ miles long and ½ mile wide), everything is so informal you don't even have to wear shoes for dinner, let alone a jacket and tie.

Indeed, we can think of nowhere better to unwind after you've tied the knot.

Where, though, do you go if you prefer something a little more adventurous?

The answer could be Hamilton Island on the Great Barrier Reef.

As well as soaking up the sun, you can fish for the Dogtooth Tuna, parasail, jet ski and tour the Barrier Reef in a catamaran.

All marvellous, of course, if you've got two or three weeks to spare. But what if you can only manage two or three days? In that case, may we suggest somewhere closer to home?

Like the Chewton Glen Hotel in New Milton. Or Middlethorpe Hall in York. Or Cliveden in Taplow perhaps. This elegant hotel is set in 370 acres overlooking the Thames, and was once home to a Prince of Wales, three Dukes and the Astor family.

But no matter where you decide to honeymoon or for how long, we can assure you of a truly memorable time together.

In fact, the only reservations you should ever have before walking down the aisle to get married, are the ones you make with us.

FOUR CORNERS

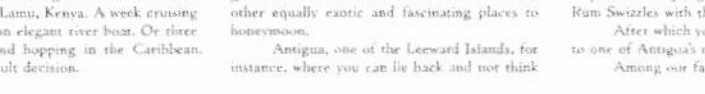

Four Corners are in the Strand, Kensington High Street, Altrincham, Bromley, Chelmsford, Croydon, Leicester, Maidstone, Reading, Whiteleys of Bayswater and Windsor. Or call one of our travel consultants on: 0622 692256.

A week by the pool with a car thrown in.

Take advantage of Sol car hire even if your client's holiday or flight isn't booked through us. Sol arrange everything at their low all-inclusive prices, and the car is always ready to drive on arrival, whichever airline or ABTA tour operator is used.

But you could drive around the resort pictured here absolutely free.

Win a week's Sol holiday for two *plus* car hire by naming: (1) The resort. (2) The holiday codes of the cars Sol rent there.

Look in the Sol "Rent-a-Car" leaflet for the chance to dive (and drive) in the sun.

Yours ever, SOL

COMPETITION RULES

- Entries must be received by Monday 30 January, 1989.
- The draw will be held on Tuesday 31st January, 1989.
- The first correct answer out of the postbag wins.
- The judges' decision is final.
- The winner will be notified by post.

Please return completed entry forms to:
Sol Holidays, Arndale House, Charles Street, Bradford BD1 1EL.
I think the resort is ______
and the holiday codes of the cars are ______
Name ______
Address ______

365

Win a Sol holiday to Pluto.

Spot Pluto's nose in our '89 Florida brochure and see all the Disneyworld characters for free.

Our prices are low, but take a look at the quality of our resorts in Orlando in Central Florida and St. Petersburg on the coast.

Do it for free by answering these questions: 1. What page does this nose appear on? 2. How many Hotels are featured in the Sol Florida '89 brochure?

Find the answers in the brochure and win a week's holiday for two that's out of this world.

Yours ever, SOL

COMPETITION RULES

- Entries must be received by Monday 6th February, 1989.
- The draw will be held on Tuesday 7th February, 1989.
- The first correct answer out of the postbag wins.
- The judges' decision is final.
- The winner will be notified by post.

Please return completed entry forms to:
Sol Holidays, Arndale House, Charles Street, Bradford BD1 1EL.
I think the nose is on page ______
and the number of Hotels in the Florida brochure is ______
Name ______
Address ______

366

365, 366
Sol Holidays
United Kingdom
Agency: Edwards Martin Thornton, London

Both ads feature competitions offering the chance to win a holiday. In one the big blue blob is Pluto's nose, Pluto being not the planet but the Walt Disney character, a denizen of Disneyworld in Florida. The holiday prize in the other competition includes free car hire.

367
British Airways
Worldwide
Agency: Saatchi & Saatchi, London
Some 4,000 extras were employed in this big-budget commercial, directed by Hugh Hudson, who made the movie *Chariots of Fire*. The BA film was made in the American Mid-West. Background music is from the opera *Lakmé* by Delibes. The agency's aim is to add 'more warmth and humanity' to the airline's image. However that may be, the commercial will stand as an impressive piece of logistics.

Visual: We open on a group of swimmers clothed in red with red goggles on, swimming towards us. ***Audio:*** MUSIC THROUGHOUT. Cut to close up of female swimmer with red lips. Cut to many swimmers in the shape of a pair of lips moving from the water on to a beach. Cut to another viewpoint of them coming out of the water. Cut to them on the beach. Cut to wide aerial shot of the lips with spectacular scenery in the background. Cut to shot of stone eagles on top of a building with a shape of blue people forming on the ground. Cut to eye with a group of blue people reflected in it, cut to shot of people moving along the street in the shape of an eye. Cut to shot of Egyptian ladies exotically dressed in blue crossing the screen. Cut to aerial shot of the people eye. Cut to many people dressed in white running together to make the shape of an ear. Cut to wide aerial shot of people ear travelling along, we see that they are in a mountainscape. Dissolve through to many red people moving from right to left across screen. Cut to wide aerial shot of many people in shapes: red lips, blue eyes, black nose, converging together, dissolve through to an even wider shot, of this odd Picasso shape. Dissolve again to reveal spectacular mountains in the distance behind the Picasso shape. Cut to two hands shaking with Union Jack undulating in the background.

A series of greeting shots then follows: Indian mother and daughter (Stars and Stripes in the background), little black children being greeted by their relatives, cheerleader greeting coach and team. MVO: *Every year . . .* Cut to Egyptians and Arabs greeting each other. . . . *the World's favourite airline . . .* Cut to BA stewardess shepherding people, smiling (French flag in the background). Cut to close up of little black girl being twirled around (Australian flag in the background). . . . *brings 24 million people . . .* Cut to BA pilot with BA stewards behind him, directing a young girl to the right place. Cut to a mother kissing her baby (Japanese flag in the background). Cut to mid shot of all the shape people in the shape of a proper face. The lip section moves to make a smile. We pan out to reveal the full face and the eye section winks. The shape changes to a globe with spectacular canyonlands in the background. . . . *together.* SUPER: British Airways. The World's favourite airline. (MUSIC ENDS WITH JET WHOOSH.)

367

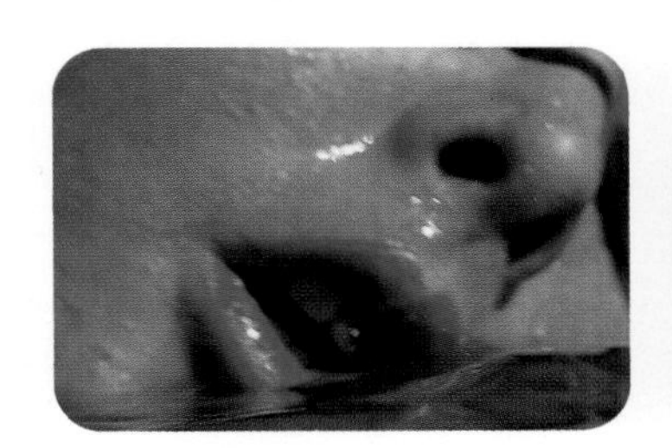

368
Central Japan Railways
Japan
Agency: Dentsu, Tokyo

The film shows a reunion between young lovers, thanks to the railway. Voice-over: 'Your coming home was the best present of all'. Central Japan Railways, one of the successor companies to Japan National Railways, which was split up and privatised in 1987, has focused in its advertising on human interest themes.

368

369
British Rail
United Kingdom
Agency: Saatchi & Saatchi, London

A beautiful film, directed by Tony Kaye, which has won a shoal of creative awards. The song *Relax*, composed and sung by the American Leon Redbone, gives the film much of its lazy charm. The agency's creative team consisted of two of its stars, with copy by Jeff Stark and art direction by creative director Paul Arden, who first came across Redbone's music several years ago in New York. As well as the little touches of visual wit, the commercial is noteworthy for its technique of using muted colour tones. British Rail believes the commercial did a first-class job in creating more positive attitudes to its InterCity services.

Visual: Open with feet walking quickly along street. Cut to wide shot of station – people boarding the train. ***Audio:*** MUSIC: *Anytime you choose. Kick off your shoes . . .* Cut to woman relaxing kicking off her high heeled shoes – the high heeled shoes 'relax' (heel curls round over shoe). *Rest your weary eyes . . .* Cut to a woman reading a newspaper. Cut to more countryside. *Catch up with the news. Her favourite cup of tea . . .* Cut to a woman reading Penguin book – penguin sighs and relaxes. *A perfect company. Relax.* Cut to Grandfather and Grandson playing chess. The chessmen sigh and relax. *Forget about the blues. You're doing fine. Leave your cares and worries down the line . . .* Cut to young man relaxing in his seat and then to his shoes changing to slippers. *Loosen up your tie . . .* Cut to InterCity train passing by. *Watch the world speed by . . .* Cut to InterCity logo stretching vertically which then comes back and relaxes into the normal BR logo. *Relax.*

369

CREDITS

ALCOHOLIC DRINKS

1, 2, 3
Smirnoff vodka
United Kingdom
Agency: Young & Rubicam, London
Art director: Ruth Owen
Copywriter: Charlotte Sillars
Photographer: Richard Mummery
Model makers: Gerry Judah (cave drawing, mosaic); Shirt Sleeves (Egyptian frieze)

4
Kronenbourg beer
France
Agency: Young & Rubicam, Paris
Art director: Patrick Fourré
Copywriter: Madeleine Danielson
Photographer: Francis Azemard

5
Malibu
United Kingdom
Agency: Burkitt Weinreich Bryant, London
Art director: Ray Barrett
Copywriter: Piers Carter
TV director: Stak
Production company: Maggie Mullen

6
Archer's Peach County schnapps
United Kingdom
Agency: Burkitt Weinreich Bryant, London
Art director: Ray Barrett
Copywriter: Patrick Collister
Photographer: Jack Bankhead

7
Johnnie Walker Black Label whisky
United Kingdom
Agency: Collett Dickenson Pearce and Partners, London
Art director: Neil Godfrey
Copywriter: Indra Sinha
Photographer: Neil Barstow

8
Castlemaine XXXX
United Kingdom
Agency: Saatchi & Saatchi, London
Art director: Peter Gibb
Copywriter: Richard Myers
Photographer: Terence Donovan

9, 10, 11
Absolut vodka
United States
Agency: TBWA, New York
Art director: Tom McManus
Copywriter: David Warren
Photographer: Steve Bronstein (San Francisco); others are stock pictures

12
Bavaria beer
Netherlands
Agency: DMB&B, Amsterdam
Art director: Peter van den Engel
Copywriter: Martijn Horvath
Photographer: Hans Kroeskamp

13
J & B Rare whisky
United Kingdom
Agency: Young & Rubicam, London
Art director: Anthony Stileman
Copywriter: Neil Patterson
Photographer: Martin Thompson
Model maker: Guy Hodgkinson

14
Tartan bitter
United Kingdom
Agency: Burkitt Weinreich Bryant, London
Art director: Ray Barrett
Copywriter: Patrick Collister
Illustrator: Kim Le Liboux

15
Grant's whisky
France
Agency: BDDP, Paris
Art director: Philippe Pollet Villard
Copywriter: Rémi Babinet
Photographer: Paul Goirand

16
Draught Bass
United Kingdom
Agency: Edwards Martin Thornton, London
Art director: Karen Hagemann
Copywriter: Keiron Simpson
Photographers: Richard Mummery, John Lawrence-Jones

17
Tennent's Super lager
United Kingdom
Agency: Edwards Martin Thornton, London
Art director: Karen Hagemann
Copywriter: Chris Martin
Photographer: Jerry Oke

18
Grand Marnier
United States
Agency: TBWA, New York
Art directors: Joe Stutts, Arnie Arlow
Copywriter: Peter Lubalin
Illustrator: Gervasio Gallardo

19, 20
1664 beer
France
Agency: BDDP, Paris
Art director: Pierre Gauthronet
Copywriter: Alain Jalabert
Photographer: Nick Knight

21
Cuervo tequila
United States
Agency: Young & Rubicam, New York
Art director: Clark Frankel
Copywriter: Mike Robertson
Photograph: stock
Retoucher: E. S. Paccione

AUDIO AND VIDEO

22, 23, 24, 25
Sanyo audio and video equipment
United Kingdom
Agency: The Leagas Delaney Partnership, London
Art directors: Steve Dunn (It's ugly; Lazy, stupid); Gary Marshall (daughter's wedding; No sex, please)
Copywriters: Tim Delaney (It's ugly; Lazy, stupid); Paul Marshall (daughter's wedding; No sex please)
Photographer: John Hammond
Typographer: Jeff Lewis

26, 27
Philips car stereo equipment
United Kingdom
Agency: Ogilvy & Mather, London
Art director: Brian Fraser
Copywriter: Simon Learman
Photographers: Martin Thompson (compact disc); Terence Donovan (loudspeakers)

28
Grundig video recorder
Italy
Agency: Bozell e Associati, Milan
Art director: Agostino Toscana
Copywriter: Paolo Savignano
Photographer: Raffaello Brà

29
Grundig M95 S/PiP TV set
Italy
Agency: Bozell e Associati, Milan
Art director: Agostino Toscana
Copywriter: Paolo Savignano
Illustrator: E.G.I.M.

30
Grundig portable TV set
Italy
Agency: Bozell e Associati, Milan
Art director: Agostino Toscana
Copywriter: Paolo Savignano
Photographer: Paolo Gandola

31
Toshiba C3 TV
Hong Kong
Agency: Ball WCRS Partnership, Hong Kong
Art director: Tan Khiang
Copywriter: Simon Hayward
Photographer: Joseph Chiu

32, 33
Maxell audio tapes
United Kingdom
Agency: Howell Henry Chaldecott Lury, London
Art director: Tim Ashton
Copywriter: Naresh Ramchandani
TV producer: Jane Fuller
Production company: The Molotov Brothers

34
Vivivideo video cassettes
Italy
Agency: Bozell e Associati, Milan
Art director: Mario Raimondi
Copywriters: Pasquale Barbella, Paolo Chiabrando
Illustrator: Marco Ventura

35, 36
Solidaire TV sets
India
Agency: Insight, Madras
Art director: Nalesh Patil
Copywriter: Gangadharan
Illustrator: Shantaram Pawar
Photographer: Suresh Cordo

AUTOMOTIVE

37
Porsche 944 S2
United Kingdom
Agency: The Leagas Delaney Partnership, London
Art director: Steve Dunn
Copywriter: Tim Delaney
Photographer: Lester Bookbinder
Typographers: Jeff Lewis, Steve Dunn

38, 39
Porsche Cabriolet 911 and 928 S4
West Germany
Agency: Wensauer & Partner, Ludwigsburg
Art director: Günther Tibi
Copywriter: Armin Schmidt
Photographer: Dietmar Henneka

40
Mitsubishi cars
Japan
Studio: Takayuki Itoh Design Office, Tokyo
Art director: Minako Ebisawa
Copywriter: Asatsu Inter
Photographer: Hideki Fuji

41
Ford Transit
United Kingdom
Agency: Ogilvy & Mather, London
Art director: Brian Fraser
Copywriter: Simon Learman
Photographer: Chris Cheetham

42, 43
Volkswagen Corrado
United Kingdom
Agency: BMP DDB Needham, London
Art director: Mark Reddy

Copywriter: Richard Grisdale
Photographer: Lester Bookbinder

44
Motorcraft service centre
United Kingdom
Agency: Ogilvy & Mather, London
Art director: Mike Comley
Copywriter: Mike Little
Photographer: James Wormser

45
Volkswagen competition
United Kingdom
Agency: BMP DDB Needham, London
Art director: Mark Reddy
Copywriter: Richard Grisdale
Photographer: David Scheinmann

46, 47
Fiat Uno
Germany, Netherlands, Belgium, Austria
Agency: Michael Conrad & Leo Burnett, Frankfurt
Art directors: John Buchner, Felix Glauner
Copywriters: Klaus Erich Küster, Christoph Herold, Georg Krause
Photographers: Albert Watson, Thomas Jung

48, 49
Fiat motor oil
Italy
Agency: Bozell e Associati, Milan
Art director: Loris Losi
Copywriter: Pasquale Barbella
Illustrators: Tom Spikic (The most opened can); Graziano Tinti (In the last 75 years)

50
Peugeot scooters
France
Agency: Young & Rubicam, Paris
Art director: Richard Claverie
Copywriter: Hervé Chadenat
Photographer: Patrick Ibanez

51
Dunlop tyres
Australia
Agency: Campaign Palace, Melbourne
Art director: Bart Palovich
Copywriter: Scott Whybin

52
BMW financing
France
Agency: BDDP, Paris
Art director: Pascal Midavaine
Copywriter: Dominique Quessada
Photographer: Thierry Legoues

53
BMW Series 3
France
Agency: BDDP, Paris
Art director: Antoine Choque
Copywriters: Gilles Grach, Martin Kolebka
Photographer: Peter Knaup

54
Alfa Romeo 75
Australia
Agency: Brand Management, Sydney
Art director: Oliver Maisey
Copywriter: Kim Mukerjee
Photograph: supplied by client

55
Toyota
United Kingdom
Agency: Collett Dickenson Pearce & Partners, London
Art director: Neil Godfrey
Copywriter: Indra Sinha
Photographer: Neil Barstow

56
Mazda 626
Austria
Agency: Demner & Merlicek, Vienna
Art directors: Klaus Erwarth, Chrigel Ott
Copywriters: Geri Aebi, Johannes Newrkla
Photographer: René Staud
Graphics: Andreas Müller

57
Volvo cars
United States
Agency: Scali McCabe Sloves, New York
Art director: Steve Montgomery
Copywriter: Mike Feinberg
Illustrator: Jim Crowell

58
Mazda 121
Switzerland
Agency: Advico Young & Rubicam, Zürich
Art director: Martin Spillmann
Copywriter: André Benker
Photographer: Peter Forster

59, 60
Audi
United Kingdom
Agency: Bartle Bogle Hegarty, London
Art director: Graham Watson
Copywriter: Mike Cozens
Photographer: John Hammond

61
Volkswagen Golf
United Kingdom
Agency: BMP DDB Needham, London
Art director: John Webster
Copywriter: John Webster
TV director: Michael Feresin
Production company: BFCS

62
Volkswagen Passat
United Kingdom
Agency: BMP DDB Needham, London
Art director: Gary Betts
Copywriters: Tony Cox, Malcolm Green
TV director: Tony Kaye
Production company: Tony Kaye Films

63
Pirelli tyres
United Kingdom
Agency: Woollams Moira Gaskin O'Malley, London
Art director: Malcolm Gaskin
Copywriter: Gerry Moira
TV director: Marek Kaneivska
Production company: RSA Films

64
Audi
United Kingdom
Agency: Bartle Bogle Hegarty, London
Art director: Gary Denham
Copywriter: Derek Payne
TV director: Chris Hartwill
Production company: RSA

CLOTHING AND FOOTWEAR

65
Hansen knitwear
United States
Agency: Frankenberry Laughlin & Constable, Milwaukee
Art director: Kris Jenson
Copywriter: Karen Ninneman
Photographers: Mike Huibregtse, Buck Miller

66
Elbeo men's socks
West Germany
Agency: R. G. Wiesmeier, Munich
Art director: Stephan Auer
Copywriter: Rita Obers
Photographer: Dieter Eikelpoth

67
Kookaï
France
Agency: CLM/BBDO, Paris
Art director: Bruno Lemoult
Copywriter: Pascal Manry
Photographer: Andrew Macpherson

68
Rodier women's clothes
France
Agency: BDDP, Paris
Art director: Dominique Bonan
Copywriter: Pascale Chadenat
Illustrator: Dominique Bonan

69
Scandale underwear
France
Agency: BDDP, Paris
Art director: Dominique Bonan
Copywriter: Clélia Dumoulin
Photographer: Mario Testino

70, 72
H & M Hennes clothing
United Kingdom
Agency: in house
Art director: Nick Scott
Copywriter: Richard Spencer
Photographers: Andrew Macpherson, Peter Brown

71
Pingouin wool kit
France
Agency: BDDP, Paris
Art director: Sophie Desmarez
Copywriter: Nicole Bristol
Photographer: Michel Comte

73
Pretty Polly stockings
United Kingdom
Agency: Bartle Bogle Hegarty, London
Art director: Marcus Vinton
Copywriter: Rianach O'Flynn
Photographer: John Swannell

74
Adidas Torsion sports shoes
Germany, France, United States
Agency: Young & Rubicam, Frankfurt
Art directors: Maria-Christina Sennefelder, Susanne Müller
Copywriter: Hartmut Bauer
Photographers: Brigitte Richter, Tom Gläser

75
Kickers shoes
United Kingdom
Agency: Ogilvy & Mather Partners, London
Art director: Noel Farrey
Copywriter: John Spinks
Illustrator: Malcolm Chandler

76
Timberland boots
United Kingdom
Agency: The Leagas Delaney Partnership, London
Art director: Steve Dunn
Copywriter: Tim Delaney
Photographer: John Claridge
Typographer: Jeff Lewis

77, 78
Inter sports shoes
Netherlands
Agency: TBWA, Amsterdam
Art director: Ton Giesbergen
Copywriter: Ton Giesbergen
Illustrator: Maurice Rosy

79, 80
Dormeuil cloth
United Kingdom
Agency: BBDO, London
Art director: Gary Martin
Copywriter: Mark Goodwin
Photographer: Andreas Heumann

81
Chantal Thomass stockings
France
Agency: Saatchi & Saatchi, Paris
Art director: Thierry Meunier
Copywriter: Christophe Trouve-Dugeny
Photographer: Lauren Hammer

82, 83
Aristoc stockings and tights
United Kingdom
Agency: WCRS Mathews Marcantonio, London
Art director: Michael Durban
Copywriter: Landsley Henry
Photographer: Horst P. Horst
Typographer: Mark Osborne

84
Levi's chinos
United Kingdom
Agency: Bartle Bogle Hegarty, London

Art director: Martin Galton
Copywriter: Will Awdry
Photograph: library picture

85, 86
Levi's jeans
Spain
Agency: Bassat, Ogilvy & Mather, Barcelona
Art director: David Ruiz
Copywriter: Paco Savio
Photographer: Cesar Lucadamo (Rebajas)

87
Etam underwear
France
Agency: Bélier/WCRS, Paris
Art directors: Guy Camillieri, Roland Della Monta
Copywriter: Agnès Thurnauer
Photographer: Valéry Assenat

88
Schaffhauser wool
Switzerland
Agency: Impuls, Küsnacht
Art directors: Felix Zimmermann, Helene Forster
Copywriter: Martin Uebele
Photographers: Ernst Wirz, Rolf Moser, Gaston Wicky

89
Candy shoes
Australia
Agency: Campaign Palace, Melbourne
Art director: Sarah Barclay
Copywriter: Mara Marich
Photographer: Robert Erdman

90
Cotton
United States
Agency: Ogilvy & Mather, New York
Art director: Grant Parrish
Copywriter: Jan Prager
TV director: Leslie Dektor
Production company: Peterman/ Dektor

91
K Shoes
United Kingdom
Agency: Bartle Bogle Hegarty, London
Art director: Dennis Lewis
Copywriter: Steve Hooper
TV director: Richard Loncraine
Production company: James Garrett & Partners

92, 93
Pingouin jumpers
France, United Kingdom
Agency: BDDP, Paris
Art director: Jean-Michel Smilenko
Copywriter: Sophie Anduze
TV director: Patrice Hadad
Production company: Première Heure

COMPUTERS AND OFFICE EQUIPMENT

94
Office furniture
Sweden
Agency: Hall & Cederquist/Y&R, Stockholm
Art director: Kjell Martinsson
Copywriter: Lars Forsberg
Photographer: Stefan Frank-Jensen

95
NEC MultiSync 4D Monitor
United Kingdom
Agency: BMP Business, London
Art director: Tony Smith
Copywriter: Hugo Kondratiuk
Photographer: John Ferrara

96
Bull information systems
Italy
Agency: RSCG Mezzano Constantini Mignani, Milan
Art director: Jaime Ambler
Copywriter: Cesare Casiraghi
Photographer: James Marsh

97
Hewlett-Packard personal computers
United Kingdom
Agency: Primary Contact, London
Art director: Robin Atkins
Copywriter: Graham Bunting
Photograph: library picture
Illustrator (hand colouring): Di Tommasso-Petrie

98, 100
Olivetti computers and other office equipment
Italy
Agency: Bozell e Associati, Milan
Art director: Mauro Marinari
Copywriter: Pasquale Barbella
Photographer: Jean-Pierre Maurer

99
GCEL telephones with electronic locks
India
Agency: Contour Advertising, Bombay
Art director: Rajan Mistry
Copywriter: Shobhan Biswas
Photographers: N. K. Sharma, Sunil Desai

101
Panasonic FX-RS505 image scanner
United Kingdom
Agency: Grange Advertising, Berkhamsted
Art director: Mark Lane
Copywriter: Peter Hayward
Photographer: Mike Hawley
Illustrator: Patrick Wright

102
Epson PC AX 3s Computer
France
Agency: BDDP, Paris
Art director: Philippe Pollet Villard
Copywriter: Rémi Babinet
Photographer: Paul Goirand
Illustrator: Philippe Cauquil

103
Bene office furniture
Austria
Agency: Demner & Merlicek, Vienna
Art director: Gerhard Plakolm
Graphics: Dana Kacetl
Copywriter: Peter Czerny
Photographer: Elfie Semotan

104
Apple computers
France
Agency: CLM/BBDO, Paris
Art director: Eric Holden
Copywriter: Grégoire Delacourt
TV director: Claude Miller
Production company: Téléma

CORPORATE

105
BHW building society
West Germany
Agency: ABC/Eurocom, Düsseldorf
Art director: Wilfried Siemes
Copywriter: Jörg Meyer
Illustrator: Thomas Kuhlenbeck

106
IBP Company
India
Agency: ASP, Bombay
Art director: Mahadeo Shetye
Copywriter: Gangadharan
Photographer: Suresh Cordo

107
Freelance creative team
Netherlands
Creative team: Herman Feberwee & Peter Meijburg, Alphen
Art director: Herman Feberwee
Copywriter: Peter Meijburg
Illustrator: Herman Feberwee

108
GBB advertising agency
Iceland
Agency: GBB/Hvíta Húsid, Reykjavík
Art director: Sverrir Björnsson
Copywriter: Sverrir Björnsson
Photographer: Sigurgeir Sigurjónsson

109
Safeway
United Kingdom
Agency: Ogilvy & Mather, London
Art director: Tan Shen Guan
Copywriter: Eugene Cheong
Illustrator: Tim Gill

110
Water industry
United Kingdom
Agency: DMB&B, London
Art director: Clive Challis
Copywriter: Peter Collingwood
Photographer: Ray Massey

111
Mazda
Worldwide
Studio: Nakamoto Design Office, Tokyo
Art director: Kunsei Nakamoto
Photographer: Nob Fukuda

112
Saatchi & Saatchi
East Germany
Agency: Saatchi & Saatchi, London
Art director: Paul Arden
Copywriter: Paul Arden
Photographer: Melanie Friend

113
Mukand
India
Agency: Rediffusion, Bombay
Art director: Dilip Warang
Copywriter: Kamlesh Pandey
Photographers: Prabhakar Panchal, Suresh Cordo

114
Toray Industries
Japan
Agency: Dentsu, Tokyo
Art directors: Masahiko Satoh, Miyako Maekita
Copywriters: Masahiko Satoh, Miyako Maekita
TV director: Shinya Nakajima
Production company: Tohokushinsha Film Company

115
BP
United Kingdom
Agency: Saatchi & Saatchi, London
Art directors: Fergus Fleming, Rupert Stubbs
Copywriter: Tom Wnek
Photographer: Ford Jenkins

116
AT&T
United States
Agency: Ayer, New York
Art directors: Ken Sausville, Walter Burek
Copywriters: Jeanne Chinard, Gordon Hasse, Rich Wagman
TV director: David Cornell
Production company: Spots Films

EXHIBITIONS AND EVENTS

117
Vienna Festival
Austria
Agency: Demner & Merlicek, Vienna
Art director: Klaus Erwarth
Graphics: Andreas Miedaner
Copywriter: Mariusz Jan Demner
Photograph: library picture

118
Bristol Animation Festival
United Kingdom
Agency: J. Walter Thompson, London
Art director: Russell Skidmore
Copywriter: Mark Adkins
Photographer: Charles Settrington

119
Nob Fukuda photographic exhibition
Japan
Studio: Keizo Matsui Design Office, Osaka
Art director: Keizo Matsui
Photographer: Nob Fukuda

120
Basketball matches
United States
Agency: Martin/Williams, Minneapolis
Art director: Wayne Thompson
Copywriter: David Whitman
Photographer: Craig Perman

121
The Empress Place
Singapore
Agency: Ball WCRS Partnership, Singapore
Art director: Tang Loi Nguang
Copywriters: Allan Tay, Seow Bee Yen

122
Vision of Britain exhibition
United Kingdom
Agency: Saatchi & Saatchi, London
Art director: Alexandra Taylor
Copywriter: Charles Hendley
Illustrator: Canaletto

123, 125
Berlin Film Festival
Germany
Agency: Volker Noth Grafik-Design, Berlin
Art director: Volker Noth

124
Takashi Kanome exhibition
Japan
Studio: Takashi Kanome, Tokyo
Art director: Takashi Kanome
Photographer: Nob Fukuda

126
International Design Exhibition
United States
Studio: Keizo Matsui Design Office, Osaka
Art director: Keizo Matsui
Designer: Keizo Matsui
Photographer: Nob Fukuda

127
Imperial War Museum
United Kingdom
Agency: Ogilvy & Mather, London
Art director: Ian Sizer
Copywriter: Alun Howell
Illustrator: Charles Thompson

128
Siemens Museum
West Germany
Agency: MC&D, Munich
Art director: Jochen Greve
Copywriter: Claudia Schlögel
TV director: Thomas Jauch
Production company: DCF, Munich

129
Giovanna D'Arco, theatre play
Italy
Agency: Armando Testa, Turin
Art directors: Armando Testa, Carlotta Soffiantino

FINANCIAL

130
Lloyds Bank
Argentina
Agency: Ayer Vazquez, Buenos Aires
Art director: Carlos Varau
Copywriter: Lily Ann Martin
Photographer: Sindo Fariña

131
First Direct
United Kingdom
Agency: Howell Henry Chaldecott Lury, London
Art director: Axel Chaldecott
Copywriter: Steve Henry
Photograph: library picture

132
Legal & General insurance company
United Kingdom
Agency: Young & Rubicam, London
Art director: Derrick Hass
Copywriter: Howard Fletcher
Photographer: Graham Ford
Model maker: Risky Ventures

133
Delta Dental insurance
United States
Agency: Zwiren Collins Karo Trusk & Ayer, Chicago
Art director: John Schmidt
Copywriter: Jeff Holinski
Photographer: Dave Jordano

134
New India Assurance
India
Agency: Contour Advertising, Bombay
Art director: Rajan Mistry
Copywriter: Shobhan Biswas
Photographers: Sunil Desai, Mahesh Kubal

135
Bain Clarkson insurance brokers
United Kingdom
Agency: Primary Contact, London
Art director: Vincent Chasteauneuf
Copywriter: Ben Friend
Illustrator: Simon Stern

136
Danske Bank
Denmark
Agency: Young & Rubicam, Copenhagen
Art director: Rolf Elsner
Copywriter: Philip Scherrer
Photographer: Station 1

137
3i
United Kingdom
Agency: Howell Henry Chaldecott Lury, London
Art director: Alex Chaldecott
Copywriter: Steve Henry
Illustrator: Larry Franklin

138, 139
National Westminster Bank
United Kingdom
Agency: Collett Dickenson Pearce and Partners, London
Art directors: Dennis Willison (house); Garry Horner (dice)
Copywriters: Julian Dyer (house); John O'Donnell (dice)
Photographers: Andre Klimonowski (house); John Claridge (dice)

140, 141
Creditanstalt bank
Austria
Agency: Demner & Merlicek, Vienna
Art director: Gerhard Plakolm
Graphics: Stefan Fuhrer, Dana Kacetl
Copywriters: Peter Czerny, Dieter Weidhofer
Photographer: Michel Comte, Paris

142, 143
Eurocard
Iceland
Agency: Hvíta Húsid, Reykjavík
Art directors: Sverrir Björnsson, Hrafnhildur Juliusdóttir
Copywriters: Ragnar Blöndal, Sverrir Björnsson
Photographer: Brian Pilkington

144
Iceland Insurance Company
Iceland
Agency: Hvíta Húsid, Reykjavík
Art director: Sverrir Björnsson
Copywriter: Sverrir Björnsson
Creative assistance: Ragnar Blöndal, Olöf Thorvaldsdóttir
Photographer: Lárus Karl Ingason

145
American Express Optima card
United States
Agency: Ogilvy & Mather, New York
Art director: Parry Merkley
Copywriter: Lynn Dangel
TV director: Leslie Dektor
Production company: Peterman/Dektor

FOOD AND NON-ALCOHOLIC DRINKS

146
Apple juice
Sweden
Agency: Hall & Cederquist/Y&R, Stockholm
Art director: Olle Matson
Copywriter: Lars Forsberg
Photographer: Lennart Durehed

147
Colombian Coffee
United States
Agency: DDB Needham, New York
Art director: Sharon L. Occhipinti
Copywriter: Doug Raboy
Photographer: James Koepnick

148
Anchor cheddar cheese
United Kingdom
Agency: Saatchi & Saatchi, London
Art director: Bob Gabriel
Copywriter: Marc Rutter
Photographer: Martin Thompson

149
Amul Ghee
India
Agency: ASP, Bombay
Art director: Nalesh Patil
Copywriter: Gangadharan
Photographer: Suresh Cordo

150
Rupp Käsle cheese
Austria
Agency: Demner & Merlicek, Vienna
Art directors: Klaus Erwarth, Chrigel Ott
Graphics: Jana Thür
Copywriter: Angelo Peer
Photographer: Udo Reisinger

151, 152
Twix
United Kingdom
Agency: DMB&B, London
Art director: Badger Smith
Copywriter: Nick Morgan
Photographer: John Swannell

153
Danone white cheese
Belgium
Agency: Young & Rubicam, Brussels
Art director: Michel Crabbe
Copywriter: Alex Rolet
Photographer: Xavier Harcq

154
Sinalco soft drink
Switzerland
Agency: Advico Young & Rubicam, Zürich
Art director: Thomas Schaub
Copywriter: Peter Schulz
Photographer: Doris Quarella

155
Saratoga mineral water
United States
Agency: TBWA, New York
Art director: Janet Trompeter
Copywriter: Jeff Linder

156, 157
Evian mineral water
United States
Agency: TBWA, New York
Art director: Janet Trompeter
Copywriter: Jeff Linder

158, 159
Kit Kat
United Kingdom
Agency: J. Walter Thompson, London
Art director: Dominic Martin
Copywriter: Fred Megerdichian
Photographers: Robert Dowling (Wimbledon); Tim O'Sullivan (hair)

160, 161
Aqua Libra
United Kingdom
Agency: Ayer, London
Art director: Gary Woodward
Copywriter: Ivor Jones
Photographer: Graham Ford

162, 163
Sugar
Austria
Agency: Demner & Merlicek, Vienna
Art director: Franz Merlicek
Graphics: Jürgen Mick
Copywriter: Angelo Peer
Photographer: Heinz Schmölzer

164, 167
Milk
Netherlands
Agency: PPGH/J. Walter Thompson, Amsterdam
Art director: Pieter van Velsen
Copywriter: Aad Kuyper
Photographer: Hans Kroeskamp

165
Eagle Snacks
Portugal
Agency: Ayer, Lisbon
Art director: Antonio Pilar
Copywriter: Maria Das Mercês Almeida
Photographer: Manuel Costa

166
Certs
United States
Agency: Young & Rubicam, New York
Art director: Gretchen Rollins
Copywriter: David Oakley
Photographer: David Bishop

168
Ikaruga dairy products
Japan
Studio: Keizo Matsui Design Office, Osaka
Art director: Keizo Matsui
Photographer: Nob Fukuda

169
Kia-Ora orange drink
United Kingdom
Agency: BMP DDB Needham, London
Art director: Ashley King
Copywriter: Louise Vanstone
Photographer: Dave Stewart

170
Tao yoghurt
Italy
Agency: Armando Testa, Turin
Art directors: Silvano Guidone, Franco Testa
Copywriter: Ennio Onnis
Photographer: Lois Greenfield

171
Milk
Sweden
Agency: Hall & Cederquist/Y&R, Stockholm
Art director: Lars Hall
Copywriter: Jan Cederquist
Photographer: Mikael Jansson

172, 173
Hellmann's Mayonnaise
United Kingdom
Agency: BMP DDB Needham, London
Art director: Eddi Greenwood
Copywriter: Marianne Little
Photographer: Charles Settrington

174
Lindt chocolates
West Germany
Agency: Michael Conrad & Leo Burnett, Frankfurt
Art director: Peter Huschka
Copywriter: Fritz Iversen
Photographer: Hubertus Hamm

175
Vittel mineral water
France
Agency: Lintas, Paris
Art director: Martine Camillieri
Copywriter: Anne Moustrou
Photographer: Ken Nahoun

176
Lesieur olive oil
France
Agency: Saatchi & Saatchi, Paris
Art director: André Bouchard
Copywriter: Marc Labrosse
Illustrator: Denise Mordan

177
Sea fish
United Kingdom
Agency: BMP DDB Needham, London
Art director: Joanna Wenley
Copywriter: Nick Gill
Photographer: John Parker

178
La Vache Qui Rit cheese
France
Agency: RSCG, Paris
Art director: Pierrette Diaz
Copywriter: Franck Tapiro
TV director: Tony Halton
Production company: 1-33

179
Mamie Nova chocolate mousse
France
Agency: CLM/BBDO, Paris
Art director: Bruno Lemoult
Copywriter: Pascal Manry
Photographer: Jean-Baptiste Mondino
TV director: Claude Miller
Production company: Téléma

180
Nestlé Gold Blend
United Kingdom
Agency: McCann-Erickson, London
Art director: David Lindsay
Copywriter: Jerry Green
TV director: Derek Coutts
Production company: Berry & Coutts

181
Batchelors Mushy Peas
United Kingdom
Agency: BMP DDB Needham, London
Art director: Joanna Wenley
Copywriter: Nick Gill
TV director: David Smith
Production company: Park Village Productions

182
Food from Andalusia
Spain
Agency: KMO-Leo Burnett, Madrid
Art directors: Concha Quiros, Pascual Heredero, Carlos Mouzo
Copywriter: Antonio Romero
TV director: Ricardo Albiñana
Production company: Ricardo Albiñana Films

183
Phileas Fogg snacks
United Kingdom
Agency: Bartle Bogle Hegarty, London
Art director: Dennis Lewis
Copywriter: Steve Hooper
TV director: John Lloyd
Production company: Limelight Commercials

184
Hershey's Kisses
United States
Agency: Ogilvy & Mather, New York
Art director: Ann Phares
Copywriter: David Apicella
TV director: Carl Willat
Production company: Colossal Pictures

HOUSE AND GARDEN

185, 186, 187
AEG household electrical appliances
United Kingdom
Agency: Young & Rubicam, London
Art director: Trevor Melvin
Copywriter: Jeanne Willis
Photographer: Richard Haughton
Illustrator: Zoltan

188
La Foire du Ventilateur electric fans
Canada
Agency: Young & Rubicam, Montreal
Art director: Roger Gariépy
Copywriter: André Paradis
Illustrator: Studio Catalpa

189
Levis paints
Belgium
Agency: Lowe Troost, Brussels
Art director: Georges Lafleur
Copywriter: Eric Kawan
Photographer: Daniel Jouanneau

190
Flou beds
Italy
Agency: Ayer, Milan
Art director: Bruno Banone
Copywriter: Pierangelo de Luca
Photographer: Franck Heroldt

191
Claire Burke home fragrances
United States
Agency: Fallon McElligott, Minneapolis
Art director: Tom Lichtenheld
Copywriter: Jamie Barrett
Photographer: Kerry Peterson

192
Sandtex masonry paint
United Kingdom
Agency: Saatchi & Saatchi, London
Art director: Paul Arden
Photographer: John Turner
Typographer: Roger Kennedy

193
Zwilling J. A. Henckels kitchen knife
Japan
Agency: Dentsu, Osaka
Art director: Wataru Ash'da
Photographer: Nob Fukuda

194
3M Safest Stripper
United States
Agency: Martin/Williams, Minneapolis
Art director: Jim Henderson
Copywriter: Pete Smith
Photographer: Ron Crofoot

195
Louis de Poortere carpets
Belgium
Agency: Young & Rubicam, Brussels
Art director: Willy Coppens
Copywriter: Véronique Hermans
Photographer: Xavier Harcq

196, 197
Le Creuset kitchenware
United Kingdom
Agency: Saatchi & Saatchi, London
Art director: Antony Easton
Copywriter: Adam Kean
Photographer: Sebastiao Salgado

198
Laufen bathroom ceramics
Austria
Agency: Demner & Merlicek, Vienna
Art director: Franz Merlicek
Graphics: Jürgen Mick
Copywriters: Geri Aebi, Michael Freund
Photographer: Bernhard Angerer

199, 200
Dulux Woodtones and Woodsheen
United Kingdom
Agency: WCRS Mathews Marcantonio, London
Art director: Michael Durban
Copywriter: Landsley Henry
Photographer: Graham Ford
Typographer: Keith Mackenzie

201
National washing machine
Japan
Agency: Dentsu, Toyko
Art directors: Mamoru Kusakawa, Toshiaki Nozue
Copywriters: Mamoru Kusakawa, Izuru Toi
Photographer: Toshio Tateishi
TV director: Masatake Satomi
Production company: CAP

202
Axion 2 washing powder
France
Agency: Young & Rubicam, Paris
Art director: Philippe Ducat
Copywriter: Gilbert Carsoux
TV director: Monique Laigle
Production company: Miroirs

203
Woodlife wood preservative
United States
Agency: Zwiren Collins Karo Trusk Ayer, Chicago
Art director: John Schmidt
Copywriter: Jim Doherty
TV director: Greg Hoey
Production company: Film Fair Chicago

204
Ambi-Pur room freshener
Spain
Agency: RCP/Saatchi & Saatchi, Barcelona
Art director: Pepino Garcia
Copywriter: Luis Casadevall
Photographer: Vernon Layton
TV director: Mariano Resquin
Production company: Mariano Resquin

INDUSTRIAL

205, 206
Jeyes Hygiene Services
United Kingdom
Agency: Arc International Advertising, London
Art director: David White
Copywriter: Laurence Percival
Photographer: Howard Kingsnorth

207
ICI chemical products
United Kingdom
Agency: Alliance International, London
Art director: Mark Oliver
Copywriter: Sheila Saphier
Photographer: Charles Settrington

208
Dual herbicide
United States
Agency: Martin/Williams, Minneapolis
Art director: Jim Henderson
Copywriter: Lee Schmidt
Photographer: Tom Connors

209
Ford New Holland farm machinery
United Kingdom
Agency: Butler Borg, London
Art director: Alan Spicer
Copywriter: Graeme Forster
Photographer: Brian Leggett

210
Laing Design and Construct service
United Kingdom
Agency: Cronin Morgan Stokes, Watford
Art director: Bernard Curtis
Copywriter: Maureen Purbrook
Photographer: Peter Campion

211
Rockwool roofing board
United Kingdom
Agency: McCann-Erickson Wales, Penarth
Art director: Colin Gould
Copywriter: Chris Gill
Photographer: Jonathon Metcalfe

212, 213
H. & R. Johnson tiles
United Kingdom
Agency: The Buchanan Company, Manchester
Art directors: Dave Matthews (Show us your colours); Ced Milner (Walk all over you)
Copywriter: Steve Halworth
Photographer: Jonathan Oakes

214
Filtrona cigarette filters
United Kingdom, United States, Europe
Agency: Cronin Morgan Stokes, Watford
Art director: Bernard Curtis
Copywriter: Maureen Purbrook
Photographer: Peter Campion

215
Schrack telecommunication systems
Austria
Agency: Young & Rubicam, Vienna
Art director: Charly Frei
Copywriter: Sabine Mühlberger

216
Basagran herbicide
Argentina
Agency: Ayer Vazquez, Buenos Aires
Art director: Armando Luizaga
Copywriter: Marcos Carnevale
TV director: Claudio Arbos
Production company: AC Prod.

JEWELLERY AND WATCHES

217, 218, 219
Lorenz watches
Italy
Agency: STZ, Milan
Art director: Fritz Tschirren
Copywriter: Marco Ferri
Photographer: Jean-Pierre Maurer

220
Garrard One One Two jewellery
United Kingdom
Agency: The Leagas Delaney Partnership, London
Art director: Steve Dunn
Copywriter: Tim Delaney
Photographer: Daniel Jouanneau
Typographer: Steve Dunn

221, 222, 223
Hirsch watchstraps
North America, Europe
Agency: Demner & Merlicek, Vienna
Art director: Werner Celand
Graphics: Thomas Kajaba, Sylvia Danzinger, Jana Thür
Copywriter: Johannes Krammer
Photographer: Bernhard Angerer

224, 225, 226, 227
Zeon watches and clocks
United Kingdom
Agency: Coplan Advertising, London
Art director: Glen Melrose
Photographer: Peter Griffin

228, 229
Diamond International Awards
United States
Agency: Ayer, New York
Art director: Don Zimmerman
Copywriter: Lynn McGrath
Photographer: Albert Watson

230
Pulsar watches
Netherlands
Agency: Campaign Company, Amsterdam
Art director: Bela Stamenkovits
Copywriter: Rob Floor
Photographer: Hans Kroeskamp

231
Diamonds of Distinction
United States
Agency: Ayer, New York
Art director: Jeff Odiorne
Copywriter: Morlenn Novitt
Photographer: Andrew Unangst

232
Champion watches
Brazil
Agency: Guimaraes e Giacometti, São Paulo
Art director: Adeir Rampazzo
Copywriter: Regina Brissax
TV director: Paulo Morelli
Production company: Olhar Eletrônico

MEDIA

233
Bleikt & Blatt
Iceland
Agency: Hvíta Húsid, Reykjavík
Art director: Sverrir Björnsson
Copywriters: Ragnar Blöndal, Sverrir Björnsson

234
Time magazine
United Kingdom
Agency: Saatchi & Saatchi, London
Art director: Matt Ryan
Copywriter: John Pallant
Photographer: Alan Brooking

235
VTM television news
Belgium
Agency: Young & Rubicam, Brussels
Art director: André Plaisier
Copywriter: Eric Debaene
Photographer: Jos Molenaars

236, 237
de Volkskrant
Netherlands
Agency: PPGH/J. Walter Thompson, Amsterdam
Art director: Pieter van Velsen
Copywriter: Aad Kuyper
Photographer: Hans Kroeskamp

238
Kurier leisure supplement
Austria
Agency: Demner & Merlicek, Vienna
Art director: Klaus Erwarth
Graphics: Andreas Miedaner
Copywriter: Angelo Peer
Photographer: Bert Brüggemann

239
Cash
Switzerland
Agency: Advico Young & Rubicam, Zürich
Art director: Martin Spillmann
Copywriter: Gaby Girsberger

240
Sonntagsblick
Switzerland
Agency: Advico Young & Rubicam, Zürich
Art director: Roland Scotoni
Copywriter: André Benker
Photographer: Michael Joseph

241
Yorkshire TV
United Kingdom
Agency: Young & Rubicam, London
Art director: Anthony Stileman
Copywriter: Neil Patterson

242
ITV Association
United Kingdom
Agency: J. Walter Thompson, London
Art director: Lewis Lloyd
Copywriter: Jaspar Shelbourne
Photographer: Hugh Johnson

243
Exchange & Mart
United Kingdom
Agency: Howell Henry Chaldecott Lury, London
Art director: David Buonaguidi
Copywriter: Stevie Girdlestone
Photographer: John Londei

244
Trend
Austria
Agency: Demner & Merlicek, Vienna
Art director: Klaus Erwarth
Graphics: Jana Thür
Copywriter: Angelo Peer
Photographer: Heinz Schmölzer

245
ARD and ZDF
West Germany
Agency: Young & Rubicam, Frankfurt
Art director: Heribert Burkert
Copywriter: Günter Sendlmeier
Photographer: Hermann Fünfgeld

246
KTCZ-FM radio station
United States
Agency: The Edison Group, Minneapolis
Art director: Wayne Thompson
Copywriter: Cathy Ostlie
Photographer: Patrick Fox

247
El Mundo
Spain
Agency: TAPSA/Ayer, Madrid
Art director: Christoph Becker
Copywriter: Tony Fernandez

Photographer: Jesus Chamizo
TV director: Peter Pullon
Production company: Key Bay

248
WXRT radio station
United States
Agency: Young & Rubicam, Chicago
Art director: Faye Kleros
Copywriter: Scott Burns
TV producer: Ellen Israel
TV director: David Wild
Production company: Highlight Commercials

249
Ekonomik Panorama
Turkey
Agency: Young & Rubicam/ Reklamevi, Istanbul
Copywriter: Gokhan Ozgun
TV director: Ece Acarlar
Production company: Senkron

MISCELLANEOUS

250
Mitsubishi pencils
Japan
Agency: Dentsu, Tokyo
Art directors: Masamichi Yoshino, Keiji Kawasaki
Copywriter: Ryoichi Akiba
Photographer: Takayuki Watanabe

251
3M Image Graphics
United States
Agency: Martin/Williams, Minneapolis
Art director: Pam Conboy Mariutto
Copywriter: Christopher Wilson
Photographer: Rick Dublin

252
Cross writing instruments
United Arab Emirates
Agency: Inca Tanvir Advertising, Sharjah
Creative director: Tanvir Kanji
Designer: Max D'Lima
Copywriter: Pinky Daniels
Illustrator: Rajan Amrute

253
Kodansha paperback novels
Japan
Agency: Dentsu, Tokyo
Art directors: Tetsu Goto, Hiroshi Katsumura
Copywriter: Masaaki Tsuruho
Photographer: Takashi Seo

254
London Fields, novel by Martin Amis
United Kingdom
Agency: Bartle Bogle Hegarty, London
Art director: Martin Galton
Copywriter: Will Awdry
Photographer: Don McCullin

255
Estoffi eyewear
Singapore
Agency: Ketchum Advertising, Singapore
Art director: Heintje Moo
Copywriter: Jim Aitchinson
Photographer: Melvin Lee

256, 257
Robert La Roche
International
Agency: Robert La Roche (in house), Vienna
Art director: Christian Satek
Photographer: Gerhard Heller

258
Ophthalmic treatment
Spain
Agency: TAPSA/Ayer, Madrid
Art director: Juan Ignacio Beltran
Copywriter: Manuel Olano

259
Pittsburgh Laser Center
United States
Agency: The Edison Group, Minneapolis
Art director: Wayne Thompson
Copywriter: David Whitman
Illustration: stock picture

260
Metropolitan Police recruitment
United Kingdom
Agency: Collett Dickenson Pearce & Partners, London
Art director: Neil Godfrey
Copywriter: Indra Sinha
Photographer: Don McCullin

261, 262
Royal Air Force recruitment
United Kingdom
Agency: J. Walter Thompson, London
Art director: Peter Celiz
Copywriter: Richard Saunders
Photographer: John Londei

263
Coal fires
United Kingdom
Agency: Saatchi & Saatchi, London
Art director: Adrian Kemsley
Copywriter: Charles Hendley
Photograph: still from film directed by Tony Kaye

264
Federal Express
Europe
Agency: KHBB, London
Art director: Clive Parsley
Copywriter: Justine Walker
Photographer: Peter Lavery

265
Vidal Sassoon salons
Scotland
Agency: DMB&B, London
Art director: Jo Hodges
Copywriter: Ruth Shabi
Photographer: Jonathan Rae

266, 267
Luncheon vouchers
United Kingdom
Agency: Simons Palmer Denton Clemmon & Johnson, London
Art directors: Paul White (crocodile); Mark Denton (pig)
Copywriters: Trevor de Silva (crocodile); Chris Palmer (pig)
Photographer: Paul Bevitt

268
British Telecom
United Kingdom
Agency: J. Walter Thompson, London
Copywriter: Richard Phillips
TV director: Richard Phillips
Production company: McMillan & Hughes

269
Pedo diapers
Turkey
Agency: Young & Rubicam/ Reklamevi, Istanbul
Art director: Bulent Erkmen
Copywriter: Serdar Erener
TV director: Sahin Kaygun
Production company: Art Film

PHOTOGRAPHIC

270
Olympus AZ-200
United Kingdom
Agency: Collett Dickenson Pearce & Partners, London
Art director: Paul Briginshaw
Copywriter: Malcolm Duffy
Photographer: John Swannell

271, 272
Kodacolor Gold film
Denmark
Agency: Young & Rubicam, Copenhagen
Art director: Franek Zajaczkowski
Copywriter: Philip Scherrer
Photographer: Göran Ortegren

273, 274, 275, 276
Kodacolor gold film
Switzerland
Agency: Advico Young & Rubicam, Zürich
Art director: Roland Scotoni
Copywriter: Hansjörg Zürcher
Photographer: Hans Feurer

277
Kodak disposable cameras
France
Agency: Young & Rubicam, Paris
Art director: Richard Claverie
Copywriter: Madeleine Danielson
Photographer: Willy Biondani

278
Kodak Ektachrome
Germany, Austria, Switzerland, Japan
Agency: Young & Rubicam, Frankfurt
Art director: Jürgen Däuwel
Copywriter: Johannes Klenk
Photographer: Dietmar Henneka

279
Kodak
France
Agency: Young & Rubicam, Paris
Art director: Richard Claverie
Copywriter: Hervé Chadenat
Photographer: Jean-Baptiste Mondino

280
Kodacolor Gold film
France
Agency: Young & Rubicam, Paris
Art director: Richard Claverie
Copywriter: Hervé Chadenat
TV director: Jean-Baptiste Mondino
Production company: Bandits

281
Polaroid high definition film
France, United Kingdom
Agency: BDDP, Paris
Art director: Philippe Pollet Villard
Copywriter: Rémi Babinet
Agency TV producer: Vincent Meyer
TV director: Gilles Gallu
Production company: Gedeon

PUBLIC SERVICE

282
Friends of the Earth
United Kingdom
Agency: Burkitt Weinreich Bryant, London
Art director: Robin Smith
Copywriter: Robin Weeks
Photographer: John Wallace

283
Royal National Institute for the Deaf
United Kingdom
Agency: Ogilvy & Mather, London
Art directors: Pete Bradly, Marc Hatfield
Copywriters: Pete Bradly, Marc Hatfield
Photographer: Paul Windsor

284
Dental health education
Singapore
Agency: Ketchum Advertising, Singapore
Art director: Heintje Moo
Copywriter: Jim Aitchinson
Illustrator: Sim Kwang Theng

285
River Po Protection Association
Italy
Agency: Armando Testa, Turin
Art directors: Armando Testa, Aurelio Rizzo

286
Red Cross
Belgium
Agency: Young & Rubicam, Brussels
Art director: André Plaisier
Copywriter: Guillaume Van Der Stighelen
Illustrator: André Plaisier

287
Anti-smoking
United States
Agency: Martin/Williams, Minneapolis
Art director: Wendy Hansen
Copywriter: Lyle Wedemeyer
Photographer: Rick Dublin

288
Business in the Community
United Kingdom
Agency: Young & Rubicam, London
Art director: Colin Morris
Copywriter: Stuart Blake
Photographer: Graham Fox

289
'Work less' campaign
Japan
Agency: McCann-Erickson Hakuhodo, Tokyo
Art director: Kazuya Mototani
Copywriter: Masashi Kato
Illustrator: Ayami Hayashima

290
Anti-drugs campaign
India
Agency: Rediffusion, Bombay
Art director: Dilip Warang
Copywriter: Kamlesh Pandy
Illustrator: Avinash Godbole

291
Anti-smoking
New Zealand
Agency: Adventure, Wellington
Art director: Paul Anderson
Copywriter: Mark di Somma
Illustrator: Fane Flaws

292
Women's Counselling Service
West Germany
Agency: Grey, Düsseldorf
Art directors: Lindsay Cullen, Marina Lörwald
Copywriter: Tania Schickert
Photographer: Harry Vorsteher
Special effects: Bernd Bauer

293
Environmental protection
Japan
Studio: Takayuki Itoh Design Office, Tokyo
Art director: Miwako Ebisawa
Copywriter: Jim McDonald
Illustrator: Chikako Ogawa

294
Anti-vivisection
United Kingdom
Agency: BMP DDB Needham, London
Art director: Anita Davis
Copywriter: Anita Davis
TV director: John Swannell
Production company: John Swannell Films

295
Campaign against drunk driving
Spain
Agency: Bassat, Ogilvy & Mather, Barcelona
Art directors: Carles Graell, Curro Astorza
Copywriters: Xavier García, Ignasi Clará

296
Environmental protection
Brazil
Agency: MPM, Rio de Janeiro
Art director: Adeir Rampazzo
Copywriter: Wanderley Doro
TV director: Enzo Barone
Production company: Cinema Centro do Brasil

RETAIL AND RESTAURANTS

297
Monoprix
France
Agency: CLM/BBDO, Paris
Art directors: Bruno Lemoult, Stéphane Richard
Copywriter: Pascal Manry
Photographer: Gérard Beaulet

298
Forum des Halles
France
Agency: CLM/BBDO, Paris
Art director: Anne de Maupéou
Copywriter: Eric Galmard
Photographer: Manuel Prouteau
Illustrator: Gilles Maribaur

299
Leclerc
France
Agency: CLM/BBDO, Paris
Art directors: Bruno Lemoult, Stéphane Richard
Copywriters: Serge Fichard, Thomas Reichlin Meldegg
Photographer: Gérard Beaulet

300
Virgin Megastore
France
Agency: BDDP, Paris
Art director: Philippe Pollet Villard
Copywriter: Rémi Babinet
Photographer: Paul Goirand

301
Liberty
United Kingdom
Agency: Bartle Bogle Hegarty, London
Art director: Robbert Jansen
Copywriter: Tom Hudson
Photographer: Andreas Heumann

302
Asprey
United Kingdom
Agency: Edwards Martin Thornton, London
Art director: Karen Hagemann
Copywriter: Keiron Simpson
Illustrator: Neil Gower

303
Boots
United Kingdom
Agency: Collett Dickenson Pearce & Partners, London
Art director: Garry Turner
Copywriter: John O'Donnell
Photographer: Steve Cavalier

304
Truffles restaurant
Singapore
Agency: Ketchum Advertising, Singapore
Art director: Heintje Moo
Copywriters: Jim Aitchinson, Garry Abbott
Photographer: David Foo

305
Daimaru department store
Japan
Agency: Dentsu, Osaka
Studio: Hills Design Office
Art director: S. Yorioka
Photographer: Nob Fukuda

306
Riachuelo department store
Brazil
Agency: Guimaraes e Giacometti, São Paulo
Art director: Adeir Rampazzo
Copywriter: Regina Brissac
TV director: José Possi Neto
Production company: Noar Filmes

307
JCPenney
United States
Agency: Ayer, Dallas
Art director: Don Sedei
Copywriter: Jim Hradecky
TV director: Mark Coppos
Production company: Coppos Films

308
Kentucky Fried Chicken
New Zealand
Agency: Young & Rubicam, Auckland
Art director: Nic Hall
Copywriter: Lynn Smith
TV director: Nigel Hutchinson
Production company: Motion Pictures, Wellington

309
McDonald's
France
Agency: BDDP, Paris
Art director: Pierre Gauthronet
Copywriter: Alain Jalabert
Agency TV producer: Françoise Korb
TV director: Jean-Claude Garcia
Production company: Il Est En Reunion

310
Burger King
United States
Agency: Saatchi & Saatchi, New York
Art director: Craig Miller
Copywriter: Norm Weill
TV director: Fred Peterman
Production company: Peterman/Dektor

TOBACCO

311
Fortuna cigarettes
Spain
Agency: TAPSA/Ayer, Madrid
Art director: Roberto Ruiz
Copywriter: Carlos Navarro
Photographer: Jesus Chamizo

312, 313, 314, 315
Dames cigarettes
Austria
Agency: Young & Rubicam, Vienna
Art director: Charly Frei
Copywriters: Sabine Mühlberger, Peter Dirnberger
Photographer: Uli Burtin

316, 317
Benson & Hedges Special Filter cigarettes
United Kingdom
Agency: Collett Dickenson Pearce & Partners, London
Art director: Nigel Rose
Photographers: John Parker (axe); Graham Ford (camera)

318, 319
Silk Cut cigarettes
United Kingdom
Agency: Saatchi & Saatchi, London
Art director: Graham Fink
Copywriter: Jeremy Clarke
Photographer: Barney Edwards

320, 321, 322, 323, 324
Old Holborn tobacco
United Kingdom
Agency: J. Walter Thompson, London
Art director: David May
Copywriter: Steve Jenkinson
Photographers: John Claridge (bone); James Cotier (mackerel, flower, tea strainer)
Illustrators: David May, Peter Owen

TOILETRIES, COSMETICS, PHARMACEUTICALS

325
Respons shampoo
Denmark, Sweden, Norway
Agency: Young & Rubicam, Copenhagen
Art director: Sonja Rasmussen
Copywriter: Philip Scherrer
Photographers: Claës & Tony Lewenhaupt

326, 327
Revlon cosmetics
United Kingdom
Agency: The Leagas Delaney Partnership, London
Art director: Steve Dunn
Copywriter: Tim Delaney
Photographer: Peter Lindburgh
Typographer: Steve Dunn

328
Franka M. Berger perfume foam
France
Agency: Saatchi & Saatchi, Paris
Art director: Anne Duchêne
Copywriter: Michel Cohen
Photographer: Francis Giacobetti

329
Eurax
United Kingdom
Agency: Woollams Moira Gaskin O'Malley, London
Art director: Lynn Kendrick
Copywriter: Peter Souter
Photographer: Horst P. Horst

330, 331, 332, 333
Tri-Ac
United Kingdom
Agency: Woollams Moira Gaskin O'Malley, London
Art director: Lynn Kendrick
Copywriter: Peter Souter
Photographer: Brad Branson
Typographer: Barry Brand

334
Lux toilet soap
United Kingdom
Agency: J. Walter Thompson, London
Art director: Dick Poole
Copywriter: Tim John
Photographer: Terence Donovan

335
Hawaiian Tropic sun tan lotion
United Kingdom
Agency: J. Walter Thompson, London
Art director: Bill Mawhinney
Copywriter: Harry De Zitter

336
Right Guard deodorant
United Kingdom
Agency: Saatchi & Saatchi, London
Art director: Matt Ryan
Copywriter: Rod Lyons
Photographer: James Cotier

337
Clinica Lion toothpaste
Japan
Agency: Dentsu, Tokyo
Art director: Takehiko Miura
Copywriters: Takehiko Miura, Ichiro Kamata, Akira Matsumoto
Photographer: Morio Saegusa
TV director: Kazuyoshi Hayakawa
Production company: TYO Productions

338, 339
Margaret Astor cosmetics
West Germany
Agency: Michael Conrad & Leo Burnett, Frankfurt
Art director: Angelika Lang
Copywriter: Veronika Classen
TV director: Lester Bookbinder
Production company: RSA, London

340
Cutex Strong Nail varnish
United States
Agency: Ogilvy & Mather, New York
Art director: Mark Webb
Copywriter: Lynn Welsh
TV director: Bryce Atwell
Production company: Sant Andrea Productions

TRAVEL AND TOURISM

341
Northern Territory Tourist Commission
Australia
Agency: Saatchi & Saatchi, Sydney
Art director: Alan Morden
Copywriter: Philip Putnam

342
All Nippon Airways
Japan
Agency: Dentsu, Tokyo
Art directors: Kohji Mizutani, Ichiro Mitani, Masatoshi Ikeda
Copywriter: Naoto Ohdate
Photographer: Sachiko Kuru

343, 344
Singapore Airlines/NTTC
United Kingdom
Agency: Edwards Martin Thornton, London
Art director: Dave Weller
Copywriter: Jak Burrell
Illustrator: Jean Christian Knoff

345, 346, 348
Austrian National Tourist Office
Europe
Agency: Demner & Merlicek, Vienna
Art director: Tomek Luczynski
Graphics: Gerald Walter
Copywriters: Peter Czerny, Dieter Weidhofer
Photographer: Hans Wiesenhofer

347
Air Canada
United Kingdom
Agency: Young & Rubicam, London
Art director: Colin Morris
Copywriter: Stuart Blake
Photographer: Mike Parsons

349
British Airways Super Shuttle
United Kingdom
Agency: Saatchi & Saatchi, London
Art director: Russell Ramsey
Copywriter: John O'Keeffe
Photography: Owen & Potts

350, 351, 352, 353
Air France
United Kingdom
Agency: Ayer, London
Art director: Roddy Kerr
Copywriter: Arthur Parshotam
Illustrators: Warren Madill (legs); Richard Prideaux (Magritte man); Jean Larcher (routes); Ziggy (traffic jam)

354, 355, 356, 357
Condor charter flights
West Germany
Agency: Michael Conrad & Leo Burnett, Frankfurt
Art directors: Wolfgang Leihener, Angelika Lang
Copywriter: Veronika Classen
Photographer: Michael Ehrhart

358, 359
Maharashtra Tourism Development Corporation
India
Agency: Rhizic, Bombay
Art director: Rumi Mistry
Copywriter: Rumi Mistry

360, 361
Lauda Tours
Austria
Agency: Young & Rubicam, Vienna
Art director: Charly Frei
Copywriters: Sabine Mühlberger, Walter Robisch

362
Young Persons Railcard
United Kingdom
Agency: Saatchi & Saatchi, London
Art director: Mark Collicott
Copywriter: Patricia Doherty
Photographer: Clive Arrowsmith

363
Trans World Airlines
United Kingdom
Agency: Young & Rubicam, London
Art director: Alan Herring
Copywriter: Mike Wharton
Photographer: Mike Parsons

364
Four Corners
United Kingdom
Agency: The Leagas Delaney Partnership, London
Art director: Gary Marshall
Copywriter: Paul Marshall
Typographer: Jeff Lewis

365, 366
Sol Holidays
United Kingdom
Agency: Edwards Martin Thornton, London
Art director: Dave Weller
Copywriter: Jak Burrell

367
British Airways
Worldwide
Agency: Saatchi & Saatchi, London
Art director: Graham Fink
Agency producer: Martha Greene
Copywriter: Jeremy Clarke
TV director: Hugh Hudson
Production company: Hudson Film

368
Central Japan Railways
Japan
Agency: Dentsu, Tokyo
Art director: Takehiko Miura
Copywriters: Takehiko Miura, Mitsuhiro Wada, Takeaki Kojima
Photographer: Fumio Iwamoto
TV director: Kazuyoshi Hayakawa
Production company: TYO Productions

369
British Rail
United Kingdom
Agency: Saatchi & Saatchi, London
Art director: Paul Arden
Copywriter: Jeff Stark
Agency producer: Arnold Pearce
TV director: Tony Kaye
Production company: Tony Kaye Films

INDEX OF PRODUCTS AND SERVICES

1664 beer 19, 20
3i 137
3M Image Graphics 251
3M Safest Stripper 194

Absolut vodka 9, 10, 11
Adidas Torsion sports shoes 74
AEG household electrical appliances 185, 186, 187
Air Canada 347
Air France 350, 351, 352, 353
Alfa Romeo-75 54
All Nippon Airways 342
Ambi-Pur room freshener 204
American Express Optima card 145
Amul Ghee 149
Anchor cheddar cheese 148
Anti-drugs campaign 290
Anti-smoking 287, 291
Anti-vivisection 294
Apple computers 104
Apple juice 146
Aqua Libra 160, 161
Archer's Peach County schnapps 6
ARD and ZDF 245
Aristoc stockings and tights 82, 83
Asprey 302
AT&T 116
Audi 59, 60, 64
Austrian National Tourist Office 345, 346, 348
Axion 2 washing powder 202

Bain Clarkson insurance brokers 135
Basagran herbicide 216
Basketball matches 120
Batchelors Mushy Peas 181
Bavaria beer 12
Bene office furniture 103
Benson & Hedges Special Filter cigarettes 316, 317
Berlin Film Festival 123, 125
BHW building society 105
Bleikt & Blatt 233
BMW financing 52
BMW Series-3 53
Boots 303
BP 115
Bristol Animation Festival 118
British Airways 349, 367
British Rail 369
British Telecom 268
Bull information systems 96
Burger King 310
Business in the Community 288

Campaign against drunk driving 295
Candy shoes 89
Cash 239
Castlemaine XXXX 8
Central Japan Railways 368
Certs 166
Champion watches 232
Chantal Thomass stockings 81
Claire Burke home fragrances 191
Clinica Lion toothpaste 337
Coal fires 263
Colombian Coffee 147
Condor charter flights 354, 355, 356, 357

Cotton 90
Creditanstalt bank 140, 141
Cross writing instruments 252
Cuervo tequila 21
Cutex Strong Nail varnish 340

Daimaru department store 305
Dames cigarettes 312, 313, 314, 315
Danone white cheese 153
Danske Bank 136
de Volkskrant 236, 237
Delta Dental insurance 133
Dental health education 284
Diamond International Awards 228, 229
Diamonds of Distinction 231
Dormeuil cloth 79, 80
Draught Bass 16
Dual herbicide 208
Dulux Woodtones and Woodsheen 199, 200
Dunlop tyres 51

Eagle Snacks 165
Ekonomik Panorama 249
El Mundo 247
Elbeo men's socks 66
Empress Place, The 121
Environmental protection 293, 296
Epson PC AX 3s computer 102
Estoffi eyewear 255
Etam underwear 87
Eurax 329
Eurocard 142, 143
Evian mineral water 156, 157
Exchange & Mart 243

Feberwee & Meijburg, freelance creative team 107
Federal Express 264
Fiat motor oil 48, 49
Fiat Uno 46, 47
Filtrona cigarette filters 214
First Direct 131
Flou beds 190
Food from Andalusia 182
Ford New Holland farm machinery 209
Ford Transit 41
Fortuna cigarettes 311
Forum des Halles 298
Four Corners 364
Franka M. Berger perfume foam 328
Friends of the Earth 282

Garrard One One Two jewellery 220
GBB advertising agency 108
GCEL telephones with electronic locks 99
Giovanna D'Arco 129
Grand Marnier 18
Grant's whisky 15
Grundig M95 S/PiP TV set 29
Grundig portable TV set 30
Grundig video recorder 28

H & M Hennes clothing 70, 72
H. & R. Johnson tiles 212, 213
Hansen knitwear 65
Hawaiian Tropic sun tan lotion 335
Hellmann's Mayonnaise 172, 173

Hershey's Kisses 184
Hewlett-Packard personal computers 97
Hirsch watchstraps 221, 222, 223
Hvíta Húsið advertising agency: see GBB

IBP Company 106
Iceland Insurance Company 144
ICI chemical products 207
Ikaruga dairy products 168
Imperial War Museum 127
Inter sports shoes 77, 78
International Design Exhibition 126
ITV Association 242

J & B Rare whisky 13
JCPenney 307
Jeyes Hygiene Services 205, 206
Johnnie Walker Black Label whisky 7

K Shoes 91
Kentucky Fried Chicken 308
Kia-Ora orange drink 169
Kickers shoes 75
Kit Kat 158, 159
Kodacolor Gold film 271, 272, 273, 274, 275, 276, 280
Kodak 279
Kodak disposable cameras 272
Kodak Ektachrome 278
Kodansha paperback novels 253
Kookaï 67
Kronenbourg beer 4
KTCZ-FM radio station 246
Kurier leisure supplement 238

La Foire du Ventilateur electric fans 188
La Vache Qui Rit cheese 178
Laing Design and Construct service 210
Lauda Tours 360, 361
Laufen bathroom ceramics 198
Le Creuset kitchenware 196, 197
Leclerc 299
Legal & General insurance company 132
Lesieur olive oil 176
Levi's chinos 84
Levi's jeans 85, 86
Levis paints 189
Liberty 301
Lindt chocolates 174
Lloyds Bank 130
London Fields 254
Lorenz watches 217, 218, 219
Louis de Poortere carpets 195
Luncheon Vouchers 266, 267
Lux toilet soap 334

Maharashtra Tourism Development Corporation 358, 359
Malibu 5
Mamie Nova chocolate mousse 179
Margaret Astor cosmetics 338, 339
Maxell audio tapes 32, 33
Mazda 111
Mazda-121 58
Mazda-626 56

McDonald's 309
Metropolitan Police recruitment 260
Milk 164, 167, 171
Mitsubishi cars 40
Mitsubishi pencils 250
Monoprix 297
Motorcraft service centre 44
Mukand 113

National washing machine 201
National Westminster Bank 138, 139
NEC MultiSync 4D Monitor 95
Nestlé Gold Blend 180
New India Assurance 134
Nob Fukuda photographic exhibition 119
Northern Territory Tourist Commission 341

Old Holborn tobacco 320, 321, 322, 323, 324
Olivetti computers and other office equipment 98, 100
Olympus AZ-200 270
Ophthalmic treatment 258

Panasonic FX-RS505 image scanner 101
Pedo diapers 269
Peugeot scooters 50
Phileas Fogg snacks 183
Philips car stereo equipment 26, 27
Pingouin jumpers 92, 93
Pingouin wool kit 71
Pirelli tyres 63
Pittsburgh Laser Center 259
Polaroid high definition film 281
Porsche 944 S2 37
Porsche Cabriolet 911 and 928 S4 38, 39
Pretty Polly stockings 73
Pulsar watches 230

Red Cross 286
Respons shampoo 325
Revlon cosmetics 326, 327
Riachuelo department store 306
Right Guard deodorant 336
River Po Protection Association 285
Robert La Roche 256, 257
Rockwool roofing board 211
Rodier women's clothes 68
Royal Air Force recruitment 261, 262
Royal National Institute for the Deaf 283
Rupp Käsle cheese 150

Saatchi & Saatchi 112
Safeway 109
Sandtex masonry paint 192
Sanyo audio and video equipment 22, 23, 24, 25
Saratoga mineral water 155
Scandale underwear 69
Schaffhauser wool 88
Schrack telecommunication systems 215
Sea fish 177
Siemens Museum 128
Silk Cut cigarettes 318, 319

Sinalco soft drink 154
Singapore Airlines/NTTC 343, 344
Smirnoff vodka 1, 2, 3
Sol Holidays 365, 366
Solidaire TV sets 35, 36
Sonntagsblick 240
Sugar 162, 163
Swedish office furniture 94

Takashi Kanome exhibition 124
Tao yoghurt 170
Tartan bitter 14
Tennent's Super lager 17
Timberland boots 76
Time magazine 234
Toray Industries 114
Toshiba C3 TV 31
Toyota 55
Trans World Airlines 363
Trend 244
Tri-Ac 330, 331, 332, 333
Truffles restaurant 304
Twix 151, 152

UK water industry 110

Vidal Sassoon salons 265
Vienna Festival 117
Virgin Megastore 300
Vision of Britain exhibition 122
Vittel mineral water 175
Vivivideo video cassettes 34
Volkswagen competition 45
Volkswagen Corrado 42, 43
Volkswagen Golf 61
Volkswagen Passat 62
Volvo cars 57
VTM television news 235

Women's Counselling Service 292
Woodlife wood preservative 203
'Work less' campaign 289
WXRT radio station 248

Yorkshire TV 241
Young Persons Railcard 362

Zeon watches and clocks 224, 225, 226, 227
Zwilling J. A. Henckels kitchen knife 193

INDEX OF AGENCIES AND STUDIOS

ABC/Eurocom, Düsseldorf 105
Adventure, Wellington 291
Advico Young & Rubicam, Zürich 58, 154, 239, 240, 273, 274, 275, 276
Alliance International, London 207
Arc International Advertising, London 205, 206
Armando Testa, Turin 129, 170, 285
ASP, Bombay 106, 149
Ayer
  Dallas 307
  Lisbon 165
  London 160, 161, 350, 351, 352, 253
  Milan 190
  New York 116, 228, 229, 231
Ayer Vazquez, Buenos Aires 130, 216

Ball WCRS Partnership
  Hong Kong 31
  Singapore 121
Bartle Bogle Hegarty, London 59, 60, 64, 73, 84, 91, 183, 254, 301
Bassat, Ogilvy & Mather, Barcelona 85, 86, 295
BBDO, London 79, 80
BDDP, Paris 15, 19, 20, 52, 53, 68, 69, 71, 92, 93, 102, 281, 300, 309
Bélier/WCRS, Paris 87
BMP Business, London 95
BMP DDB Needham, London 42, 43, 45, 61, 62, 169, 172, 173, 177, 181, 294
Bozell e Associati, Milan 28, 29, 30, 34, 48, 49, 98, 100
Brand Management, Sydney 54
Buchanan Company, Manchester 212, 213
Burkitt Weinreich Bryant, London 5, 6, 14, 282
Butler Borg, London 209

Campaign Company, Amsterdam 230
Campaign Palace, Melbourne 51, 89
CLM/BBDO, Paris 67, 104, 179, 297, 298, 299
Collett Dickenson Pearce and Partners, London 7, 55, 138, 139, 260, 270, 303, 316, 317
Contour Advertising, Bombay 99, 134
Coplan Advertising, London 224, 225, 226, 227
Cronin Morgan Stokes, Watford 210, 214

DDB Needham, New York 147
Demner & Merlicek, Vienna 56, 103, 117, 140, 141, 150, 162, 163, 198, 221, 222, 223, 238, 244, 345, 346, 348
Dentsu
  Osaka 193, 305
  Tokyo 114, 201, 250, 253, 337, 342, 368
DMB&B
  Amsterdam 12
  London 110, 151, 152, 265

Edison Group, Minneapolis 246, 259
Edwards Martin Thornton, London 16, 17, 302, 343, 344, 365, 366

Fallon McElligott, Minneapolis 191
Frankenberry Laughlin & Constable, Milwaukee 65

GBB, Reykjavík: see Hvíta Húsið
Grange Advertising, Berkhamsted 101
Grey, Düsseldorf 292
Guimaraes e Giacometti, São Paulo 232, 306

Hall & Cederquist/Y&R, Stockholm 94, 146, 171
Herman Feberwee & Peter Meijburg, Alphen 107
Howell Henry Chaldecott Lury, London 32, 33, 131, 137, 243
Hvíta Húsið, Reykjavík 108, 142, 143, 144, 233

Impuls, Küsnacht 88
Inca Tanvir Advertising, Sharjah 252
Insight, Madras 35, 36

J. Walter Thompson, London 118, 158, 159, 242, 261, 262, 268, 320, 321, 322, 323, 324, 334, 335
Keizo Matsui Design Office, Osaka 119, 126, 168
Ketchum Advertising, Singapore 255, 284, 304
KHBB, London 264
KMO-Leo Burnett, Madrid 182

Leagas Delaney Partnership, London 22, 23, 24, 25, 37, 76, 220, 326, 327, 364
Lintas, Paris 175
Lowe Troost, Brussels 189

Martin/Williams, Minneapolis 120, 194, 208, 251, 287
MC&D, Munich 128
McCann-Erickson, London 180
McCann-Erickson Hakuhodo, Tokyo 289
McCann-Erickson Wales, Penarth 211
Michael Conrad & Leo Burnett, Frankfurt 46, 47, 174, 338, 339, 354, 355, 356, 357
MPM, Rio de Janeiro 296

Nakamoto Design Office, Tokyo 111

Ogilvy & Mather
  London 26, 27, 41, 44, 109, 127, 283
  New York 90, 145, 184, 340
Ogilvy & Mather Partners, London 75

PPGH/J. Walter Thompson, Amsterdam 164, 167, 236, 237
Primary Contact, London 97, 135

RCP/Saatchi & Saatchi, Barcelona 204
Rediffusion, Bombay 113, 290
R. G. Wiesmeier, Munich 66
Rhizic, Bombay 358, 359
RSCG, Paris 178
RSCG Mezzano Constantini Mignani, Milan 96

Saatchi & Saatchi
  London 8, 112, 115, 122, 148, 192, 196, 197, 234, 263, 318, 319, 336, 349, 362, 367, 369
  New York 310
  Paris 81, 176, 328
  Sydney 341
Scali McCabe Sloves, New York 57
Simons Palmer Denton Clemmon & Johnson, London 266, 267
STZ, Milan 217, 218, 219

Takashi Kanome, Tokyo 124
Takayuki Itoh Design Office, Tokyo 40, 293
TAPSA/Ayer, Madrid 247, 258, 311
TBWA
  Amsterdam 77, 78
  New York 9, 10, 11, 18, 155, 156, 157
Thompson, J. Walter: see J. Walter Thompson

Volker Noth Grafik-Design, Berlin 123, 125

WCRS Mathews Marcantonio, London 82, 83, 199, 200
Wensauer & Partner, Ludwigsburg 38, 39
Wiesmeier, R. G.: see R. G. Wiesmeier
Woollams Moira Gaskin O'Malley, London 63, 329, 330, 331, 332, 333

Young & Rubicam
  Auckland 308
  Brussels 153, 195, 235, 286
  Chicago 248
  Copenhagen 136, 271, 272, 325
  Frankfurt 74, 245, 278
  London 1, 2, 3, 13, 132, 185, 186, 187, 241, 288, 347, 363
  Montreal 188
  New York 21, 166
  Paris 4, 50, 202, 277, 279, 280
  Vienna 215, 312, 313, 314, 315, 360, 361
Young & Rubicam/Reklamevi, Istanbul 249, 269

Zwiren Collins Karo Trusk & Ayer, Chicago 133, 203

HEINRICH HOFFMANN & PARTNER

Un style de vie équilibré était pour Béa aussi important que d'avoir l'air séduisante sur la plage. (La campagne pour les couteaux Gerber joue avec les différents sens des mots "sharp" et "balance" (équilibre/balance). Balance est d'ailleurs le nom de ces couteaux spéciaux.) A: Hoffmann York & Compton, Milwaukee : Mark Drewek : Howard Halaska : Mike Huibregtse

Lürzer's Archive

Lürzer's Archive

sharpens your

aiguise votre

view of advertising

sens de la publicité

Bi-monthly, Lürzer's Archive publishes approximately 150 of the best new print ads, posters and TV spots from all over the world. Translations are provided that include explanations of plays on words and double meanings in both English and French. Long before the publication of national annuals, or the Cannes and Clio reels, you get a chance to see what's new and exciting in advertising. Has your view of advertising been sharpened already? Then pick up your scissors - more appropriate than a knife in this case - and a pencil and order your free copy.

Tous les deux mois, Lürzer's Archive publie environ 150 nouveaux spots télévisés, affiches et réclames parmi les meilleurs du monde entier. Avec l'explication des jeux de mots en anglais, allemand et français. Vous connaissez ainsi ce qui est nouveau et différent, bien avant la parution des "Annuals" nationaux et des bobines de Cannes ou de Clio. Au cas ou votre jugement serait déjà un peu aiguisé, prenez sans tarder vos ciseaux (plutôt qu'un couteau!) et votre stylo et commandez un numéro spécimen gratuit en nous renvoyant le coupon dûment complété.

Please send me a free copy/Je désire recevoir un numéro spécimen ☐ in English ☐ en français ☐ in deutsch.

Name/Nom

Company/Société

Street/Rue

(Postcode) City/(Code postal) Ville

Please send to/Veuillez envoyer à: Lürzer's Archive, Hamburger Allee 45, 6000 Frankfurt/M. 90, RFA.

Only one magazine shows you exciting new advertising six times a year.

Une seule revue vous présente tous les deux mois la meilleure publicité du monde entier.